CW00587942

Come and join the Yummy Mummy's Revolution at the most exciting and innovative new child friendly coffee shop in the Midlands....We have created a family friendly space with 21st Century comforts inc.

Buggy Park, Toilet and baby changing facilities (unisex for dads!) The Trademark Yummy Mummy's Mini Diner for Pre-Schoolers, Wooden toys Mini Library, Colouring Activities, Themed Children's Events/Seasonal Events/Story Telling, 100% Organic Baby & Children's Menus, Digital TV, Organic Lunches & Teas to go.

All Yummy Mummy's food will be available to eat in or take away in 100% biodegradable packaging, all our cups, bags and take out paper products are biodegradable and recycled.

Our fully trained Baristas (nominated recently for a top National Beverage Association Award) will make you any coffee you like how you like it using only the best freshly roasted organic, fairtrade and Rainforest Alliance beans available in the UK today.

We have a wide range of organic and fairtrade teas, gluten and nut free products, super fresh juices and funky immune boosting smoothies powered by amazing ingredients, white and dark hot chocolate with organic marshmallows, freshly made all natural milkshakes - in fact too much to tell you about here! So why not come along and see us for yourselves - yes we really are that good & if you bring this advertisement with you we will knock 10% off your bill

Wi-fi/Hi-Fi/Air Con/TV/Music/Sunday Brunch Coming Soon/Outside Catering/Kids Parties

Charlotte Bond
Founder, Owner of Yummy Mummy
Coffee Shops (Mother of 3)
Autumn 2007.

real coffee . real people . real passion .

Yummy Mummy's Coffee Shop . 10 Queen Street . Southwell . NG25 0AA .
Tel: 01636 815597
Opening : Monday to Friday 08.30 - 5.30. Saturday: 09.00 - 5.00
lottebond@hotmail.com   www.yummymummyscoffeeshops.com

introduction

Welcome to The Baby Directory for the East Midlands

It is fascinating to see how much the British entrepreneurial spirit has flourished amongst parents over the last ten years. The Baby Directories have witnessed seed ideas become serious businesses and for many, the advent of parenthood brings a new determination and confidence to try new things. This directory incorporates all the hard work that Rachel Blackwell and Louisa Priestley have carried out over the last four years with the Absolute Guide to Parenting plus the latest year's research.

We have listed every day nursery and independent school. We list all the shops you could possibly want to visit for you, your baby and your toddler.

Stuck for new ideas? We list activities, days out, music and gym sessions.

Don't forget to add www.babydirectory.com to your list of favourites, which includes the Encyclopedia of Pregnancy and our guide to Children's Health. We also have a monthly e-newsletter which keeps you informed about new product launches, special offers and giveaways - so don't forget to register!

If we have left anything out which you think deserves a slot next time, then please don't hesitate to email me at editor@babydirectory.com.

Whether you are pregnant, a very new parent or planning your life with a toddler - we hope you will use this guide to make life that much easier! And remember, if you are moving out of the East Midlands we have other regional publications and a London directory covering the whole of the UK.

Clare Flawn-Thomas
editor@babydirectory.com

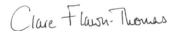

WONDERLAND
Pleasure Park
Adventure Play Education

Stratstone

Sainsbury's

CHILD BASE
Nurseries

We would also like to thank all the sponsors of the guide and the East Midlands Baby and Toddler Show 2007.

Edited, designed and published by
Brockwell Publishing Limited

Tel +44 (0)845 466 0262

Fax +44 (0)20 7733 4988

Editors	Clare Flawn-Thomas
	Rachel Blackwell
Researchers	Kirsty Holme
	Kathryn Rea
	Susie Delabilliere
Advertising Sales	Rachel Blackwell
	Louisa Priestley
	Patricia Belotti
	Geeta Chamdal
Design and Production	Caroline Mills

All Images © The Baby Directory except: cover © Phunky Photos, page 1, page 19, page 49, page 113, page 155 and page 163 © PRshots.com page 29 ©Naturaland, page 39 ©Julia Laderman.

ISBN: 978-1-903288-24-5

0% APR TYPICAL ON THE VOLVO C30

Visit our stand at the East Midlands Baby and Toddler Show.
Call 0115 942 5500 or visit Stratstone.com

On The Road Price	£14,750	24 Monthly Payments of	£305
Customer Deposit	£7430	Total Charge for Credit	£0
Amount of Credit	£7320	Total Amount Payable	£14,750

0.0% APR Typical

volvo. for life

Stratstone

Stratstone.com

need a **helping** hand?
want more for **your money**?

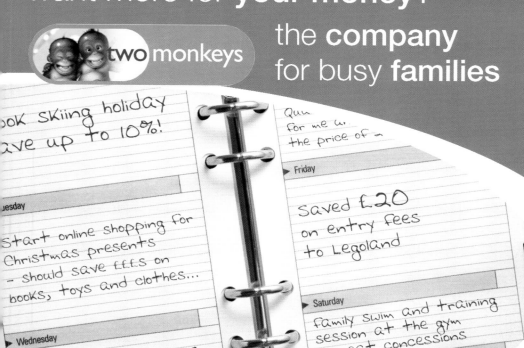

twomonkeys

the **company**
for busy **families**

contents

LOOK OUT FOR DETAILS
OF THE 2008 SHOW

The East Midlands

Baby
and toddler show

A fun day out for all the family!

BEAUTIFUL CLOTHES FOR YOU AND YOUR CHILDREN
EXPERT ADVICE & INFORMATION
FASHION SHOW ■ **ENTERTAINERS** ■ ARTS & CRAFTS
CAR SEAT SAFETY CHECKS BY NOTTINGHAM FIRE BRIGADE
CHILD MODEL COMPETITION
4D SCANS ■ FACE PAINTING ■ **MEET THE MIDWIVES**
SPECIAL OFFERS & AMAZING SAVINGS
HUGE CHARITY PRIZE DRAW & COMPETITIONS

If you would like to exhibit, attend or find out about
sponsorships for the 2008 event, please contact:

LRK Events 0115 9410 889

toddler activities

As every mother will know, idle little hands and minds need channelling. A mix of physical and creative activities will help develop confidence, co-ordination, concentration, creativity and individual skills. Our listings will give you loads of inspiration and guide you to the multifarious classes, clubs and centres that abound. For active kids, we list gym clubs, dance classes, swimming classes, football and more; for creative youngsters there are arts and crafts clubs, drama classes, musical activity groups and ceramic cafes. Add a soupçon of French language here and a shot of mini-tennis there, and your toddler will be the most accomplished in town

Age range	Activity ideas and when to introduce them
First **6** weeks	Lots of **physical contact**, **gentle voices**, **faces** to look at.
6 weeks to **3** months	Put toys within **touching** distance; use **bouncing** chairs; **massage**; **stretching** exercises and kicking; holding **rattles** (soft so they don't bash themselves); and **rolling** over onto tummy. Encourage baby **babble** by repeating the sounds they make/peek-a-boo.
3 months to **6** months	Looking at picture **books**, **sitting** and **bouncing** on your knee, introduce an **activity mat** with dangling toys with interesting textures/colours; if good head control introduce **baby bouncers**. Start socialising within **music** groups (see pg 16) and **baby swimming** (see pg 18).
6 months to **10** months	Encourage **sitting** up with support and getting more **active** (see gym groups on pg 13). Provide interestingly shaped **objects** (ie keys that rattle) and encourage **passing** from one hand to another. Introduce **signing actions** with songs (see pg 16).
10 months to **1** year	Practise **waving bye-bye** and **clapping hands**; encourage use of **finger** and **thumb** to pick up small objects (such as string attached to a toy); encourage **standing up** with your support; **dropping** things and seeing where they go; **filling** and **emptying** containers.
1 year to **18** months	First real **words** appear at this stage so continue with nursery rhymes; play with **sand** and **water**; **copying** games (such as making faces in a mirror); introduce push-along toys, **ball** throwing, **stacking** bricks and shape **sorting**; begin to **stand** and **walk** or **cruise** between furniture.
18 months to **2** years	Provide **ride**-on toys; go **climbing** and **sliding** in the playground or in indoor activity playcentres (see pg 3); jigsaws (lift-out and inset); introduce **playdough** (see our recipe opposite); encourage **colouring** and continue going to **music** clubs (see pg 10).
2 years to **3** years	Introduce ball games such as **football** or **skittles** (and emphasise **taking turns**); help with **construction** toys; encourage **sentences** and remembering songs; develop **turning** one page at a time whilst **reading books**. Practise **cutting** out with scissors.
3 years to **5** years	Hold a **crayon** between **first two fingers and thumb** and draw **shapes** not scribble; encourage **dressing up** and **make believe**. Introduce **numbers** and **letters** (particularly in their own name); try **listening games** or **cooking** (eg decorating biscuits); encourage **swimming** without aids; start **dance**, **drama** classes, football groups or **foreign** language clubs.

activity centres

DERBYSHIRE

Bumpi's Big Adventure **01332 204 292**
Goodward Park, Derby, DE24 8GW
www.bumpi.co.uk
There's a warm welcome at Bumpi's play and party centres at Derby and Leicester, plus a free coffee term time when you come before 11am*. Tuesday or Thursday morning term time we'll keep your little treasures occupied with busy bambino activities specially planned by a qualified member of our friendly team – while you relax with a real Italian coffee! If your little one is still a baby...bring them along….there's a baby ball pit and soft play – plus you'll love our Blue Cloud Café. Don't forget to bring your older ones too; our frame is 3 story's high -lots of fun. Max height 4ft 9ins. We'd love to see you! *some conditions apply.

Chucklebutties Play Centre **01773 880 123**
Riverside Suite, Belper Mills, Bridgefoot, Belper, DE56 1YD

Crazy Crocodiles **0115 944 1555**
Abbey Street, Ilkeston, DE7 8DN
www.crazycrocodiles.co.uk
All year round indoor adventure play centre for children 0-10yrs.

Easy Tigers **01246 260 011**
Nurture House, Dunston Trading Estate, Foxwood Road, Chesterfield, S41 9RF
www.easytigers.co.uk
Easy Tigers™ are committed to providing the highest quality play environment for your children, whilst ensuring that your needs as a parent are met. Our play areas are designed to provide the maximum fun, with the highest visibility for parents to be able to supervise their child. Open 7 days a week 9.30am until 6.30pm; enjoy one of our Parent and Toddler sessions exclusive to the under 5's, Monday, Wednesday and Fridays mornings (9.30am until 12pm (term-time only)). Experience a wonderful party, planned, organised and delivered with both your child and you in mind. Book early to avoid disappointment.

Freddy's Play Kingdom **01332 662 322**
50 Nottingham Road, Spondon, Derby, DE21 7NL
www.freddythedragon.co.uk
Children's activity play centre. Discos and parties catered for - cafeteria service food and drink.

Hudy's Play Barn **01283 732 083**
High Street, Woodville, Swadlincote, DE11 7EH

Pirates Play Island **01332 875 000**
44 Derby Road, Draycott, DE72 3NJ

Planet Happy **01773 748 600**
Heague Road Ind Estate, Ripley, DE5 3GH

Tubby Bear's Play Den

An indoor soft play centre for children and a relaxing place for adults too.

Tubby Bear's Play Den is open 7 days a week:
Monday 10.00am – 4.00pm
Tuesday – Saturday 10.00am – 6.00pm
Sunday and Bank Holidays 10.00 am – 4.00pm

The entrance price includes one complementary hot drink for the adult and a squash for the child.

After 3.45pm, children can play for £1.75. Tubby's menu is available until 4.45pm so you can stay for tea too.

Carrington Court, Great Nothern Road, Derby DE1 1LR
Telephone: 01332 341355   www.tubbybears.co.uk

The Cats Whiskers Playhouse   01457 855 552
Units 3, & 4 Surrey St, Glossop, SK13 7AH

Tubby Bear's Play Den   01332 341355
Carrington Court, Great Northern Road, Derby, DE1 1LR
www.tubbybears.co.uk
At Tubby Bear's Play Den, parties are our speciality! There's loads for the children to do, they'll love our slides, ballpools and our large playframe. Let us organise your party for you! All of our party packages include; invitations, a dedicated host, reserved tables at our café and exclusive use of our fantastic party room. We are located at the rear of Carrington Court on Great North Road. Opening times Mon 10am-4pm, Tues-Sat 10am-6pm and Sun and Bank Holidays 10am-4pm.

LEICESTERSHIRE
Bumpi's Big Adventure   0116 282 5822
Meridian Leisure Park, Braunstone
www.bumpi.co.uk
There's a warm welcome at Bumpi's play and party centres at Derby and Leicester, plus a free coffee term time when you come before 11am*. Tuesday or Thursday morning term time we'll keep your little treasures occupied with busy bambino activities specially planned by a qualified member of our friendly team – while you relax with a real Italian coffee! If your little one is still a baby...bring them along....there's a baby ball pit and soft play – plus you'll love our Blue Cloud Café.
*some conditions apply

Braunstone Adventure Play   0116 291 9700
8 Court Crescent, Braunstone, Leicester, LE3 1QZ

LINCOLNSHIRE
Captain Kids Adventure World   01754 760 600
Skegness Pier, Grand Parade, Skegness, PE25 2UE
Open every day of the week from 10am – 7pm in the winter and 10am-10pm in the summer. There is a special area for under fours. Sign up for a toddler group on Wednesdays.

Crazee Bongos   01529 410 808
Unit 4, Sellwood Court, Sleaford Enterprise Park, East Road, Sleaford, NG34 7EH
Take the kids along to Crazee Bongos for all-weather fun. They have a soft play area for under 5s and a separate area for 5-12 year olds. There is a café and they do Birthday parties. Open Tue-Sun 10am-6pm.

JJ's Playmania   01427 677 974
Middlefield Lane, Gainsborough, DN21 1UU
www.playmania.co.uk
Soft play for the under fives. Mother and toddler mornings are held on Tuesday, Wednesday and Thursday mornings from 10am –12 noon with cheaper entry and free drinks!

Kids Adventure World   01507 477 310
High Street, Spanish City, Mablethorpe, LN12 1AD
This indoor play centre is open on weekends and school holidays and has a soft play area for the under 5s. Food and drinks are available in the café.

Lets Play — 01778 425 444
Station Yard, South Road, Bourne PE10 9LU

There is something for everyone here; soft play area for the under 3s, pirate ship for older children and a café for the parents. Open Mon-Sat 9.30- 6pm and 10am-6pm on Sundays, the café is open until 4.30.

Lincoln Toy Library — 01522 546 215
Withham Park, Waterside South, Lincoln, LN5 7JN

As well as the toy library there is a soft play area and an under 1's play area. There is coffee and tea available and they have a picnic room for those who want to bring their own lunch. Open Tue to Fri 10.30am-3pm, Sat 10am- 1pm. Second Saturday of each month is reserved for a special needs afternoon.

Playzone Lincoln — 01522 539 999
The Old Gymnasium, Cross St, Lincoln LN5 7LF

Parent and toddlers' specials are offered Mon-Fri 10am-1.30pm (Tuesday 11am- 1.30pm). There is a soft play area for the under fours and a separate area for the over 4s which can be used by toddles if accompanied by a parent. While the children are amusing themselves, you can relax in the café or seating area. They also do Birthday parties. Open all week 10am-7.15pm.

Fun Farm — 01406 373 444
High Road, Weston, Spalding PE12 6JU
www.funfarm.co.uk

The outdoor play area, indoor soft play area and dedicated under 5's area are all free for children under 1 and adults! They do Birthday parties and have full maternity and disabled facilities, a café, a licenced bar and a gift shop. They also do tenpin bowling and laser tags. Open all week 10am- 6pm.

Funtasia Fun House — 01522 695 553
Stephenson Road, North Hykeham Technology Park, North Hykeham, Lincoln LN6 3QU

The fun never stops in the Funtasia Fun House, let them run riot in the toddler only play area with slides and a ball pool. Tots and toddlers get cheaper sessions during term time during the week from 10am- 3pm, this includes free drinks for children and parents. There is a café selling hot and cold food. Birthday parties. Open Mon-Fri 10am-6.30pm, Sat 10.30am-7pm and Sun 11am-5pm.

Rascals the Fun Factor — 01778 480 610
Unit 2, West Street, Stamford, PE9 2PR

Come and join in the fun at the Fun Factory soft play centre, there is a section for the under 2's. There is a café and a parking area. Discounts are offered for groups of 10 or more children. Open Mon-Fri 10am- 5.30pm and Sat 10.30am-4.30pm.

The Play Barn — 01775 766 393
Springfield Outlet Centre, Camel Gate, PE12 6ET
www.springfieldshopping.co.uk

The Play Barn offers both an outdoor play area with mini golf, mechanical diggers, bumper cars and a remote control boat on a lake, and an indoor soft play barn with a toddler area. There is a café and an eating area. Open 10am-6pm.

NOTTINGHAMSHIRE

Cyril's Nut Hut — 01159 736 532
Unit 3 Acton Road, Long Eaton, NG10 1FR
www.cyrilsnuthut.co.uk

Cyril's Nut Hut is a fabulous indoor play centre, with adventure play and soft play equipment designed to keep kids of all ages happy - from tots just starting to crawl, right up to active kids of 11 years old (4ft 11 max). Conveniently located in Long Eaton, they are easy to reach from Nottingham, Derby and the surrounding East Midlands - just minutes away from the A50 / M1 junction at Castle Donnington.

Denz Children's Play Centre — 0115 925 5007
131 Queens Road, Beeston, NG9 2FE
www.denz.ltd.uk

Looking for somewhere to take the kids for a couple of hours or longer, then why not try Denz's Indoor play centre? While the children let off steam on the four level play frame you can enjoy a cup of coffee and a bite to eat or if you want something more substantial try one of our reasonably priced, freshly prepared meals. We are open 7 days a week from 9.30am to 6.00pm so just pop along when you want, no need to book. We can also arrange your child's party in one of our private themed rooms.

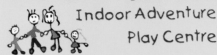
Hoods Hideout   **0115 9151575**
Beechdale Swimming Centre, Billborough, NG8 3LL
Nottingham City Council
A relaxed and friendly play centre that just enables you to drop by for an hour or two and allows the children to work off some steam. Throughout the holidays the Hideout is open from 10 am all day.

Kool Kids Indoor Adventure   **0115 950 0125**
Play Centre
Carlton Road, Nottingham, NG3 2NR
Indoor fun and adventure including a ball crawl, soft play ground, bouncy castle and snooker tables. A great way to tire out energetic kids big and small, and when they get hungry there is food available in the café. Also does Birthday parties.

Lanky Bill's Fun Shack   **01773 767 050**
Unit 6, Cromford Road Industrial Estate,
Nottingham, NG16 4FL
www.lankybills.com
At Lanky Bill's Fun Shack we cater for children from 6 months to 11 years. We have a large main frame and soft play for the 4's and under. We offer three party rooms and during term time Parent and Toddler Groups. Ofsted registered childcare; Holiday club, After-school Club. Home cooked meals and qualified staff all creates a friendly environment in which to spend a few hours and let off some steam. Please contact us for further information.

WONDERLAND
Pleasure Park
Adventure Play Education

Children's rides & attractions
Indoor play area
Tropical House
Train ride
Pitch 'n' Put
Picnic areas
Licensed bar/café
Garden centre and much more!

www.wonderlandpleasurepark.com

CHECK OUT OUR WEBSITE

Open daily from 10am to 5pm
Please call or visit our website
for details of opening times for November to January.

Wonderland Pleasure Park,
White Post, Farnsfield, Newark, Notts, NG22 8HX.
Call 01623 882773 for more information

enjoy england
excellence
awards
2005

Silver Award Winner

WELCOME HOST

English Tourism Council
QUALITY ASSURED
VISITOR
ATTRACTION

Playland **01623 654 712**
Unit 1a Botany Commercial Park, Botany Avenue,
Mansfield, NG18 5NF

Run Riot **0115 981 4027**
Rugby Road, West Bridgford, Nottingham, NG2 7HY
www.rushcliffe.gov.uk
See advert opposite contents page

The White Post Farm Centre **01623 882 977**
Mansfield Road, Farnsfield, NG22 8HL
www.whitepostfarmcentre.co.uk
The White Post Farm is a popular tourist attraction 12 miles
north of Nottingham. Open every single day of the year, there
is something for everyone; a truly hands on experience. Daily

events include baby animal holding, meet-a-reptile, baby goat
bottle-feeding, as well as acres of animals to stroll around,
feeding a variety of breeds. With special seasonal events
throughout the year, every visit is different. PLUS Farm shop
full of fresh local produce and Pet Centre with everything you
need for a happy, healthy pet.

Wonderland Pleasure Park **01623 882 773**
White Post, Farnsfield, Newark, NG22 8HX
www.wonderlandpleasurepark.com
Set in 30 acres of parkland in the heart of Nottinghamshire
Wonderland Pleasure Park makes the perfect day out for all
the family.

art workshops

The Creation Station **0845 050 8743**
215 Ashby Road, Loughborough, LE67 5UG
www.thecreationstation.co.uk
The award-winning Creation Station inspires imagination
through a range of creative sessions, birthday parties and
products. Since 2002, over 10,000 children and parents have
already benefited from our 'Exploration' structured
educational program. Each child develops their own journey
of exploration, discovery and development using a wide
range of art & craft materials, tools & ideas, with a little bit of
magic and a lot of laughter. In a recent survey, 100% of
parents who attend the 'Exploration' sessions stated that
their child's concentration had increased after 5 sessions.
'There are reasons why you don't do this sort of thing at
home…and they're all reasons why you come to The
Creation Station. It's messy fun- not sure who enjoys it
more- the children or the mums (& dads!). Great ideas that
inspire the imagination- Brilliant' Hannah's Mummy.

Derby Play and Reclycling **01332 299 165**
Centre
6-10 Werburgh Street, Derby, Derbyshire, DE22 3QG
www.derbyplayandrecyclingcentre.co.uk
This centre takes in donations of craft materials from local
businesses [ie fabrics, wood, plastic] and offers drop in
workshops for children on Saturday mornings. Children do
need to be accompanied by an adult. Alongside the
workshop is a craft store, which is open on Tues/Wed from
10am-3pm, Thurs 10am-5pm. There are lots of creative
ideas on hand and plenty of advice.

Splodge and Splat **0115 913 0006**
www.splodgeandsplat.co.uk
Welcome to Splodge & Splat the home of CREATIVE MESS
and FANTASTIC FUN! Our themed sessions enable the
children to explore messy materials and activities that aim to
stimulate a variety of their senses. The starting point of a
session might be a song, rhyme, story character or prop to
spark their imagination. It is then through a wide range of
materials that we hope to support the development of the
individual's needs. We aim to inspire the children's creativity
whilst developing their curiosity, and build a sense of awe
through their enjoyment of the sessions.

Playdough

The texture of playdough is fascinating for toddlers of about 18mths. But if your shop bought playdough has hardened you can rustle up your own from our recipe below. Initially kids will need to be shown how to squeeze and squash it into recognisable shapes – and later you can provide implements for cutting. It's also a useful activity if you are in the kitchen cooking and they want to copy you.

Recipe
- 2 x teaspoons cream of tartar
- 1 x cup plain flour
- 1 x tablespoon oil
- 1 x cup water

Mix to form a smooth paste. Put in a saucepan and cook slowly, until the dough comes away from the side of the pan and forms a ball. When cool enough knead the dough for 3-4 minutes. When not in use keep in an airtight container in the fridge. Food colouring can be added to the water or the dough for colour variety.

Potty Picassos Ceramic Café 01623 556 813
92 Outram Street, Sutton in Ashfield, NG17 4FS
www.pottypicassos.co.uk
Have some fun at this ceramic cafe where you can take a print of your baby's hands and feet, have a children's birthday party, or simply come in and if you are stuck for inspiration the friendly and helpful staff have lots of suggestions.

dance

Most ballet classes are for children from 2½ yrs-3yrs or 'out of nappies'. They are great for posture, co-ordination and for graceful confidence. Some children will progress to professional ballet schools but many more will experience dance as a pleasure and a cherished childhood memory. It will also encourage an appreciation of dance throughout adult life.

The Baby Ballet Song & 0870 143 0063
Dance Academy
www.babyballet.co.uk
Baby Ballet is a wonderfully exciting educational movement to music programme for pre-school boys and girls. Designed to encourage babies and young children to enjoy the benefits and joys of song and dance, Baby Ballet has built up a fantastic reputation for providing children with the opportunity to express themselves within a fun, safe and caring environment.

Royal Academy of Dance 020 7326 8000
www.rad.org.uk
Based in London, the RAD is an internationally recognised body for teaching, training and setting exam syllabus for classical dance. Teachers who qualify can apply for membership and parents can request details or send an SAE.

gym

Tumble Tots: 01623 635 197
www.tumbletots.com/northnottingham
peter.rogers@tumbletots.com
Peter covers Mapperley, Mansfield Woodhouse, Newark and Ravenshead.

Tumble Tots 0115 958 9767
www.tumbletots.com/nottingham
jayne.chadburn@tumbletots.com
Jayne covers Gamston, Bramcote, West Bridgford, Radcliffe-on-Trent and Bottesford.

Tumble Tots 0116 272 0057
Mobile 07050 266 355
www.tumbletots.com/leicesterwest
smita.ghelani@tumbletots.com
Smita covers Hinckley, Glenfield, Lutterworth, Enderby, Thurmaston and opening soon in Beaumont Leys.

Skills for Life

The springboard to confidence for your child

Tumble Tots is Britain's leading National Active Physical
Play Programme for children from 6 months to 7 years

◆ Using specifically designed equipment your child will learn
  agility, balance, climbing and co-ordination skills appropriate
  to their age

◆ A structured programme designed to build self confidence and
  develop essential listening and language skills

◆ Supervised by trained staff in a fun and caring environment

For your nearest Tumble Tots centre
call **0121 585 7003**
www.tumbletots.com

DERBY CITY COUNCIL

Springtots

Pre-school gymnastics for 6 months up to 5 years

Try Before You Buy Special Offer!
Book your child in for a Springtots taster
session and pay just £1.
Please contact one of the centres listed below to check
availability and book your child's place,
quoting Absolute Guide to Parenting. Cut out this
coupon and take it to the sports centre to claim
your £1 session.
£1 Taster sessions are subject to availability.
Offer expires August 2008

Springwood Leisure Centre, Oakwood, Derby, **tel 01332 664433**, Minicom 01332 663809
Moorways Sports Centre, Allenton, Derby, **tel 01332 363686**, Minicom 01332 294526
Shaftesbury Sports Centre, Normanton, Derby, **tel 01332 255603**, Minicom 01332 715171

www.derby.gov.uk/sportsfacilities

leisure centre

Leisure Centres provide enjoyable exercise for both you and your child. It is never too early to teach your child to swim and most leisure centres will hold classes for the very young in the form of aqua-babies. You will also find that the vast majority hold activity placements for young children from 1-6 weeks during school holidays.

DERBYSHIRE

Albion Leisure Centre 0115 944 0200
East Street, Ilkeston, Derbyshire

Alfreton Leisure Centre 01773 834 617
Church Street , Alfreton, DE55 7BD
www.dcleisurecentres.co.uk

Amber Valley Leisure 01773 841 438
PO Box 17 Town Hall,Market Place, Ripley, Derbys, DE5 3TU

Ashbourne Leisure Centre 01335 343712
Clifton Road, Ashbourne, Derbyshire

Belper Leisure Centre 01773 825285
Kilbourne Road, Belper, Derbyshire

Chester Green Community Group 01332 360342
Darley Playing fields, City Road, Derbyshire

Derby City Council 01332 715 671
5th Floor Celtic House, Derby, DE1 1QX
www.derby.gov.uk/sportsfacilities

Green Bank Leisure Centre 01332 297444
Civic Way, Swadlincote, Derbyshire

Heanor Leisure Centre 01773 769 711
Hands Road, Heanor, DE75 7HA
www.dcleisurecentres.co.uk

Meadowside Leisure Centre 01283 508 865
High Street, Burton-On-Trent, Derbyshire

Meadowside Leisure Centre 01283 508865
High Street, Burton On Trent

Melbourne Leisure Centre 01332 863522
High Street, Melbourne, Derbyshire

Queens Leisure Centre 01332 716620
Cathedral Road, Derby

Ripley Leisure Centre 01773 746 531
Derby Road, Ripley, DE5 3HR
www.dcleisurecentres.co.uk

Shobnall Leisure Centre 01283 516180
Shobnall Road, Burton On Trent

Springwood Leisure Centre 01332 664433
Oakwood, Derbyshire

Willows Sports Centre 01332 204004
1 Willow Row, Derbyshire

LEICESTERSHIRE

Aylestone Leisure Centre 01162 333 040
2 Knighton Lane East, Leicester

Braunstone Recreation Centre 01162 333 085
Winforde Crescent, Leicester

Coalville Gymnastics 01530 811001
Ravenstone Road, Coalville, Leicestershire

Derby Leisure Centre 01162 750 234
Mill Lane, Derby, Leicester

East Leake Leisure Centre 01509 852 956
Lantern Lane, Loughborough, Leicester

Elizabeth Park Sports & Community Centre 01162 602 519
Checkland Road, Thurmaston, Leicester

Evington Swimming Pool 01162 995 575
Downing Drive, Leicester

Fleckney Sports & Leisure Centre 01162 403 755
Recreation Ground Leicester Road, Fleckney, Leicester

Goals Soccer Centre Ltd 01162 490 555
Wakeley Road, Leicester
Soccer at weekends for kids and kids parties.

Harborough Leisure Centre 01858 410 115
Northampton Road, Market Harborough, Leicester

Hermitage Leisure Centre 01530 811 215
Silver Street, Whitwick, Coalville, Leicester

Hood Park Leisure Centre 01164 122 181
North Street, Ashby De La Zouch, Leicester

Huncote Leisure Centre 01162 750 246
Sportsfield Lane, Huncote, Leicester

Kibworth Sports Centre 01162 796 971
Sneeton Road, Kibworth Beauchamp, Kibworth, Leicester

Leicester Leys Leisure Centre 01162 333 070
Beaumont Way, Beaumont Leys, Leicester

Loughborough Leisure Centre 01509 611 080
Browns Lane, Loughborough, Leicester

Megazone Laser Centre 01162 531 153
171 Belgrave Gate, Leicester

Melton Leisure Centre 01664 851 111
Asfordby Road, Melton Mowbray, Leicester

New Park Leisure Centre 01162 333 080
St. Oswalds Road, New Parks, Leicester

Parklands 01162 720 789
Wigston Road, Oadby, Leicester

St. Margarets Pastures 01162 333 095
St. Margaret Way, Leicester

Southfields Drive Sports Centre 01162 839 047
Southfield Drive, Leicester

Spence Street Sport Centre 0116 2995584
Spence Street, Leicester

Sport In Desford Clubhouse 01455 828 786
Peckleton Lane, Desford, Leicester

Sports-League Leicester Ltd 01162 470 221
16 Commercial Square, Leicester

Soar Valley 01162 275 267
Off Kingfisher Road, Mount Sorrel, Leicestershire

NOTTINGHAMSHIRE

Bingham Leisure Centre 01949 838 628
The Banks, Bingham, Nottinghamshire
www.leisure-centre.com

Bramcote Leisure Centre 01159 173 000
Derby Road, Bramcote, Nottingham

Chilwell Olympia Sports Centre 0115 9 173 333
Bye Pass Road, Chilwell, Nottingham

Clifton Leisure Centre 0115 9 152 333
Southchurch Drive, Clifton, Nottingham

Calverton Leisure Centre 01159 653 781
Flatts Lane, Calverton, Nottingham

Cotgrave Leisure Centre 01159 892 916
Woodview, Cotgrave, Nottingham
www.leisure-centre.com

Harvey Hadden Sports Centre 01159 151 515
Bilborough Park, Wigham Road, Bilborough

Hucknall Leisure Centre 01159 568 750
Linby Road, Hucknall, Nottinghamshire

John Carroll Leisure Centre 01159 151 535
Denham Street, Radford, Nottingham

Keyworth Leisure Centre 01159 375 582
Church Drive, Keyworth, Nottingham
www.leisure-centre.com

Kimberley Leisure Centre 01159 173 366
Newdigate Street, Kimberley, Nottingham

Lenton Leisure Centre 01159 150 095
Willoughby Street, Lenton, Nottingham

Noel Street Leisure Centre 01159 151 545
Ken Martin's Swimming Centre
Hucknall Lane, Bulwell, Nottinghamshire

Redhill Leisure Centre 01159 569 996
Redhill Road, Arnold, Nottingham

Richard Herrod Leisure Centre 01159 612 949
Foxhill Road, Carlton, Nottingham

Rushcliffe Leisure Centre 01159 234 921
Boundary Road, West Bridgford, Nottingham
www.leisure-centre.com

Sandiacre Freisland Sports Centre 01159 490 400
Nursery Avenue, Nottingham

Selston Leisure Centre 01773 781 800
The Matthew Holland Complex, Chaple Road, Nottinghamshire

Victoria Leisure Centre 0115 915 5600
Gedling Road, Sneinton, Nottingham

West Park Leisure Centre 0115 946 1400
Wilsthorpe Road, Nottingham

Portland Leisure Centre 0115 915 0015
Muskham Street, The Meadows, Nottingham

Southglade Leisure Centre 0115 915 1595
Southglade Road, Bestwood, Nottinghamshire

Musical fun with Jo Jingles!
♫ Music ♫ Singing ♫ Movement

Fun with music from the UK's leading children's music group!
For babies and children from 6 months to 5 years

Jo Jingles Classes:

- Fun & educational
- Interactive - children & parents join in!
- Structured & age specific
- Stimulate imagination & learning
- Develop speech & listening skills
- Encourage children to socialise
- Available in over 500 centres

Jo Jingles Classes Offer:

- Active music making
- Proven educational themes
- Safe, learning environment
- High quality visuals & instruments
- Introduction to routine & discipline
- Fun range of musical merchandise to use at home

For details on local classes please contact:

Sam Preston
Meridian Park, Narborough, Enderby, Hinckley, Burbage, Lutterworth & Nuneaton
Tel: 01455 611110
www.jojingles.com/swleicester

Mari-Vic Gomez
Lichfield, Tamworth, Burton-on-Trent & Derby
Tel: 01283 791067
www.jojingles.com

Gaynor Smith
Wollaton, West Bridgford, Gamston, Long Eaton, Bingham, Melton Mowbray & Hucknall
Tel: 0870 900 4567
www.jojingles.com/nottingham

Sally Davey
Loughborough, Mountsorrel, Kegworth, Shepshed, Thringstone, Sutton Bonington & East Leake
Tel: 01530 814083
www.jojingles.com/loughborougharea

Jo Jingles Birthday Parties!

Fun filled parties also available.
Contact your local teacher for full details.

Musical Fun for Everyone!

Jo Jingles is a Full Member of the British Franchise Association

THE MUSIC & MOVEMENT EXPERIENCE

music

There's nothing like a good sing song to lift the spirits and even the smallest baby can benefit from the classes we have listed.

Caterpillar Music   **0870 199 8732**
www.caterpillarmusic.com
Music activity sessions for 0-4 years olds. Also how about invite us to your party and we will bring our music, instruments, puppets and bubbles to make your party really special! Suitable for 1-4yrs. We will provide a fun-filled hour and even bring a pass the parcel and a present for the birthday boy/girl.

Jo Jingles   **0870 900 4567**
www.jojingles.com
Who is this happy little fellow, all dressed in red and yellow?...It's Jo Jingles! Jo Jingles is the UK's leading national provider of music and singing classes for young children aged from 6 months to 5 years. We are passionate about providing quality, fun, educational, musical sessions for the very young and have classes available throughout the Leicestershire, Nottingham and Derby areas. All Jo Jingles sessions are age specific from babies to 5 years of age and are well structured with a carefully developed class program incorporating pre-school learning themes – but don't tell the children, as they have so much fun they do not realise they are learning at the same time! See class details left.

Caterpillar Music activity sessions for 0-4 year olds encourage learning in a fun atmosphere. Our carefully planned sessions have a variety of activities to stimulate and entertain.

Call us today for a free information pack with details of local classes, discounts and free sessions.
Telephone: 0870 199 8732

Sing and Sign   01273 550 587

www.signandsign.com

Baby signing helps your baby to communicate before speech. Traditional and original songs. Classes make use of puppets and musical instruments. Classes for babies aged 7-18mths are held in North Leicester and Loughborough with Nicola Arkley Tel: 01530 244 538, Coventry with Holly Kindness Tel: 07912 892 908, in South Leicester, Rugby & Hinckley with Katy Duckett Tel: 01455 289 202 and in Nottingham West Bridgford with Adele Johnson Tel: 0115 847 1877.

Swimming classes

East Midlands Swimming   07813 892 108
Academy

www.em-sa.co.uk

The East Midlands swimming school was founded by Sally Parkin in 1998 and runs excellent classes throughout the year for mothers and babies as well as children. The classes are held at the Marriott Hotels in Leicester, Morley, Sheffield, Grantham and Meriden; the Renaissance Hotel in Derby/Nottingham; the Legacy Hotel in Chesterfield and the Loughborough Quality Hotel. They also offer weekly classes at West Bridgford School in Nottingham. Visit this excellent website to see the pools and great testimonials, and contact Sally for availability and class times.

Water Babies Nottingham   01937 522 517

9 Priesthill Gardens, Nottingham, LS22 7UD
www.waterbabies.co.uk

You'll find that a Water Babies course is very different to traditional swimming lessons. With the main emphasis on having fun, the course is also highly structured, with a carefully designed, progressive lesson plan for each of the four 10 week courses. Our unique methods will enable your baby to feel at ease swimming both above and below the water's surface, and they'll also learn some water safety techniques along the way. More information is available on www.waterbabies.co.uk

Aqua Zone Swimming   0115 989 2916

www.leisure-centre.com

Baby and toddler swimming at Bingham, Cotgrave, Keyworth and Rushcliffe leisure centres.

parties

Birthdays, for children, are synonymous with parties. And so, whether you like it or not, you will be throwing one for at least the first five years of your child's life. Fear not: here we offer enough tips, ideas and resources to make it a breeze, with listings of party entertainers, cake-makers and sources of party-bag fillers, bouncy castles and themed tableware. If it all gets too much, you can always call in a party organiser, who will take care of the whole event for you!

baby parties

First Birthdays

The first birthday party is a baptism by fire for most first-time parents. Plan to hold it at home with family, a few friends, and not too many competing babies - this is an excuse for grown-ups to shower an angel or urchin with adoration and gorgeous baby gifts. NB Presents should be targeted to delight mum rather than baby, who will invariably find the wrapping paper more interesting. The key to making the party flow is to provide lots of Champagne and food for the grown-ups.

Second and Third Birthdays

A tea party at home with small tables and chairs will ensure that the catering aspect of the party contains itself to one room and not your carpet. A ball pond or a few tunnels will provide plenty of excitement for 2yr olds – but remember to put away toys that you don't want to be played with (especially the favourites or new presents). Party games like "pass the parcel" don't really work at 2yrs – so you can leave that one for another year.

Things begin to get serious by the age of 3. The party needs orchestrating and guests corralling, to avoid tears and tantrums before your party fairy or Spiderman has got as far as cutting the cake. We highly recommend a musical party (see music groups on page X).

You must plan to cater for parents as well – and make it clear whether siblings can come. We recommend that you just invite children from your child's age group otherwise you will find you have older children getting bored and running riot.

Fourth and Fifth Birthdays

If your child attends a nursery or playgroup, then you will find that this becomes a whole class event.

Parents are not expected to stay and you can let them know what time to pick the children up afterwards. You also need space if you want to hold the party at home – so many opt for an indoor activity centre (see toddler activities), or a party venue that has a party programme pre-prepared (see party venues). Themed parties with dressing up are very popular. You can also play traditional party games or try making things (see arts and crafts pg X or cooking pg X).

Party entertainers are in their element with 4-5yr olds. Magic, silly songs, puppets, balloon modelling, bubble machines, face painting, white rabbits, doves, snakes – all delight and entrance;

and such is their popularity you need to book around 6 weeks ahead, particularly during festive seasons such as Christmas. Entertainers normally attend for around 2 hrs with a 45 minute session whilst you are getting the food ready, then another 45 minutes after the meal. What makes a good entertainer? Getting all the children to remain seated, fully engaged and responsive for the whole session – and they're worth every penny.

Tips from the experts:

• Book your entertainer well ahead. If you haven't found a venue locally then many party organisers, such as Twizzle, have a whole range at their fingertips for every postcode. Let them know how many children they are entertaining and what the age range will be.

• Try and orientate parties around your child's natural mealtimes so that everyone has a good appetite. For 2-3yrs they recommend 11-1pm or 12-2pm rather than afternoons, and for 3-5yrs 12.30-2.30pm or 3.30-5.30pm.

• Liaise with other parents if children's birthdays in the same class clash across one weekend.

• Make sure the sweet things aren't on the table before the savoury – and decide whether to put the cake in the party bag or serve it at the table. Ask parents to mention allergies before the day so you can cater accordingly.

• Party bags are becoming ever more sophisticated, but stick to your budget and you'll be surprised how much you can find that delights the under 5s (see party supplies online).

For additional entertainers in other areas of the UK check the www.babydirectory.com website for our recommendations.

bouncy castles

DERBYSHIRE
Abi's Inflatables   **0788 795 0119**
6 Bladen View, Stretton, DE13 0JE
info@abis-inflatables.com

Bouncy Castle Hire Co   **0133 254 4501**
6 Merthyr Court, Oakwood, Derby, DE21 2RJ

LEICESTERSHIRE
Jump and Bumps   **0116 241 5639**
Bouncy Castle
66 Wintersdale Road, Leicester, LE5 2GL

The Factory of Fun   **0116 283 2709**
47 Lutterworth Road, Leicester, LE2 8PH

Abi's Inflatables

Adult and Children's Bouncy Castle and Inflatable Slide Hire.

Art and Craft Parties

Birthday Party Packages
SPECIAL RATES FOR SCHOOL HOLIDAY HIRES.

Kay Bentley

Phone: **07887950119**
E-mail: info@abis-inflatables.com

LINCOLNSHIRE

Aztec Bouncy Castle Hire   0800 043 1225
14 Lincoln Rd, Ruskington, Sleaford, NG34 9AW

Wobbly's Bouncy Castle Hire   0147 6404 790
1 Reedings Close, Barrowby, Grantham, NG32 1AX

NOTTINGHAMSHIRE

Art Leisure   **0115 961 1567**
21 Balmoral Road, Colwick, NG4 2GF
www.artleisure.co.uk

Electric Rainbow   **0115 927 3322**
35 Severn Street, Bulwell, Nottingham, NG6 8LQ
www.electricrainbow.co.uk

Electric Rainbow **0115 927 3322**
35 Severn Street, Bulwell, Nottingham, NG6 8LQ
www.electricrainbow.co.uk

Jack In The Box **0115 913 8431**
50 Westwick Road, Bilborough
Fully insured bouncy castles for party hire, fetes and schools.

party catering

DERBYSHIRE
Chocolate Art **0162 958 1291**
Woodbine Cottage, Riber Road, Starkholmes,
Matlock, DE4 5JB

Delicious Dishes **0128 355 0359**
2 Delph Centre, Market Street, Swadlincote, DE11
9DA

LINCOLNSHIRE
Something Special **0152 252 9885**
45 Rookery Lane, Lincoln, LN6 7PX

NOTTINGHAMSHIRE
A Cake to Celebrate **0772 932 2958**
10 Poplar Avenue, Sherwood, Nottingham, NG5
1DJ

Horspools **0115 981 8307**
22 Tudor Square, West Bridgford, Nottingham, NG2
6BT

party entertainers

Twizzle **020 8789 3232**
www.twizzle.co.uk
Organisers of children's parties from 2yrs+, offering a range
of different activities and themes for small children.

DERBYSHIRE
Buzz Ceramics **0115 875 3664**
Ilkeston
www.buzzceramics.co.uk
Buzz Ceramics is a mobile pottery painting studio; They
come to your party. For children of all ages and in all
locations, it's time to get creative! Party food and drink are
included. Several party packages are available.

Coe Coe the Clown **0133 266 8024**
23 Cleveland Avenue, Chaddesden, Derby, DE21 6SB

Fairy Tales on Strings **0124 655 1170**
4 Alford Close, Brampton, Chesterfield, S40 1YP

LEICESTERSHIRE
Chuckle Chops and Chums **0153 045 7786**
253 Hall Lane, Whitwick, Coalville, LE67 5PH
www.chucklechops.co.uk
Children's Entertainment for all occasions: Birthdays,
Christenings, Weddings, or simply as a special surprise treat!
Taking the pressure off the parents and helping to ensure that

the children have a lot of fun throughout the party, Chuckle
Chops and Chums provide lots and lots of activities including;
balloon modeling, comedy magic, face painting, Santa Claus
and more.

Mr and Mrs Custard **0153 677 1881**
www.bluenose.co.uk
For silly magic, music and games and all sorts of
entertainment that small children love. Mr and Mrs Custard
cover Lincolnshire and Leicestershire.

LINCOLNSHIRE
Olliwiz **0177 842 2094**
89 Kingsway, Bourne, PE10 9DJ
Children's magic shows, Birthday parties and functions for
children 3 - 7 years.

Party's At Yours! **0152 279 2625**
64 Sleaford Rd, Branston, Lincoln, LN4 1LL

NOTTINGHAMSHIRE
Arty Antics **0115 840 1350**
Arty Antics offer an exciting arty experience for girls and boys
aged from 3 years upwards. For more details contact Tania
on 0115 840 1350.

Glitzy Girls Parties **0162 363 3963**
19 Lincoln Drive, Mansfield

Jolly Jingles Funtime **0845 009 0848**
103 Douglas Rd, Long Eaton, Nottingham, NG10 4BE
www.jollyjingles.co.uk

Jollys Face Painting **0115 950 4411**
39 Longbeck Avenue, Mapperley, Nottingham, NG3 6LT

Pogo the Clown **0115 961 1190**
48 Conway Crescent, Carlton, Nottingham, NG4 2PZ
www.pogotheclown.co.uk

party ideas/themes

Murals by Tess Willoughby **0797 278 5469**
www.tesswilloughby.com

party shops

Balloon & Party Ideas **0133 282 4268**
Unit 2 Bio House, Derwent St, Derby, DE1 2ED
Also have a shop in Nottingham (Glasshouse Street) 0115
924 2345.

party supplies

Party Ark **0153 677 2523**
www.partyark.co.uk
Party Ark is a family-run business designed to make party
shopping easier for parents. From traditional pirate and fairy
themes to the latest film, television and book characters,
Party Ark offers parents an ever-expanding range of party
tableware, gifts and accessories for children between 0-
10yrs.

party venues

DERBYSHIRE

Bumpi's Big Adventure   **01332 204 292**

Goodward Park, Derby, DE24 8GW
www.bumpi.co.uk
There's a warm welcome at Bumpi's play and party centres at Derby and Leicester, plus a free coffee term time when you come before 11am*. Tuesday or Thursday morning term time we'll keep your little treasures occupied with busy bambino activities specially planned by a qualified member of our friendly team – while you relax with a real Italian coffee! If your little one is still a baby...bring them along....there's a baby ball pit and soft play – plus you'll love our Blue Cloud Café. Don't forget to bring your older ones too; our frame is 3 story's high -lots of fun. Max height 4ft 9ins. We'd love to see you! *some conditions apply.

Cats Whiskers   **0145 785 5552**

Units 3 & 4, Surrey Street, Glossop, SK13 7AJ

Chucklebutties Play Centre   **01773 880 123**

Riverside Suite, Belper Mills, Bridgefoot, Belper, DE56 1YD

Crazy Crocodiles   **0115 944 1555**

Abbey Street, Ilkeston, DE7 8DN
www.crazycrocodiles.co.uk
All year round indoor adventure play centre for children 0-10yrs.

Easy Tigers   **01246 260 011**

Nurture House, Dunston Trading Estate, Foxwood Road, Chesterfield, S41 9RF
www.easytigers.co.uk
Easy Tigers™ are committed to providing the highest quality play environment for your children, whilst ensuring that your needs as a parent are met. Our play areas are designed to provide the maximum fun, with the highest visibility for parents to be able to supervise their child. Open 7 days a week 9.30am until 6.30pm; enjoy one of our Parent and Toddler sessions exclusive to the under 5's, Monday, Wednesday and Fridays mornings (9.30am until 12pm (term-time only)). Experience a wonderful party, planned, organised and delivered with both your child and you in mind. Book early to avoid disappointment.

Freddy's Play Kingdom   **01332 662 322**

50 Nottingham Road, Spondon, Derby, DE21 7NL
www.freddythedragon.co.uk
Children's activity play centre. Discos and parties catered for - cafeteria service food and drink.

Hudy's Play Barn   **01283 732 083**

High Street, Woodville, Swadlincote, DE11 7EH

Pirates Play Island   **01332 875 000**

44 Derby Road, Draycott, DE72 3NJ

Planet Happy   **01773 748 600**

Heague Road Ind Estate, Ripley, DE5 3GH

Smilee Faces 01283 563 999
Hawkins Lane, Burton-on-Trent, DE14 1PT

The Cats Whiskers Playhouse 01457 855 552
Units 3, & 4 Surrey St, Glossop, SK13 7AH

Tubby Bear's Play Den 0133 234 1355
Carrington Court, Great Northern Road, Derby, DE1 1LR
www.tubbybears.co.uk
At Tubby Bear's Play Den, parties are our speciality! There's lots for the children to do, they'll love our slides, ball pools and our large play frame. Let us organise your party for you! All of our party packages include; invitations, a dedicated host, reserved tables at our cafe and exclusive use of our fantastic party room. We are located at the rear of Carrington Court on Great North Road. Opening times Mon 10am-4pm, Tues-Sat 10am-6pm and Sun and Bank Holidays 10am-4pm.

LEICESTERSHIRE

Bumpi's Big Adventure 0116 282 5822
Meridian Leisure Park, Braunstone
www.bumpi.co.uk
There's a warm welcome at Bumpi's play and party centres at Derby and Leicester, plus a free coffee term time when you come before 11am*. Tuesday or Thursday morning term time we'll keep your little treasures occupied with busy bambino activities specially planned by a qualified member of our friendly team – while you relax with a real Italian coffee! If your little one is still a baby...bring them along....there's a baby ball pit and soft play – plus you'll love our Blue Cloud Café. Don't forget to bring your older ones too; our frame is 3 story's high -lots of fun. Max height 4ft 9ins. We'd love to see you! *some conditions apply

Braunstone Adventure Play 0116 291 9700
8 Cort Crescent, Braunstone, Leicester, LE3 1QZ

LINCOLNSHIRE

Captain Kids Adventure World 01754 760 600
Skegness Pier, Grand Parade, Skegness, PE25 2UE
Open every day of the week from 10am – 7pm in the winter and 10am-10pm in the summer. There is a special area for under fours. Sign up for a toddler group on Wednesdays.

Crazee Bongos 01529 410 808
Unit 4, Sellwood Court, Sleaford Enterprise Park, East Road, Sleaford, NG34 7EH
Take the kids along to Crazee Bongos for all-weather fun. They have a soft play area for under 5s and a separate area for 5-12 year olds. There is a café and they do Birthday parties. Open Tue-Sun 10am-6pm.

JJ's Playmania 01427 677 974
Middlefield Lane, Gainsborough, DN21 1UU
www.playmania.co.uk
Soft play for the under fives. Mother and toddler mornings are held on Tuesday, Wednesday and Thursday mornings from 10am –12 noon with cheaper entry and free drinks!

Kids Adventure World 01507 477 310
High Street, Spanish City, Mablethorpe, LN12 1AD
This indoor play centre is open on weekends and school holidays and has a soft play area for the under 5s. Food and drinks are available in the café.

Lets Play 01778 425 444
Station Yard, South Road, Bourne PE10 9LU
There is something for everyone here; soft play area for the under 3s, pirate ship for older children and a café for the parents. Open Mon-Sat 9.30- 6pm and 10am-6pm on Sundays, the café is open until 4.30.

Lincoln Toy Library 01522 546 215
Withham Park, Waterside South, Lincoln, LN5 7JN
As well as the toy library there is a soft play area and an under 1's play area. There is coffee and tea available and they have a picnic room for those who want to bring their own lunch. Open Tue to Fri 10.30am-3pm, Sat 10am- 1pm. Second Saturday of each month is reserved for a special needs afternoon.

Playzone Lincoln 01522 539 999
The Old Gymnasium, Cross St, Lincoln LN5 7LF
Parent and toddlers' specials are offered Mon-Fri 10am-1.30pm (Tuesday 11am- 1.30pm). There is a soft play area for the under fours and a separate area for the over 4s which can be used by toddles if accompanied by a parent. While the children are amusing themselves, you can relax in the café or seating area. They also do Birthday parties. Open all week 10am-7.15pm.

Fun Farm 01476 562 228
Dysart Road, Grantham, NG31 7LE
The Fun Farm has both and indoor and outdoor play area and an area for under 4s. Open all week 10am-6pm.

Fun Farm 01406 373 444
High Road, Weston, Spalding PE12 6JU
www.funfarm.co.uk
The outdoor play area, indoor soft play area and dedicated under 5's area are all free for children under 1 and adults! They do Birthday parties and have full maternity and disabled facilities, a café, a licenced bar and a gift shop. They also do tenpin bowling and laser tags. Open all week 10am- 6pm.

Funtasia Fun House 01522 695 553
Stephenson Road, North Hykeham Technology Park, North Hykeham, Lincoln LN6 3QU
The fun never stops in the Funtasia Fun House, let them run riot in the toddler only play area with slides and a ball pool. Tots and toddlers get cheaper sessions during term time during the week from 10am- 3pm, this includes free drinks for children and parents. There is a café selling hot and cold food. Birthday parties. Open Mon-Fri 10am-6.30pm, Sat 10.30am-7pm and Sun 11am-5pm.

Rascals the Fun Factor 01778 480 610
Unit 2, West Street, Stamford, PE9 2PR
Come and join in the fun at the Fun Factory soft play centre, there is a section for the under 2's. There is a café and a

parking area. Discounts are offered for groups of 10 or more children. Open Mon-Fri 10am- 5.30pm and Sat 10.30am-4.30pm.

The Play Barn   **01775 766 393**
Springfield Outlet Centre, Camel Gate, PE12 6ET
www.springfieldshopping.co.uk
The Play Barn offers both an outdoor play area with mini golf, mechanical diggers, bumper cars and a remote control boat on a lake, and an indoor soft play barn with a toddler area. There is a café and an eating area. Open 10am-6pm.

NOTTINGHAMSHIRE
Cotgrave Leisure Centre   **0115 989 2916**
Woodview, Cotgrave, NG12 3PJ
www.leisure-centre.com
Kids parties and activities.

Denz Children's   **0115 925 5007**
Play Centre
131 Queens Road, Beeston, NG9 2FE
www.denz.ltd.uk
Looking for somewhere to take the kids for a couple of hours or longer, then why not try Denz's Indoor play centre? While the children let off steam on the four level play frame you can enjoy a cup of coffee and a bite to eat or if you want something more substantial try one of our reasonably priced, freshly prepared meals. We are open 7 days a week from 9.30am to 6.00pm so just pop along when you want, no need to book. We can also arrange your child's party in one of our private themed rooms.

Hoods Hideout   **0115 915 1575**
Beechdale Swimming Centre, Billborough, NG8 3LL
Nottingham City Council
If you are looking for a opportunity to take a deep breathe whilst your child is entertained by toddler climbing frames and colourball pits then this could be a good port of call. A relaxed and friendly atmosphere that just enables you to drop by for an hour or two and allows the children to work off some steam. Throughout the holidays the Hideout is open from 10 am all day.

Kool Kids Indoor Adventure   **0115 950 0125**
Play Centre
Carlton Road, Nottingham, NG3 2NR
Indoor fun and adventure including a ball crawl, soft play ground, bouncy castle and snooker tables. A great way to tire out energetic kids big and small, and when they get hungry there is food available in the café. Also does Birthday parties.

Lanky Bill's Fun Shack   **01773 767 050**
Unit 6, Cromford Road Industrial Estate,
Nottingham, NG16 4FL
www.lankybills.com
At Lanky Bill's Fun Shack we cater for children from 6 months to 11 years. We have a large main frame and soft play for the 4's and under. We offer three party rooms and during term time Parent and Toddler Groups. Ofsted registered childcare; Holiday club, After-school Club. Home cooked meals and qualified staff all creates a friendly environment in which to spend a few hours and let off some steam. Please contact us for further information.

Playland   **01623 654 712**
Unit 1a Botany Commercial Park, Botany Avenue, Mansfield, NG18 5NF

Party Mania   **0115 923 4921**
Rushcliffe Leisure Centre, Boundary Road, West Bridgford, Nottingham, NG2 7BY
(see advert above for listings)

Run Riot   **0115 981 4027**
Rugby Road, West Bridgeford, Nottingham, NG2 7HY
www.rushcliffe.gov.uk

The White Post Farm Centre   **01623 882 977**
Mansfield Road, Farnsfield, NG22 8HL
www.whitepostfarmcentre.co.uk
The White Post Farm is a popular tourist attraction 12 miles north of Nottingham. Open every single day of the year, there is something for everyone; a truly hands on experience. Daily events include baby animal holding, meet-a-reptile, baby goat bottle-feeding, as well as acres of animals to stroll around, feeding a variety of breeds. With special seasonal events throughout the year, every visit is different. PLUS Farm shop full of fresh local produce and Pet Centre with everything you need for a happy, healthy pet.

Wonderland Park   **01623 882 773**
White Post, Farnsfield, Newark, NG22 8HX
www.wonderlandpleasurepark.com

days out

Youngsters in the East Midlands are brought up to the great outdoors, with fertile fields and some of England's finest forests. But for those who prefer their nature tamed, there are farms, country houses, zoos and theme parks to visit. Information and inspiration for fun days out can be found in this section.

castles

DERBYSHIRE
Bolsover Castle   **0124 682 2844**
Nr Chesterfield, S44 6PR
www.english-heritage.org.uk
Set on a hilltop overlooking the Vale of Scarsdale, Bolsover
Castle enjoys panoramic views over the beautiful Derbyshire
countryside. Children can learn about the fairy tale castle,
made easy by the colouring in and activity sheets provided.
Outside in the grounds the ruined terrace is perfect for a
game of 'hide and seek' and there is lots of green space for
them to charge around. You will find even more activities in
the Discovery Centre; audio-visual displays and the re-
created 'Little Castle' for the little ones! On a warm day the
grounds make an excellent place for a picnic or, pop into the
cafe where you will find a variety of sandwiches, soups and
light bites and the 'Little Squires' box for your little Squire's
lunch. There are baby-changing facilities provided and a
parking area. The castle is located 6 miles east of
Chesterfield on the A632, off the M1 at junction 29
(signposted.) Open daily from May-September, 10am-6pm.
Closed on Tuesdays and Wednesdays in the winter and
24th-26th of Dec and 1st Jan.

LEICESTERSHIRE
Belvoir Castle   **01476 871 002**
Belvoir, NG32 1PE
www.belvoircastle.com
The castle, home to the Duke and Duchess of Rutland, sits
on a hilltop commanding stunning views over the Vale of
Belvoir. As well as the magical castle there are beautiful,
green gardens to explore. During the opening season,
(check the website or call for dates) events take place every
weekend, including Medieval jousting, teddy bears picnics,
family days, Morris dancing and open air concerts and
theatre. Open 11am - 5pm (last entry 4pm) Saturdays 11am
- 4pm (last entry 3pm.)

LINCOLNSHIRE
Lincoln Castle   **01522 511 068**
Castle Hill, Lincoln, LN1 3AA
www.lincolnshire.gov.uk/castle
Built by William the Conqueror in 1068, Lincolnshire Castle is
an imposing structure that has in the past been a court and a
prison with many being executed on the ramparts! Every
year Lincoln Castle presents a full and varied events program,
(usually runs from April to the end of August.) Expect to be
entertained by medieval jousting, historical re-enactments
and children's fun days. There is a cafe, a picnic area and a
car park. Open throughout the year (closes for Christmas
and New Year.) Mon - Sat, 9.30am to 5.30pm, Sun,
11.00am to 5.30pm.

NOTTINGHAMSHIRE
Nottingham Castle   **0115 915 3700**
Off Maid Marion Way, Nottingham, NG1 6EL
This magnificent 17th century ducal mansion built on the site
of the original Medieval Castle boasts spectacular views
across the city. The cave tours of the passageways tell the

story of Nottingham. The castle is a great place for children,
with interactive displays, and an activity-led gallery
(specifically for the under 5s) that brings paintings to life.
There is also a medieval - style playground in the grounds
and a covered picnic area. Just 10 minutes walk from the
centre or, if you're in the car, there is parking nearby. Mon to
Sun, March-Sept 10.00am-5.00pm, last admissions 4.30pm.
Oct-Feb 11.00am-4.00pm last admission 3.30pm.

cinemas

DERBYSHIRE
Metro Cinema   **01332 347 765**
Green Lane, Derby, DE1 1SA

Showcase Cinema   **0871 220 1000**
Osmaston Park Road, Derby, DE23 8AG
www.showcasecinemas.co.uk

UCI-United Cinemas   **0871 224 4007**
The Meteor Centre, Mansfield Rd, Derby, DE21 4SY

LEICESTERSHIRE
City Cinema   **0116 251 9699**
27 Abbey Street, Leicester

Odeon Leicester   **0871 224 4007**
90 Aylestone Rd, Leicester, LE2 7LB

Piccadilly Leicester   **0116 251 8880**
2 Green Lane Road, Evington, Leicester,LE5 3TP

Reel Cinema   **01509 212 261**
Cattle Market, Loughborough, LE11 3DL
www.reelcinemas.co.uk

LINCOLNSHIRE
Boston West End   **01205 363 634**
West Street, Boston, Lincolnshire, PE21 8QH
www.savoycinemas.co.uk/bosto

Odeon Lincoln   **0871 224 4007**
Brayford Wharf North, Lincoln, LN1 1YW

Tower Cinema   **01754 763 938**
111 Lumley Rd, Skegness, PE25 3LZ

NOTTINGHAMSHIRE
Savoy Nottingham   **0115 9475812**
Derby Road, Nottingham, NG7 1QN
www.savoycinemas.co.uk/notts

Showcase Cinema   **0871 220 1000**
Redfield Way, Nottingham, NG7 2UW

The Corner House   **0115 950 5168**
Burton Street, Nottingham, NG1 4DB
www.cornerhouse.tv
The Cornerhouse is a major leisure complex in Nottingham.
Cinema, restaurants, hair and beauty salons, shops - and
with a Cornerhouse card you get fantastic discounts.

farms

DERBYSHIRE

Chatsworth Farmyard & **01246 583 139**
Adventure Playground
Chatsworth Estate, Nr Bakewell, DE45 1PP
www.chatsworth.org
Chatsworth House is a stunning family home. Set in a 105 acre garden and vast grounds there is a lot for the children to see and do. On a warm day they can explore the maze or paddle in the cascade. The farmyard will be popular with the little ones with its wide variety of animals and their babies! There are milking demonstrations and daily animal handling sessions at the farm while in the woodland playground the more adventurous can test their skill on the towers, ropewalks and spiral slides. Look out for seasonal displays and activities including; new life weeks, rural skills week, harvest week and Christmas Nativity weeks from mid November. If you visit the farmyard in December you will get the chance to see wonderful family nativity plays in the barn. Chatsworth is open every day until the 23rd Dec 2007; it re-opens on the 12th March 2008. Under 5's are admitted free of charge to the house and garden, and under 3's to the farmyard and playground.

LEICESTERSHIRE

Stonehurst Farm and Museum **01509 413 216**
Bond Lane, Mountsorrel, LE12 7AR
www.stonehurstfarm.co.uk
Stonehurst is a working farm and a great place to bring the family. Once they have made friends with the farmyard animals, the kids can have a ride on the tractor and trailer. Also on offer are pony rides and both indoor and outdoor play areas. You can stock up on home grown, free range and organic farm produce here too. For older children there is a Motor Museum. The "Farmers Den" teashop serves homemade cakes, cream teas, hot food and light lunches (all made with home-grown produce.) Open daily all year round, 9.30am - 5.00pm, closed 25th Dec through to 2nd Jan.

Manor Farm **01509 852525**
Animal Centre
Castle Hill, Loughborough, LE12 6LU
www.manorfarm.info
Manor farm is a beautiful animal rescue centre with donkey paddocks, pond dipping and nature trails. The centre offers rides on converted milk floats through the park as well as donkey rides. Young children have a special indoor soft play facility, activity room and dressing up boxes in the pirate ship. There is also an indoor play barn and an outdoor playground with live willow structures. Children can get involved with feeding the ducks, Teddy Bear picnics or animal bedtime. Open 10am-4pm weekdays and winter and 10am-5pm weekends and summer.

LINCOLNSHIRE
Hardys Animal Farm   **01522 694 353**
Anchor Lane, Ingoldmells, Skegness, PE25 1LZ
Hardy's Animal Farm offers an interesting and fun way to view a modern-day farm at work and is a great way to learn about the history and traditions of the countryside. There are plenty of animals for the children to meet including; sheep, cattle, goats, ducks, chicks and hens. They can watch the pigs and piglets through a specially glazed viewing area. Then while the children are letting off steam in the adventure playground, you can enjoy a drink in the tearoom (also serves meals.) Opens at Easter until the beginning of October, 10am to 6pm daily.

NOTTINGHAMSHIRE
Ferry Farm Country Farm   **0115 966 4512**
Boat Lane, Hoveringham, NG14 7JP
www.ferryfarm.co.uk
Ferry Farm is a purpose-built farm centre for children. The farm stands in extensive fields in Hoveringham and is attached to a working farm. There is plenty to keep them entertained here; tractor rides and the indoor and outdoor play centers. There is always a variety of animals for the children to handle and, depending on the season, they may be lucky enough to cuddle the piglets and baby rabbits. The farm has a small restaurant serving home cooked meals for both adults and children. Open during the wintertime Thurs - Sun, October until the 18th of December then, 5th of Feb until the 2nd of April. Between the 4th of April and the 1st of October the farm is open daily. Closed Mondays except Bank Holidays and now open on Mondays in holidays. Open half-term holidays in October and Feb. Opening hours are 10.00am to 5.30pm.

Sherwood Forest Farm Park   **01623 823 558**
Lamb Pens Farm, Edwinstowe, Mansfield, NG21 9HL
www.sherwoodforestfarmpark.co.uk
Sherwood Forest Farm Park is a centre approved by the Rare Breeds Survival Trust for the breeding of rare and protected farm animals. There are over 40 breeds of animal in the park, which is also home to a few more unusual additions; exotic birds, wallabies, water buffalo, and some very cute Kune Kune pigs. Once the children have met the animals you can relax in the beautiful water gardens. The tea-room serves locally-baked cakes, light snacks and ice creams. Open April - Oct inclusive, daily from 10.30am to 5.15pm.

The White Post Farm Centre 01623 882 977
Mansfield Road, Farnsfield, NG22 8HL
www.whitepostfarmcentre.co.uk
The White Post Farm is a popular tourist attraction 12 miles north of Nottingham. Open every single day of the year, there is something for everyone; a truly hands on experience. Daily events include baby animal holding, meet-a-reptile, baby goat bottle-feeding, as well as acres for animals to stroll around, feeding a variety of breeds. With special seasonal events throughout the year, every visit is different. PLUS Farm Shop full of fresh local produce and Pet Centre with everything you need for a happy, healthy pet.

ice rinks
National Ice Centre   **0870 120 0332**
Bolero Square, The Lace Market, Nottingham, NG1 1LA
www.national-ice-centre.com
If you're looking for a new and healthy activity for your toddler why not consider a session on skates? From 18mths-5yrs toddlers can take to the ice under the care of expert coaches, lots of toys and huge encouragement. Learning balance and co-ordination as well as taking lots of exercise sounds like fun. Parents can enjoy a peaceful coffee in the T&D Cafe Bar or you can join in and skate yourself. If you run a parent and toddler group, get in touch with Matt Bradbury (Tel: 0115 853 3064) who can provide a mini-bus to collect and return up to 14 people for just £5 per toddler/parent. There is also Christmas skating in Nottingham's Old Market Square from 21st Nov-13thJan.

museums
NOTTINGHAMSHIRE
Denby Pottery Visitor's Centre 01773 740 799
Denby, Ripley, DE5 8NX
www.denbyvisitorcentre.co.uk
Craftroom tours (available daily) are suitable for all ages and include paint a plate and make a frog. Or, you can watch traditional glass making methods on a Glass Studio Tour (Monday to Fridays). Children's Party Tours, for children 4-10 years are available throughout the year. There are also hand and footprint days where you can capture your baby's prints on a Denby plate along with the message of your choice. For details of the above and special events see the website What's On page. Denby has a small museum, shops, restaurant and coffee shop, outdoor play area and picnic benches.

LEICESTERSHIRE
National Space Centre   **0870 607 7223**
Exploration Drive, Leicester, LE4 5NS
www.spacecentre.co.uk
The National Space Centre is the UK's largest attraction dedicated to space. Bring the children along to see amazing space rockets, satellites and capsules and to take part in hundreds of interactive hands-on activities. Open 10.00am to 5.00pm (last entry 3.30pm.) Closed on Mondays.

NOTTINGHAMSHIRE

City of Caves   0115 952 0555
126 Broadmarsh Centre, Nottingham, NG1 7LN
www.cityofcaves.com
Located beneath the bustling city streets you will find this unique labyrinth of man made caves, there are over 400 in total! At The Caves of Nottingham you get the chance to explore them and experience the medieval tannery, air raid shelter and a Victorian slum. You and the kids can experience the city's past in an exciting and interactive way and watch history come to life. Opening Times: Monday - Friday 11.30am to 4.30pm. Sat / Sun 10.30am to 4.30pm. Last admission 30 minutes prior to closing time.

Green's Windmill and Science   0115 915 6878
Centre
Windmill Lane, Sneinton, Nottingham, NG10 1BQ
www.greensmill.org.uk
This windmill was once home to George Green who made important discoveries about electricity, light and magnetism. If you take a tour the windmill, you will see grain turn into flour. There are a few hands-on activities for the children and an under fives soft play area. There is no cafe so bring supplies. The organic flour produced in the windmill is available to buy in the shop. See website for details on children's activities; baking, jewelry making, play dough and drawing (all for 3+.) Open Wed-Sun, 10am-4pm.

Museum of Nottingham Life   0115 915 3600
Castle Boulevard, Nottingham, NG7 1FB
www.nottinghamcity.gov.uk/museums
Go back in time and experience everyday life in Nottingham. There are plenty of hands-on activities for the little ones, they can have a go at pumping water, sit at a desk in a Victorian classroom, root through kitchen cupboards and visit the wartime air raid shelter in the caves. Open daily 10am-4.30, last admission is at 4pm.

The Tales of Robin Hood   0115 948 3284
30-38 Maid Marion Way, Nottingham, NG1 6GF
www.robinhood.uk.com
The Tales of Robin Hood is a fun and creative indoor environment designed specifically for young children. Little outlaws will enjoy the sight and smells of medieval Nottingham, which they can experience through the exciting adventure ride. Kids activities include; falconry displays, brass rubbing and archery. Ideal for a half-day outing or a great location for children's birthday parties. Open daily, 10am-5.30 in the summer, 10am-5pm in the winter. Last admission is 90 minutes before closing. Closed on the 24th, 25th and 26th of Dec.

nature reserves

LINCOLNSHIRE
Natural World Centre   01522 688 868
Whisby Nature Park, Moor Lane, Thorpe-on-the-Hill, LN6 9BW
www.naturalworldcentre.com
This man-made Nature Park is managed by the Lincolnshire Wildlife Trust. The park, woods, lakes and wetlands are a haven for wildlife. Come and enjoy one of the many walks in the countryside along the marked footpaths. Arts and crafts workshops are provided for children during the school holidays. The Boardwalk Cafe serves up a variety of foods with a distinct local flavour. The cafe is baby-friendly offering children's options and high chairs for toddlers. There are baby changing facilities in all the toilets. They also provide a baby food warming area in the cafe, along with a child's play area with comfortable seating. Winter opening hours (Oct-Feb): Weekdays 10am-4.30pm, weekends 10am-5pm. School holidays (Feb-Oct): Daily 10am-5pm, summer opening hours (Feb-Oct): Daily 10am-5pm.

Woodside Falconry and   01522 754 280
Conservation Centre
Newball, Near Langworth, Lincoln, LN3 5DQ
www.woodsidefalconry.com
Discover the mystical world of the birds of prey. Come and watch the magnificent birds fly and feed. Also to keep the kids entertained there are a wealth of activities on offer; pig and ferret racing, fun fishing, a butterfly house, reptile handling and conservation walks. Light refreshments in the form of homemade cakes, tea and coffee, soup and a roll, and sandwiches are served throughout the day in the cafe. Open 10am-5.30pm, from the beginning of February half term to end October half term.

NOTTINGHAMSHIRE

Attenborough Nature Centre   **0115 9721777**
Chilwell, Nottingham, NG9 6DY
www.attenboroughnaturecentre.co.uk
The Attenborough Nature Centre is a haven for wildlife. Built in an old quarry, it offers woods, meadows, lakes and twisting pathways to wander down and explore. There are monthly tiny tots sessions with games, activities and crafts, as well as a Wild Kids group. (Book ahead for both of these.) Nursery groups use the facilities for educational sessions and during the holidays there is a club for 4+ year olds. Open 10am-5pm.

outings

DERBYSHIRE

John Nike Leisure Sport   **01283 217 200**
Hill Street, Swadlincote, DE11 8LB
www.jnll.co.uk
For fantastic value skiing, snowboarding and a great place for the kids to experience the excitement of snow sports in a safe environment. If you want to introduce your youngster to the delights of snow and skiing, tots lessons for budding skiers are offered on Saturday morning at 10.30. The more adventurous parent/toddler teams can have a go at tobogganing. Booking required. Catering facilities overlook the slopes and offer a wide choice of popular foods.

NOTTINGHAMSHIRE

Jumicar   **0115 9669000**
www.jumicar.co.uk
Designed to improve concentration and co-ordination in a fun outdoor environment. Jumicar offers children the chance to drive amidst traffic lights, signs and signals whilst learning about the rules of the road. The track is supervised by enthusiastic teachers who make the experience both fun and educational and is ideal for parties or individual sessions. No need to book. Open daily in school holidays 10am-6pm. Open weekends during term time 10.30am-5pm. Close 24th, 25th and 26th of Dec and the whole of January.

parks and gardens

DERBYSHIRE

Ilam Park   **01335 350 503**
Ilam, Ashbourne, DE6 2AZ
www.nationaltrust.org.uk
This beautiful area of open park and woodland runs along both banks of the river Manifold offering spectacular views of the countryside towards Dovedale. The park has baby changing and feeding facilities; pushchairs and baby back-carriers are admitted. Children can enjoy their own guide and quiz/trail. The tearoom has a children's menu. The park is open all year round however the tearoom is closed on weekdays in the winter.

LEICESTERSHIRE

Bradgate Country Park   **0116 2362713**
Newtown Linford, Leicester, LE8 5UA
If you are looking for a place to enjoy a picnic and for the

children to play in the great outdoors then this beautiful country park that offers twisting pathways through bracken and the peace and quiet of nature could be ideal. With small streams and great picnicking spots, it's a lovely place for the children to see wildlife in its natural environment and for you to enjoy some time away from all the hustle and bustle. Open daily, dawn 'till dusk.

LINCOLNSHIRE

Hartsholme Country Park   **01522 873577**
Skellingthorpe Road, Lincoln, LN6 0EY
Beautiful Victorian landscaped gardens surrounding a large reservoir, woodlands and grasslands. There are children's activities on offer as well as the children's play area. Both picnic areas and cafe are available as are public toilets and a handy car park.

NOTTINGHAMSHIRE

Rushcliffe Country Park   **0115 921 5865**
Mere Way, Ruddington, Nottingham, NG11 6JS
Set in the beautiful south Nottinghamshire countryside and only half a mile south of Ruddington, Rushcliffe Country Park is an ideal place to get away from it all. With a network of over 8 kilometres of footpaths, conservation and landscaped areas, the park is excellent for walking and spotting wildlife. Bring a picnic and encourage your children to let off steam by visiting the extensive play area, which has some 20 pieces of modern and exciting equipment.

bambinos

- additive-free bambino menu, only £3.50 (*two courses + a pomegranate juice*)
- free balloon, colouring book + crayons
- electric door access for pushchairs
- baby changing facilities
- 15+ highchairs
- private room + enclosed, safe patio area for parties
- mother + baby groups welcome
- bambinos bedtime 8pm

fire&ice

www.fireandicewb.co.uk
40 Bridgford Road | West Bridgford | Nottingham | NG2 6AP | 981 9000 | bambinos@fireandicewb.co.uk

---

Bestwood Country Park   0115 9273674
Alexandra Lodge, Bestwood Village, NG6 8UF
Set amidst 700 acres of woods, grassland and lakes, Bestwood Country Park offers a relaxing day out for the whole family. Whether you want to feed the ducks, see local wildlife or just stroll amongst the tress it's a great place to bring the children. Look out for teddy bear picnics and toddler waddles through the year. Open daily (10am-5pm) in all winds and weathers. Has its own parking facilities.

Wollaton Hall and Park   0115 915 3900
Wollaton, Nottingham, NG8 2AE
www.wollatonhall.org.uk
Wollaton Hall is a spectacular Tudor building set in 500 acres of park and grazing deer. The Natural History Museum within the hall has lots for children to do. Meet George the Gorilla, hissing cockroaches and creatures from days gone by, then venture out to the playground. The hall, industrial museum and yard gallery are open from 11am to 5pm every day while the park gates open at 8am (9am on weekends) and close at 7.30pm. There is a car park.

restaurants and cafés

Pizza Express   08453 899 489
www.pizzaexpress.com
Derby Tel 0133 234 9718; Leicester Tel 0116 254 4144; Lincoln Tel 0152 254 4701; Newark Tel 0163 670 3073; NottinghamTel 0115 912 7888; Stamford   Tel 0178 076 7902; West Bridgford Tel 0178 076 7902.

Fire and Ice   0115 982 0166
40 Bridgford Road, West Bridgford, NG2 6AP
Fire and Ice is stylish and ambient. Its Mediterranean dishes are made with freshly prepared, locally supplied organic food cooked in Nottingham's only traditional wood fired Italian oven. The kids menu (served until 7pm) offers a choice of meals including; lasagne, pizza, chargrilled chicken and cottage pie. The kitchen is open and the chefs will keep the children entertained by flamboyantly tossing and juggling the pizzas.

John Lewis   0115 941 8282
Victoria Centre, Nottingham, NG1 3QA
Healthy, value-for-money options for children. Free jars of food for baby. Hot and cold healthy options available. Highchairs and booster seats available. Practical, comfortable surroundings with easy access. Also mother and baby rooms.

Yummy Mummy's Coffee Shop   01636 815 597
10 Queen St, Southwell, Nottingham, NG25 0AA
www.yummymummyscoffeeshops.com
Yummy Mummy's is the product of one exhausted Mother of three's over active imagination. Having given up a successful career in PR and demobbed from the Big Smoke to greener pastures back home in the East Midlands; Charlotte quickly discovered a large gap in the local Market. Where can I get my fix of a really great Cappuccino NOW, and can I bring the kids? The answer to those questions was of course the birth

Come and join the Yummy Mummy's Revolution at the most exciting and innovative new child friendly coffee shop in the Midlands....We have created a family friendly space with 21st Century comforts inc.

Buggy Park, Toilet and baby changing facilities (unisex for dads!)
The Trademark Yummy Mummy's Mini Diner for Pre-Schoolers, Wooden toys Mini Library, Colouring Activities, Themed Children's Events/Seasonal Events/Story Telling, 100% Organic Baby & Children's Menus, Digital TV, Organic Lunches & Teas to go.

All Yummy Mummy's food will be available to eat in or take away in 100% biodegradable packaging, all our cups, bags and take out paper products are biodegradable and recycled.

Our fully trained Baristas (nominated recently for a top National Beverage Association Award) will make you any coffee you like how you like it using only the best freshly roasted organic, fairtrade and Rainforest Alliance beans available in the UK today.

We have a wide range of organic and fairtrade teas, gluten and nut free products, super fresh juices and funky immune boosting smoothies powered by amazing ingredients, white and dark hot chocolate with organic marshmallows, freshly made all natural milkshakes - in fact too much to tell you about here! So why not come along and see us for yourselves - yes we really are that good & if you bring this advertisement with you we will knock 10% off your bill

Wi-fi/Hi-Fi/Air Con/TV/Music/Sunday Brunch Coming Soon/Outside Catering/Kids Parties

Charlotte Bond
Founder, Owner of Yummy Mummy Coffee Shops (Mother of 3)
Autumn 2007.

real coffee . real people . real passion .

Yummy Mummy's Coffee Shop . 10 Queen Street . Southwell . NG25 0AA .
Tel: 01636 815597
Opening : Monday to Friday 08.30 - 5.30. Saturday: 09.00 - 5.00
lottebond@hotmail.com   www.yummymummyscoffeeshops.com

of Yummy Mummy's Coffee Shop. Too unique to do justice to in 100 words here, you'll just have to come and see for yourself!

theatres

DERBYSHIRE

Derby Playhouse   **01332 363 271**
15 Theatre Walk, Eagle Centre, Derby, DE1 2NF
www.derbyplayhouse.co.uk
The theatre runs Playhouse Kids, a theatre group for the under 9s. It offers training in acting, singing and performance skills in its Saturday morning sessions that are led by professional tutors. These sessions really are very popular and children may have to go on a waiting list.

LEICESTERSHIRE

The Leicester Haymarket   **0116 253 0021**
Suite 1A Rutland Centre, 56 Halford Street, Leicester, LE1 1TQ
www.lhtheatre.co.uk

LINCOLNSHIRE

Theatre Royal   **01522 519 999**
Clasketgate, Lincoln, LN2 1JJ
www.theatreroyallincoln.com
Showing Peter Pan from Fri 14th December 2007 until 20th Jan 2008. It's a spectacular show, full of music, magic and mayhem, it is the perfect treat for all the family! The theatre runs a theatre school for budding actors (5+) at weekends, see website for details.

NOTTINGHAMSHIRE

Lakeside Arts Centre   **0115 8467777**
University Park, Nottingham, NG7 2RD
www.lakesidearts.org.uk
Set in a quiet park next to a lake teaming with birds, Lakeside arts Centre is a modern oasis with both a theatre and a gallery. Particularly suited to young Children, their Tiny Fingers and Tiny Toes theatre sessions are very popular as well as the numerous performances aimed at young audiences. June sees the annual International Children's festival for Theatre and Dance where children are invited to participate as well as watch. Booking is required and the Box office is open daily.

Nottingham Arena   **0115 853 3000**
Bolero Square, The Lace Market, Nottingham, NG1 1LA
www.nottingham-arena.com
Shows for the even the smallest of tots including CBeebies Live and Mickey and Minnie in Disney On Ice (see website for details.)

Nottingham Playhouse   **0115 941 9419**
Wellington Circus, Nottingham, NG1 5AF
www.nottinghamplayhouse.co.uk
Cultural and intellectual it may be sometimes considered, but here it is also for the under 8's. The Nottingham Theatre Saturday Club has productions from Krazy kats and Non Sense theatre and is both interactive and stage based

forming the basis of a stimulating and exciting activity for your little ones. Two performances every Saturday morning at 11am and 1pm, booking essential.

Theatre Royal   **0115 989 5555**
The Royal Centre, Theatre Square, Nottingham, NG1 5ND
www.royalcentre-nottingham.co.uk
A hot bed of creative interpretation and imaginative wanderings, the Theatre Royal is moving through the new season with a sprinkle of this and a dash of that. The theatre plays host to a number of family friendly shows throughout the calendar including (of course) the annual festive pantomime, as well as ballet, adaptations of best-selling children's books and children's entertainers and children's TV favourites. Upcoming shows include: Peter Pan (Fri 7th Dec 2007 - Sun 20th Jan 2008) and Lazy town, a show packed with action, energy and a powerful message that will energise and inspire children everywhere (Sat 16th - Sun 17th Feb 2008.)

theme parks

The following attractions have amusements especially geared for young children. Check out their membership packages if you plan to visit frequently.

Drayton Manor Park   **08708 725252**
Nr Tamworth, B78 3TW
The theme park is celebrated for its range of white knuckle rides however there are lots of activities for the little ones too. Toddler friendly rides include; the super dragon roller coaster, the frog hopper, vintage cars and the flying jumbos. Fun for the whole family comes in the form of pirate adventure and the Wild West shoot out. Not forgetting the zoo; big cats, reptiles, monkeys, owls, eagles and lots more. A wide selection of eateries are scattered around the park. Height restrictions apply; children under 1meter tall will need to be accompanied by an adult on many rides. Open from the end of March-October. Gates open at 9.30am, rides open at 10.30am. Tickets can be bought online.

Gulliver's Kingdom   **01925 444 888**
Temple Walk, Matlock Bath, Matlock, DE4 3PG
Gulliver's Kingdom is nestled in the stunning hillside with amazing scenery and views. There is a whole host of rides and activities. Activities for the under 5s include; the animal farm, castles, sand pit, indoor soft play areas, ball crawls, horse carousel, and their own special play area. Children under 90cm get in for free. Baby changing facilities are dotted around the site. Check their website or call 01925 444 888 for opening times.

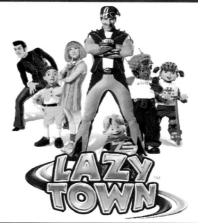

Melton Mowbray • Leicestershire
Tel:01664 567777 • www.twinlakespark.co.uk

Pleasure Island Family Theme Park   01472 211 511

Kings Road, Cleethorpes, Lincolnshire, DN35 0PL
www.pleasure-island.co.uk
There's plenty of choice here for those who are too small for the white knuckle rides; undercover play areas, mini roller coasters, mini dodgems, pony rodeo, clown slide, mini pirate ship. There is a choice of catering outlets throughout the park. They also put on indoor shows, and over the Christmas period, Father Christmas himself will be in his Pleasure Island Grotto (see website for details.) Open daily from 1st April until 4th Sept, during the low season the park is only open at the weekend. The gates open at 10.30am and close at 4pm or 5pm depending on the season.

Twinlakes Leisure Park   01664 567 777

Melton Mowbray, LE14 4SB
www.twinslakespark.co.uk
Once a farm, Twinlakes is now a theme park. You will still find farmyard animals to befriend; teeny baby chicks and black and pink piggies, shire horses and falcon displays. Bigger kids will enjoy the rides, slides, toboggan run, bumper boats, labyrinth and kart tracks. As well as the indoor and outdoor adventure playgrounds, there are mock castles and a child-size Wild West town. Peacocks roam around the numerous picnic areas (there are snack bars dotted around the park.) Easy parking close to the gates. Check their website for seasonal activities and opening times.

ZOOS

DERBYSHIRE

Chestnut Conservation Park   01298 814 099

Castleton Road, Chapel-en-le-Frith, SK12 6PE
www.chestnutcentre.co.uk
Set in 50 acres of landscaped grounds, the conservation park is home, not only to a unique collection of birds and animals, but to many wild birds and mammals. Come and see Europe's largest gathering of otters, 16 species of owls and other indigenous wildlife all in their natural surroundings including, buzzards, pine martens, polecats, foxes, Scottish wildcats and deer. Open 10.30-5.30 every day. Free for 3yrs and under in January and February.

LEICESTERSHIRE

Twycross Zoo   0182 788 0250

Burton Road, Atherstone,
Warwickshire/Leicestershire borders, CV9 3PX
www.twycrosszoo.com
The 40 acre zoo is set in open countryside. Once a modest collection of animals, it has grown into one of the major British zoos and is famous for its collection of primates. With lions, elephants, leopards, giraffes, crocs, snakes and a pigmy goat there really is loads for the kids to see. There is also a pirate themed outdoor adventure playground. Baby changing facilities are provided, there are picnic benches around the zoo, a covered picnic area and a self service cafeteria. Open daily throughout the year from 10am (Closed Christmas day). Closes at 5.30pm during the summer season and 4pm during the winter season (1st November-4th March.)

LINCOLNSHIRE

Natureland Seal Sanctuary   01754 764 345

North Parade, Skegness, Lincolnshire, PE25 1DB
www.skegnessnatureland.co.uk
The resident seals at the sanctuary are joined from time to time by seal pups found washed up on the beaches of the Lincolnshire coast. These abandoned babies are rescued, reared back to health and eventually reintroduced to the wild. As well as seals, there are penguins and a whole aquarium of tropical fish. Once the children have seen the seals and penguins being fed, they can have a go themselves in the Pets Corner, where the Koi carp, tortoises, rabbits and guinea pigs are all waiting to be fed and/or cuddled. Opens at 10am everyday except for Christmas Day, Boxing Day and New Year's Day. Closing times vary throughout the year, for more information call 01754 764 345.

or visit us online at
www.babydirectory.com

Once the elation of finding out you're pregnant dies down, a zillion questions and concerns flood in. This section may not provide all the answers but it points you to someone who can. You'll find listed the best ante-natal classes, where to get private scans, advice and support on breastfeeding, a full list of NHS and private hospitals and where to hire a pool for a water birth.

EMBODY
body painting for pregnant women

Celebrate your pregnancy
T: 07803 121923   e: info@embody.org.uk
www.embody.org.uk

Becoming a parent is a new and completely different phase in your life. You will have to take so many decisions during pregnancy and when your baby arrives that it can be very overwhelming. And those decisions have lots of social, cultural and financial implications, eg.breastfeeding or bottle feeding, mountain buggy or compact stroller, nanny or day nursery and, when they're older – football or rugby?

This guide provides some answers as well as the choice of whose service or product to select when you've made your decision.

Questions

Who do you want to see during your pregnancy for your ante-natal care?

- [ ] Your GP or a midwife at your GP's surgery
- [ ] A midwife or consultant in a maternity hospital
- [ ] A private midwife
- [ ] A private obstetrician or gynaecologist
- [ ] A private obstetrician at a private hospital

Where do you want to have your baby?

- [ ] In an NHS hospital
- [ ] In a private wing of an NHS hospital
- [ ] In a private hospital
- [ ] At home

Who do you want to guide you during labour and is there anything I need to get for it?

- [ ] Hospital: obstetrician or midwife
- [ ] Home: NHS midwife or a private midwife
- [ ] Birthing pool
- [ ] TENS machine

Where can you go to learn about giving birth and options for pain relief?

(see listings opposite)
- [ ] NHS parentcraft classes
- [ ] NCT [National Childbirth Trust] classes
- [ ] Luxury hotel weekend classes
- [ ] Active Birth classes
- [ ] Gentle Birth classes
- [ ] Maternity yoga classes
- [ ] Hypno-birthing classes

What else can I do during pregnancy?

- [ ] Take specialist exercise classes [yoga, aquayoga, buggyfit]
- [ ] Take a cast of your bump or have some pregnancy photographs taken
- [ ] Treat yourself to a pregnancy massage
- [ ] Have a 3D or 4D scan of your baby
- [ ] Go shopping for maternity wear and baby equipment or book a personalised shopping service
- [ ] Book a holiday before your 32nd week of pregnancy!

What might I need when the baby arrives?

- [ ] A maternity nurse or doula
- [ ] Breastfeeding help and support
- [ ] A birth cushion
- [ ] Equipment: there are key essentials [eg. a car seat]
- [ ] An online grocery account!

WE RECOMMEND

What to expect when you're breastfeeding and what if you can't?
[Vermillion]

What to Expect When You're Expecting
[Simon & Schuster]

My Pregnancy Journal
[Ryland, Peters & Small]

ante-natal classes

NHS CLASSES
National Health Service   **0845 4647**
(NHS) Classes
If you have chosen a hospital birth you will be offered NHS ante-natal or parentcraft classes at the hospital or at a midwife-led clinic. The ante-natal teachers are midwives who will cover waterbirth (if available at the hospital), breastfeeding, labour and pain relief available, complications in labour and caesareans. The classes are not very flexible in terms of when they are held, and classes are large so it may be difficult to get to know other mums-to-be. You can also just go on a hospital tour to see where you need to come when in labour.

NCT CLASSES
National Childbirth Trust   **0870 444 8707**
www.nctpregnancyandbabycare.com
The NCT has over 40 years experience of providing ante-natal and post-natal courses across the UK. The teachers have been trained by the NCT and the classes tend to be informal and are generally held in the teacher's home. There are couples courses, women-only courses, 8 week courses and weekend courses. The courses include relaxation and practising different positions for labour as well as information on pain relief, life with a new baby and post-natal care. There are often only 5-7 couples per course so you have a chance to get to know other people with a similar due date. NCT classes cost about £70+ per course depending on where you live. If you would like to attend but cannot afford it then the NCT will happily accept a contribution. They are popular so we recommend that you book early.

LUXURY HOTEL WEEKENDS/DAYS
Baby Gurus   **01786 826 550**
www.thebabygurus.com
Luxury ante-natal weekends held in 4 and 5 star hotels in Scotland.

ACTIVE BIRTH
Active Birth Centre   **020 7281 6760**
25 Bickerton Road, London, N19 5JT
www.activebirthcentre.com
Active Birth classes are centered around gentle yoga from your 12th week of pregnancy to help strengthen your body for birth preparation and life with a new baby. A typical class will include how to use breathing and relaxation to relieve stress, and reduce the strains of pregnancy by improving posture and circulation. Many Active Birth teachers also provide post-natal classes, baby massage and hire out waterbirth pools. Below are the Active Birth Teachers in London.

- **Janey Harvey**   **01636 681 120**
  Newark

- **Olivia Lester**   **01142 678 948**
  Nottingham

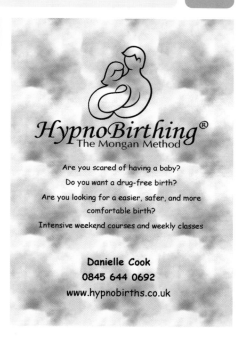

GENTLE BIRTH
Gentle Birth Programme   **020 8530 1146**
34 Cleveland Road, South Woodford, E18 2AL
www.gentlebirthmethod.com
Founded by Dr Gowri Motha in 1987, the Gentle Birth Programme prepares you for a natural delivery by teaching you how to be 'birth fit'. The emphasis of the programme is to make you physically fit and supple, and have a positive and confident frame of mind to manage your own labour. You can purchase her month-by-month guide as well as other complementary products from her website.

INDEPENDENT BIRTH PREPARATION CLASSES
HypnoBirths   **0845 644 0692**
    Mob 01773 810 517

www.hypnobirths.co.uk
Danielle uses The Mongan Method, for Hypnobirthing. Offers classes at her home limited to 2/3 couple Cost is £150 per couple. Also offers private classes, weekends and some week nights at cost of £250 (usual cost for courses in her area are £300). Fee includes The book, cd's handouts and phone/email support until birth of the baby.

Hypnobirthing   0845 644 0692
www.hypnobirths.co.uk
Now in its seventeenth year, Hypnobirthing is a complete ante-natal education. These birthing classes are intended to help you have the most natural childbirth possible, using easily-learned self hypnosis and breathing techniques.

Wendy Nichols, Derby	01332 201 767
Mia ScotlandAylestone, Leicester	0845 868 590
Justine Allen Saxilby, Lincoln	01522 703 225
Claire Atkinson, Rutland	0800 093 1219

Birth Matters 01773 826 055
74 Nottingham Road, Belper, Derbyshire
www.birthdoula.co.uk
Offering maternity reflexology and Doula support.

Bushra Finch 01283 535 818
266 Wyggeston Street, Burton on Trent, Derbyshire
www.firstbreathdoulas.co.uk
Compassionate birth support at home or hospital throughout
the Midlands. Nursing bras, slings homeopathic remedy kits
and more!

Baby Dolly 01455 441 036
PO Box 8275, Hinckley, Leicestershire, LE10 9AP
www.babydolly.org
Luxury day or weekend antenatal classes held at the
Paramount Island Hotel in Hinckley.

Birth Talk 0116 270 2592
17 Chapel Lane, Leicester, Leicestershire, LE2 3WF
www.birthtalk.co.uk
Feel happy, confident and well prepared to approach birth and
welcome your new baby. Birth Talk provides unique midwifery
support for you and your baby. Choose from creative and
interesting birth and parenting skills workshops, yoga,
complementary therapies, baby massage, a postnatal support
service and the Baby Circle. Small groups, comfortable
surroundings and a warm welcome from the midwives.

ante-natal scanning

The following are private ante-natal testing services
which offer a range of scans and blood tests not
necessarily available to you on the NHS without
referral. Alternatively you may wish to have a 3D or 4D
scan and preserve images of you baby for prosperity.

Face2Face 01455 250 021
Suite 1, 9-11 Regent Street, Hinckley,
Leicestershire, LE10 0AZ
www.face2facebabyscans.co.uk
Face2Face specialises in relaxed and unhurried 3/4D
pregnancy ultrasound scans, from a yawn to a kick see your
baby's face for the first time in 3D.

Pro-Scan 0115 941 3516
30 Regent Street, Nottingham, Nottinghamshire,
NG1 5BT
www.proscan-uk.com

Window to the Womb 0115 877 6945
www.windowtothewomb.co.uk
Ultrasound and scanning studio taking 3D pictures of your
baby. The studio is situated in Wollaton, Northamptonshire.

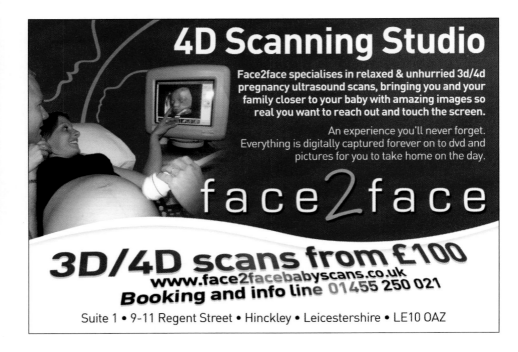

body painters

Julia Francis   **07803 121 923**
www.embody.org.uk
Become a canvas for the day and remember your pregnancy forever (see pg39).

breastfeeding

All parents want the best they can for their children from the start. The decision to breastfeed has lifelong health benefits for both mother and baby. Breastfeeding is a learned skill and it is important to be able to turn to others with experience for advice and support. Finding the right support at this time can help to make this a positive experience for the whole family.

Amber Medical   **01823 336 362**
www.ambermedical.co.uk
Rent a Ameda dual electric breastpump directly from Amber Medical who are now the exclusive distributor of the Ameda brand of products which include electric and manual breastpumps as well as a comprehensive range of breastfeeding accessories. We are the first choice for Health Care Professionals. Order at www.ameda.com or by telephone 01823 336 362.

Breastfeeding Heaven   **01475 704 245**
www.breastfeedingheaven.co.uk
Mastitis, blocked ducts, nipple pain, thrush, engorgement and low milk supply are some of the common problems which interfere with successful breastfeeding. Breastfeeding Heaven aims to provide mums with the products they require to continue breastfeeding, at very competitive prices.

La Leche League   **0845 120 2918**
129a Middleton Boulevard, Wollaton Park, Nottingham, Nottinghamshire, NG8 1FW
www.laleche.org.uk
This line aims to help mothers to breastfeed through mother-to-mother support, encouragement, information and education.

Baby Feeding, Education and Support Services
07717 068 645

25 Long Moor Road, Long Eaton, Nottingham, Nottinghamshire, DE7 8NP
www.feedingbaby.co.uk
Lactation Consultants are health professionals with a specialist qualification in breastfeeding. Denise has worked as a midwife since 1985 and a lactation consultant since 1999. Until 2005 she was Infant Feeding Advisor at Nottingham's Queen's Medical Centre. Her experience includes supporting families where babies are born preterm, are ill, or need extra support with feeding, often multiples. She is available for a consultation in your home by appointment for difficulties feeding your baby or during pregnancy if you would like to discuss particular issues. She also runs antenatal workshops with the aim of helping parents to enter parenthood with confidence in their ability to feed their baby.

Clare Byam-Cook
020 8788 8179

Clare is a leading breastfeeding consultant with years of hands-on experience. She's published and excellent book called "What to expect when you're breastfeeding and what if you can't?" as well as a practical DVD which helps guide new mums through the essential early weeks.

cord blood collection

Cord Blood Banking
www.rcog.org.uk
The collection of cord blood is from the placenta and umbilical cord and is totally painless. The blood, which contains stem cells, is stored for any potential medical treatments in the future, such as blood, immune and metabolic diseases. You must ask your hospital about its policy towards cord blood collection as, under current NHS guidelines, it is not possible for your midwife or consultant to collect the cord blood on your behalf. Instead, your birth support partner collects the cord blood as set out by the companies below or you can ask an independent midwife. There is some very helpful information published by the Royal College of Gynaecologists on cord blood collection under Patient Information.

Future Health Technologies
0870 874 0400

www.futurehealth.co.uk
Stem cell collection.

Virgin Health Bank
0845 620 9665

www.virginhealthbank.com
Many scientists believe that stem cells collected from a baby's umbilical cord could be used one day to treat a whole range of illnesses and injuries. If you choose to save your baby's stem cells with Virgin Health Bank you can receive a £150 discount until 5th September 2008 by quoting BD0907. Call now for your information pack.

doulas

The roles of a doula can be split into two – birth and post- natal. Birth doulas support a mother through the birthing process, often together with the father, and can act as an advocate between them and the midwife. They offer the comfort and calm that a female relative could give at this emotionally and physically trying time. Research has suggested that where a doula is present at a birth the labour is shorter, the need for medical intervention is lessened, and mothers were found to be more responsive to their babies. This is particularly reassuring if mum has had a previously poor experience of childbirth.

Postnatal doulas assist the new mother after the baby is born by helping her to establish breastfeeding, running a few errands, doing some light housework, helping with the care of any other children and providing opportunities for her to rest and recover from the birth. The doula also provides emotional support by encouraging mum to discuss her feelings about the birth and her new role, discussing aspects of babycare and by providing a shoulder to cry on if required. These are all tasks that in days gone by would have been provided by relatives who all lived nearby but today for various reasons, i.e. geography, work commitments, this is not always possible.

Camille Ramshaw   **07977 094 333**
www.doitwithdoulas.co.uk
The support offered by Camille is for labour and birth: this involves 2 ante-natal/2 post-natal visits, continuous support throughout labour until after the birth (however long it takes) and unlimited telephone calls to ensure adequate support.

Confident Mother Doulas   **0115 973 3474**
www.confidentmotherdoulas.co.uk
I am a trained and experienced Post Natal Doula who can draw alongside you and your family in a caring and professional way to give you help and guidance when you need it most.

hospitals: nhs

DERBYSHIRE
Chesterfield and North   **01246 277 271**
Derbyshire Royal Hospital
Chesterfield Road, Chesterfield, Derbyshire, S44 5BL
More than 2 500 babies are born each year at this hospital. Parenting and ante-natal classes are offered for all parents-to-be.

Derby City General Hospital   **01332 340 131**
Uttoxeter Road, Derby, Derbyshire, DE22 3NE
More than 4 500 babies are born each year at this hospital. Services offered include pregnancy day care and ante-natal assessment.

LEICESTERSHIRE
Leicester General Hospital   **0116 249 0490**
Gwendolen Road, Leicester, Leicestershire, LE5 4PW
Almost 4 000 babies are born each year at the Leicester General. Ante-natal classes are available and the unit offers various pain relief methods to help you remain comfortable and relaxed during your labour.

Leicester Royal Infirmary   **0116 254 1414**
Infirmary Square, Leicester, Leicestershire, LE1 5WW
More than 5 000 babies are born here each year at the LRI. Anti-natal classes are available and the unit offers various pain relief methods to help you remain comfortable and relaxed during your labour.

St Mary's Hospital   **01664 854 800**
Thorpe Road, Melton Mowbray, Leicestershire, LE13 1SJ
St Mary's is a woman-centred unit comprising two en suite birth rooms (both with pools), eight postnatal beds, a quiet room with en suite and overnight facilities and showers, bathing, visitors, dining and baby-care facilities.

LINCOLNSHIRE
Grimsby Maternity Hospital   **01472 874 111**
Scartho Road,, Grimsby, Lincolnshire, DN33 2BA

Lincoln County Hospital   **01522 512 512**
Greetwell Rd, Lincoln, Lincolnshire, LN2 1QU

The Lincoln Nuffield Hospital   **0800 731 2132**
Church Lane, Lincoln, Lincolnshire, LN2 1QU

NOTTINGHAMSHIRE
King's Mill Hospital   **01623 622 515**
Mansfield Road, Sutton-in-Ashfield, Nottinghamshire, NG17 4JL
More than 2 500 babies are born annually at this hospital. The unit, which has been refurbished and renamed The Sherwood Building Unit, has an improved waiting area for women and their relatives, redecorated delivery rooms and new equipment including delivery beds, birthing balls and high dependency equipment.

Nottingham City Hospital   0115 969 1169
NHS Trust
Hucknall Road, Sherwood, Nottingham,
Nottinghamshire, NG5 1PB
More than 6 000 babies are born each year in the purpose
built maternity unit at the City Hospital. It has excellent
facilities, ante-natal classes are offered during the day, in the
evenings and at weekends.

Queen's Medical Centre   0115 924 9924
Derby Road, Nottingham, Nottinghamshire, NG7
2UH
Around 4 000 births take place at the QMC each year. The
centre is a regional referral unit for fetomaternal medicine and
other high-risk pregnancies. Other services available include
ante-natal classes, aromatheraphy and baby massage.

hospitals: private

The Lindo Wing   020 7886 1465
St Mary's Hospital, South Wharf Road, London, W2 1NY
Popular private birthing unit situated alongside one of
London's greatest teaching hospitals.

The Portland Hospital   020 7390 8269
234 Great Portland Street, London, W1W 5QT
www.theportlandhospital.co.uk
Consultant and midwife led maternity care with a specialist,
private children's hospital and other women's health services
on an in-patient or out-patient basis.

midwives: independent

For a home birth we recommend an independent
midwife. During your ante-natal care you will be
visited by your midwife at home, who in some cases
can provide complementary therapies throughout
your pregnancy and birth. They will also continue to
provide support and visits post-natally to ensure
that you are getting on well with your new baby. For
further information visit www.homebirth.org.uk.

Notts Independent Midwives   0115 8470483
8 Waterloo Road, Notingham, NG7 4AU
www.nottsindependentmidwives.co.uk
Nottingham Independent Midwives has three experienced
midwives, Nicky Grace, Andrea Lee and Kerri-Anne Gifford.
They provide professional one to one unhurried care
throughout pregnancy, birth and the post-natal period in the
home setting.

The Midlands   07980 987 341
Independent Midwifery Service
www.freewebs.com/janethaynes/
Individualised one-to-one care in the comfort of your own
home. Focusing on the natural process of childbirth. With
sensitivity and skill, Jan will gently, support and guide you
through the amazing life experience of pregnancy, birth and
early parenthood.

pregnancy essentials

Mums Essentials   0800 085 4320
www.mumsessentials.com
Ante- and post-natal nutritional supplements – especially
good for busy mums on the go.

The Valley Cushion   01709 872 137
www.valleycushions.co.uk
The Valley Cushion has two inflatable pads and a central
gusset, which allows you sit down comfortably - especially if
you've had stiches after birth.

Beauty Temple   0845 402 4003
Unit 4, Queens Street, Nottingham,
Nottinghamshire
www.beautytemple.co.uk
Walk into a world of complete sensory heaven at Beauty
Temple. Relax in our VIP room as you look up at the
twinkling ceiling lights rediscover your senses rest your mind
breathe freely as you step into our temple of exquisite aroma.
The Ritual for Mother To Be combines tried and tested
pregnancy massage techniques adapted to each stage of
pregnancy. Specialised positioning on our unique beanbag
ensures the ultimate in comfort and relaxation, helping to
relieve tension in your lower and upper back, alleviating any
swelling in the hands and feet, whilst easing your mind and
uplifting your spirit.

TENS hire

Pain relief without drugs. An effective form of pain relief in labour, the TENS machine (Transcutaneous Electrical Nerve Stimulation) consists of four electrodes taped to your back which give a tingling sensation as a current passes through.

Mama Tens   **0845 230 4647**
www.mama-tens.info
Easy to use, drug-free pain relief during labour, allowing you to stay in control and keep mobile.

Maternity Tens   **01332 812 825**
www.maternitytens.com
Maternity Tens was set up by Kerry Greenland and offers Tens machines to buy or hire from £22 for a five week period, or purchase from £44.95. They are NCT approved and highly recommended. Kerry offers an efficient and flexible service, delivering anywhere within the UK. Her website has a number of other really useful ideas, such as the "Widgey" nursing pillow and tummy tubs as well as Medela breast

Birth Tens   **01455 233 808**
www.birthtens.co.uk
Ring Lucy to hire a TENS machine or birthing balls locally in the East Midlands.

waterbirth pool hire

Check to see whether you can hire a waterbirth pool from your local ante-natal unit, or use one of the independent companies listed below.

Active Birth Centre   **020 7281 6760**
25 Bickerton Road, London, N19 5JT
www.activebirthcentre.com
The largest nationwide pool hire business in the UK. Hexagonal, oval or round shapes available. Hire min 1 week.

Good Birth Company   **0800 035 0514**
www.thegoodbirth.co.uk
Affordable birth pool hire and Medela breast pumps.

Splashdown   **0845 612 3405**
www.waterbirth.co.uk
All shapes supplied as well as inflatables. Waterbirth workshops also run for Mums-to-be and couples.

Did you know that
The Baby Directory
has a comprehensive online
Encyclopedia of Pregnancy?

(it is one of our most popular sections of the website)
Visit **www.babydirectory.co.uk/encyclopedia**

health and beauty

Good health is not just about a lack of illness, but a sense of positive wellness – something overworked and stressed mums and mums-to-be can find elusive. Here we list practitioners of a variety of therapies to help you relax before, during and after labour, to deal with common ailments in both mothers and babies, and to help you regain your shape and vitality after the birth. You'll find everything from acupuncture to yoga, as well as complementary health centres, health clubs and details of professional bodies such as the International Federation of Aromatherapists, which can provide a list of therapists in your area. And if you're worried about immunisations or need tips on first aid, read on.

aromatherapy

Aromatherapy has been around for thousands of years, but the modern form was developed in the early 20th Century. Essential oils from plants and flowers are used to treat conditions including insomnia and PMT. Through massage the oils pass into the bloodstream and can influence mental and emotional functions.

Fingers To Toes   **0116 210 6712**
www.fingers-to-toes.co.uk
Nina Walker is a baby massage instructor and aromatherapist based in Loughborough.

Scents of Harmony   **01159 226 162**
23 Chilwell Road, Beeston, NG9 1EH
www.scentsofharmony.co.uk
Scents of Harmony offers aromatherapy and reflexology for pre-conception, pregnancy and early parenthood by a qualified midwife. Enjoy treatments in calm surroundings where you are made to feel special; your relaxing treatment can be given on a couch or a maternity beanbag. Oils and creams are mixed individually for you and can be made for you to take away. We also offer monthly drop-in sessions for new mums or for pregnancy and packages for pregnancy or pre-conception.-

immunisation

Children's Immunisation   **0870 161 0009**
Centre
144 Harley Street, W1G 7LD
12 Waterloo Street, Birmingham, B 25TB
19 St Johns Street, Manchester, M3 4DS
www.childrensimmunisation.com
The Children's Immunisation Centre was established 5 years ago to offer a range of vaccines not available on the NHS. The first clinic of its kind in the Northwest to receive Healthcare Commission approval. We have national coverage. With fully qualified Doctors, the centre gives peace of mind. We deliver the most effective single immunisations against a wide range of childhood diseases, against cervical cancer, meningitis and flu. For convenience, the clinic operates on Saturdays, which allows both parents to attend. Great care is taken to accommodate children with allergies.

Dr Julian Muir   **020 7235 6642**
3 Basil Street, Chelsea, SW3 1AU
General Practitioner offering all childhood immunisations, including separate measles, mumps and rubella and other general medical

NHS Immunisation Information
www.immunisation.nhs.uk
Information for parents who have concerns about childhood vaccinations. Also visit www.mmrthefacts.nhs.uk where you can order free leaflets online.

The Portland Hospital   **020 7390 8312**
234 Great Portland Street, W1W 5QT
www.theportlandhospital.co.uk
Private vaccinations service (single MMR vaccinations not available).

Vaccinations - Yes or No?   **0870 720 0067**
www.vaccinations-yesorno.co.uk
A must-have, unbiased book for parents facing the dilemma of MMR and the other childhood vaccinations

health clubs: private

As well as exercise classes for parents, many clubs also offer children's activities alongside crèche facilities, junior coaching and fun holiday activities

David Lloyd Leisure   **0113 203 4000**
www.davidlloydleisure.co.uk
Family-friendly clubs offering superb sports and crèche
facilities. East Midlands clubs in:
Riverside Rd, Pride Park, Derby   **01332 821**
306
Aspley Lane, Nottingham   **0115 900 7001**
Rugby Road, Nottingham   **0115 982 5555**

Virgin Active Health Clubs
www.virginactive.co.uk
East Midlands branches in:
Derbyshire Cricket Club   **0845 130 2666**
London Road, Nottingham   **0115 988 4747**

Branston Golf and Country Club   **01283 512211**
Burton Road, Branston, Burton-On-Trent, DE14 3DP
www.branston-golf-club.co.uk

Hoar Cross Hall Spa Resort   **01283 575 671**
Hoar Cross, Burton-On-Trent, DE13 8QS

Champneys Springs Health   **01530 273 873**
Resort
Gallows Lane, Ashby-De-La-Zouch, LE65 1AA

Eden Ladies Health/Fitness 0116 278 7343
6a Welford Rd, Blaby, Leicester, LE8 4FS

Living Well Health Clubs   **0116 281 4112**
Hilton Leicester Hotel, Junction 21 Approach,
Braunstone, Leicester, LE19 1WQ

Eden Hall Day Spa   **01636 525555**
Elston Village, Elston, Newark, NG23 5PG

Roko Health Club   **0115 982 7799**
Wilford Lane, West Bridgford, Nottingham, NG2 7RN

hypnotherapy

Hypnotherapy is a safe, gentle process that relaxes
mind and body. It can be particularly helpful in
pregnancy by helping you approach the birth in a
positive, calm frame of mind.

HypnoBirths   **0845 644 0692/**
01773 810 517
10 Park Lane, Pinxton, NG16 6PT
www.hypnobirths.co.uk
Danielle uses the Mongan Method for Hypnobirthing. She
offers classes at her home, which are limited to only 2 or 3
couples; the cost is £150 per couple. She also offers private
classes at weekends and some weeknights at a cost of
£250. (The usual cost for courses in her area is £300.) The
fee includes; the book, CD's, handouts and phone/email
support until the birth of your baby.

www.babydirectory.com

nutrition

Slimming World   **08700 754 666**
www.slimmingworld.com

massage

Massage during pregnancy is a luxury everyone
should treat themselves to. Easing tension and
boosting energy levels are two of the benefits.
Newborns and babies benefit mentally and
physically from regular massage and it's a
communicative experience for parents whilst
helping baby settle prior to sleep.

Fingers To Toes   **0116 210 6712**
www.fingers-to-toes.co.uk
Nina Walker is a baby massage instructor and aromatherapist
based in Loughborough.

The Beauty Temple   **0845 4024003**
2a Duke Temple, New Basford, NG7 7JN
www.beautytemple.co.uk
Walk into a world of complete sensory heaven at The Beauty
Temple. Relax in our VIP room as you look up at the
twinkling ceiling lights. Rediscover your senses, rest your
mind and breathe freely as you step into our temple of
exquisite aroma. The Ritual for Mother-to-be combines tried
and tested pregnancy massage techniques adapted to each
stage of pregnancy. Specialised positioning on our unique
beanbag ensures the ultimate in comfort and relaxation,
helping to relieve tension in your lower and upper back,
alleviating any swelling in the hands and feet, whilst easing
your mind and uplifting your spirit.

The Massage Room   **01159 191 530**
1 Cromwell Road, Beeston, NG9 1DE
www.themassageroom.org.uk
Learn baby massage in a warm comfortable setting in
Beeston, Nottingham. Small groups or individuals
accommodated at reasonable cost. Perfect for carers and
babies from 3 to 12 months. Groups can choose to receive
tuition in a location of their own choice. Massaging your baby
promotes bonding, aids digestion, sleep and muscle tone
and relaxes both baby and carer. Massage for Carers
(Swedish body and Indian Head) are also available.

The Natural Group   **07722 869 227**
www.thenaturalgroup.co.uk
Infant Massage has far reaching benefits and is not just
another fad! It is an ancient art that helps you as a parent or
carer to connect to your baby. It will help you learn your
baby's particular non-verbal language and respond with love
and understanding; It is a brilliant way to love and nurture a
child giving your relationship a magnificent start! Here at the
Natural Group, we have not just undergone the all-
encompassing training of instructors, by the International
Association of Infant Massage, of which we are members, but
most importantly the training that comes with being parents

ourselves. The instruction can be done either one to one or in a small group, in the comfort of your own home and security of your own surroundings.

reflexology

Reflexology is used to relieve tension and treat illness in the corresponding zones of the body. In pregnancy reflexology can alleviate morning sickness, constipation and rid the body of excess catarrah and stubborn colds. Post-natally, therapy is said to boost energy levels and increase breastmilk.

Scents of Harmony   **01159 226 162**
23 Chilwell Road, Beeston, Nottingham, NG9 1EH
www.scentsofharmony.co.uk
Scents of Harmony offer aromatherapy and reflexology for pre-conception, pregnancy and early parenthood by a qualified Midwife. Enjoy treatment in calm surroundings where you are made to feel special; your relaxing treatment can be given on a couch or a maternity beanbag. Oils and creams are mixed individually for you and can be made for you to take away. We also offer monthly drop-in sessions for new mums or for pregnancy and packages for pregnancy or pre conception.

first aid and safety

These courses offer practical tuition and peace of mind for parents and carers wanting to know the principal causes of accidents and how to prevent and treat them, including resuscitation and general first aid (burns, breaks and poisoning)

First Aid for Kids   **020 7854 2861**
www.firstaidforkids.com
First Aid for Kids is a complete CD-ROM that gives comprehensive first aid advice, tuition, reference and guidance to any parent or child carer, so that you can deal quickly, confidently and effectively with many childhood emergencies. A percentage of sales goes to Great Ormond Street and the King's College Hospital Silver Lining Appeal.

childcare

Finding the right childcare is a potential minefield. Full-time nanny, mother's help or au pair? Through word of mouth, small ad in the local paper or a scribbled card in a shop window? While such methods of finding help may yield happy results, childcare is one area where you don't want to take risks. In this section we recommend professional agencies that will find you a nanny, maternity nurse or other carer with proper qualifications, experience and references.

au pair agencies

The majority of au pairs are aged between 17-25, are admitted from EC countries and work for around 6 months. Expect to pay between £40-£55 per week in exchange for around 25hrs of light housework, childcare and 2 evenings of babysitting. They are not suitable for sole care of babies and young children. The agencies below will do a lot of the hard work for you in terms of selecting suitable and reliable candidates and verifying all their details.

Just Help   01460 30775
www.just-help.co.uk
Voted "Best agency for personal service", Evening Standard. Au pairs from Germany, Austria, Holland and Eastern Europe.

Peek-a-Boo Childcare   020 7600 9880
www.peekaboochildcare.com
Peek-a-boo matches the most suitable au-pairs and nannies with families around the UK and other parts of the world. We specialise in Scandinavian and British carers although we welcome al EU/EEC members, antipodeans and all other nationalities, who hold a valid UK work visa.

babysitters

We suggest that you develop between 3-4 babysitting contacts so that you can go out when a last-minute invitation arrives or when spontaneity strikes. For peace of mind you should check candidate references yourself to ensure that you are satisfied with any qualifications or experience.

Find a Babysitter   020 3220 0058
www.findababysitter.com
The UK's largest nanny and babysitter search tool. Search locally for your perfect carer. No agency fees. Search by location, language and availability. There is also comprehensive information on finding and hiring childcarers. Visit the website for more information.

The Baby Bank   0845 257 1901
www.thebabybank.com
Day or night, for 30 minutes or 5 hours, use your friends to babysit for free and get your life back, have a manicure, a coffee or a romantic dinner. Use the babybank.com and get time for you.

doulas

Camille Ramshaw   07977 094 333
www.doitwithdoulas.co.uk
The support offered by Camille is for labour and birth: this involves 2 antenatal/2 postnatal visits, continuous support throughout labour until after the birth (however long it takes) and unlimited telephone calls to ensure adequate support.

Confident Mother Doulas   **0115 973 3474**
www.confidentmotherdoulas.co.uk
I am a trained and experienced Post Natal Doula who can draw alongside you and your family in a caring and professional way to give you help and guidance when you need it most.

maternity nurses and nannies

Specialising in the care of newborns, a maternity nurse will look after your baby on return from hospital, allowing you to rest. Normally they are on call 24hrs a day, with one day off per week.

Tinies Childcare   **020 7384 0322**
www.tinies.com
Tinies is the country's leading childcare agency, with maternity nurses, part time & emergency child carers than anyone else.

Maternally Yours   **020 7795 6299**
www.maternally-yours.co.uk
Established in 1996 Maternally Yours is one of the UK's leading maternity nurse agencies.

Nannies Incorporated   **020 7340 9601**
www.nanniesinc.com
Specialists in maternity care.

nanny agencies

Tinies Childcare: **01332 856 396**
East Midlands
www.tinies.com
Tinies Childcare has been established for over 20 years while the Tinies Childcare and Training office has been operating in the Midlands (covering Yorkshire, Derbyshire, Nottinghamshire and Staffordshire) since March 2006. At our Midlands branch we pride ourselves on our ability to provide the very best service to our customers. Moreover, we strongly believe that we employ the very best childcare professionals. We currently have opportunities for experienced professionals in our organisation within the childcare and education sectors. At Tinies Childcare we work together with local schools, nurseries and parents when finding suitable posts for new candidates and offer both temporary and permanent positions.

First Choice for Families   **0870 010 3154**
www.firstchoiceforfamilies.co.uk
We make life easy... finding you perfect people to take care of your home and fabulous child carers to look after your children. We provide a much-needed affordable lifeline to parents, where all the hassle is taken out of finding suitable people to look after their children and homes.

Ideal Nannies   **0113 346 6099**
47 Park Square East, Leeds, LS1 2NL
www.idealnannies.com
Karen Murphy of Ideal Nannies has been running this flourishing agency since 1988. It is manned by Sensible, careful staff who are easy to talk to and have practical experience in the childcare world.

nanny payroll services

If you've never seen the small binder that encompasses the PAYE tax tables then we do recommend you value your time highly and delegate all responsibility for calculating tax to one of the services below. Sanity could at least be your upside.

Nanny Tax   **0845 226 2203**
www.nannytax.co.uk
Nannytax is the UK's leading payroll support service for nanny employers. We can help transform the hassle of being an employer into peace of mind. We specialise in nannyshares and can also advise on the new Ofsted register for nannies. Call one of our friendly advisers today for more information and if you quote The Baby Directory you will receive a 10% discount on your subscription.

Taxing Nannies   **020 8882 6847**
www.taxingnannies.co.uk
A specialist payroll service for employers of nannies including opening a PAYE scheme, calculating tax and national insurance. They provide regular pay slips, advise on Sick and Maternity pay and liaise with the Inland Revenue.

As soon as your child is born you'll be thinking about their education. And it's never too early to register for pre-school care as the most popular nurseries and childminders get booked up frighteningly early.

WHAT ARE YOUR PRE-SCHOOL CHILDCARE OPTIONS?

Day Nurseries [£8 per hour, all year round]: from 6 weeks - normally privately run and offering care from 8am-6pm or by the half-day in specially adapted and Ofsted inspected premises. Ideal for working parents who have to be at their desk by 9am.

Childminders [£8 per hour, all year round]: from 6 weeks childminders take children into their own home and have a small family sized group.

Private Nursery schools [Fee paying, termtime]: from 2½-5yrs usually attached to independent pre-prep schools.

Pre-schools/playgroups [contributions accepted, termtime]: from 2½yrs - mainly run by parent/volunteer committees that are not-for-profit and employ their own staff. Based in church halls or community centres.

Primary School nurseries [Free, termtime]: from 3-4yrs. Most of these are attached to local primary schools, although a place at nursery does not guarantee a place at the primary school. You must put your name down as soon as possible as there may well be a waiting list and you'll find parents with older siblings have got there first.

Primary Schools [Free, termtime]: from 4 rising 5 to 11yrs. You will need to apply for your child's primary school place when they are 3 rising 4 years - or at least a year before they start (which is usually the term before they turn 5yrs).

For nearly all nurseries and schools in the private sector, early registration is highly recommended, so ring, visit with babe in arms and register ahead of time, even if you later decide not to pursue that option.

For a list of state-run nurseries ie state primary schools with nursery classes contact your local Council.

Looking for childcare?

Call now for free, impartial information and advice about:

- Registered childcare and activities for young people 0-19 years.

- **Free nursery education places for 3 and 4 year olds.**

- Family support information, including details about help available with paying for childcare.

- Finding a Sure Start Children's Centre near to you, and the services avilable.

For Nottingham City Call

0800 458 4114

For Nottinghamshire Call

0800 781 2168

For online information about childcare and family support services visit www.childcarelink.gov.uk OR www.services4notts.org.uk

DERBYSHIRE
NURSERIES

DE1

Ashgate Nursery School   01332 371 769
18 Stepping Lane, Derby, DE1 1GJ

Jack 'n Jill Private Day Nursery   01332 382 364
128a Green Lane, Derby, DE1 1RY

The Orchard Garden   01332 370 497
Private Day Nursery
Haig House, 87 Green Lane, Derby, DE1 1RX

DE3

Mickleover Montessori Nursery   01332 513 444
School
Staker Flattfamr, Staker Lane, Mickleover, DE3 5DJ

Oak House Nursery   **01332 512 484**
127 Station Road, Mickleover, Derby, DE3 9FN
Oak House is a small and friendly nursery, owned and
managed by an early years teacher. Open 8am-6pm from
birth to 5 years, 50 weeks a year.

The Cottage Private   **01332 515 100**
Day Nursery
Uttoxeter Road, Mickleover, Derby, DE3 5AD
www.cottagenurseries.co.uk
0-4yrs. 7.30am-6pm. 50wks.

DE4

Cromford Bridge Hall Nursery   01629 580 238
Yonder Meadow, Lea Road, Cromford, Matlock,
DE4 5NL

Treetops Play Day Nursery   01629 581 007
Chesterfield Road, Matlock, DE4 3DQ

DE5

Clowns Day Nursery   **01773 747 983**
www.clowns-nursery.co.uk
12 Cromford Road, Ripley, DE5 3FP

Clowns Day Nursery   **01773 747 983**
www.clowns-nursery.co.uk
Butterley Park, Ripley, DE5 3AD

Ripley Nursery School   **01773 745 014**
Childcare Facility
Sandham Lane, Ripley, DE5 3HE

DE6

Mulberry Bush Day Nursery   01335 342 474
92 Belper Road, Ashbourne, DE6 1BD

Treetops Day Nursery   01335 342 712
13 Derby Road, Ashbourne, DE6 1BE

DE7

Horsley Woodhouse Pre-School   07969 964 842
Methodist Church Hall, Main Street, Horlsey
Woodhouse, Ilkeston, DE7 6AU

Clowns Day Nursery

- 🌸 Ripley
- 🌸 Sandiacre
- 🌸 Butterly
- 🌸 Ironville
- 🌸 North Wingfield
- 🌸 Clay Cross

Quality Childare in a safe and friendly environment

Head Office, Ripley, Derbyshire
Tel: 01773 747 983 www.clowns-nursery.co.uk

Lanes Play Day Nursery　　01159 440 810
155 High Lane Central, West Hallam, Ilkeston, DE7 6HU

Little Steps Day Nursery　　01159 321 345
19a Summerfields Way, Shipley View, Ilkeston, DE7 9HE

Pines Private Day Nursery　　01159 305 550
88 Station Road, Ilkenston, DE7 5FY

Rocking Horse Day Nursery　　01159 305 240
81 Heanor Road, Ilkeston, DE7 8DY

West Point Day Nursery　　01159 325 718
49 Kingston Avenue, Ilkeston, DE7 4BD
www.westpointhousedaynursery.co.uk
0-11yrs. 7am-6.30pm. 51wks.

DE11
Four Seasons Private Day Nursery　01283 551 398
55 Newhall Road, Swadlincote, DE11 0BD

DE21
Childs Play　　01332 662 175
473 Nottingham Road, Derby, DE21 6NA

Derwent Stepping Stones　　01332 372 245
Huntingdon Green, Derby, DE21 6AU

First Friends Play Day Nursery　　01332 677 660
141 Chaddesden Park Road, Chaddesden, Derby,
DE21 6HP

Honey Pot Day Nursery　　01332 830 473
Hill Top, Breadsall, Derby, DE21 4TJ

Kingfisher Day Nursery　　01332 669 686
38 Chapel Street, Spondon, Derby, DE21 7JP

Leapfrog Day Nursery　　01332 544 321
Smalley Drive, Oakwood, Derby, DE21 2SF

Oaktree Day Nursery　　01332 674 326
Reginald Road South, Chaddesden, Derby, DE21 6ND

The Whitehouse Nursery　　01332 666 414
63/65 Nottingham Road, Spondon, DE21 7NG
www.whitehousenurseries.co.uk
White House Children's Nursery caters for children from 3-5
years. Our aims are to provide a secure, loving, caring
environment in which all children have the opportunity to
reach their full potential emotionally, educationally and socially
through hands on experiences and by "having fun". We are
fully inclusive and care for and nurture children with special
needs within the nursery and are able to access professional
help and support if we need it. We have fully qualified staff
who are committed and dedicated to working with all our
children and parents in a caring and professional manner.

Treetops Day Nursery　　01332 281 978
382 Bishops Drive, Oakwood, Derby, DE21 2DF

EXTENDED OPENING HOURS 7AM-6.30PM

West Point House Day Nursery, Ilkeston

Day Nursery

www.westpointhousedaynursery.co.uk

Tel: 0115 932 5718 • info@westpointhousedaynursery.co.uk

- flexible sessions to suit individual requirement
- Small, traditional nursery with experienced mature staff
- out of school/holiday care
- good ofsted reports and free funded places for 3-4 years old
- safe onsite parking and large garden facilities

Please ring for further details or visit our website to view facilities

West Point House Day Nursery, 49 Kingston Avenue, Hallam Fields, Ilkeston, Derbyshire DE7 4BD

EXTENDED OPENING HOURS 7.00AM-6.30PM
WITH FLEXIBLE SESSIONS TO SUIT INDIVIDUAL REQUIREMENTS

Awsworth Schoolhouse Day Nursery & Out of School Club, Awsworth

www.awsworthschoolhousedaynursery.co.uk

Tel: 0115 9444114

info@awsworthschoolhousedaynursery.co.uk

... where learning never stops!

Out of School facilities now provided at local school onsite at Awsworth Primary and Nursery School.

Small traditional old schoolhouse building with small numbers of children and mature experienced staff.

Free funded places for 3/4 year olds

Please ring for further details or visite website to view facilities

Awsworth Schoolhouse Day Nursery, The Lane, Awsworth, Nottingham, NG16 2QQ
LOCATED NEAR IKEA RETAIL PARK JUNCTION 26 AND EASY ACCESS TO M1, DERBY AND NOTTINGHAM

DE22

Carlton Play Day Nursery   01332 366 223
Maxwell Avenue, Allestree, Derby, DE22 1GQ

Derby Montessori School   01332 346 333
296 Uttoxeter New Road, Derby, DE22 3LN
www.derbymontessori.co.uk
Derby Montessori School encourages its students to become
active and valuable members of the community. Using
Montessori principles and materials, each child is encouraged
to weave the different strands of the curriculum together in
their own unique way. Derby Montessori offers children
freedom to learn in an un-pressured, stimulating environment
where free thinking and problem solving are highly valued.
Academic progress is achieved alongside practical and social
skills, which develop children's confidence and foster a
positive disposition to learning. Open evenings are held
regularly throughout the year, where parents and other
interested parties can learn more about the Montessori
approach.

Discovery Day Nursery   01332 749 052
48 Bedford Street, Derby, DE22 3NL

Little Acorns Day Nursery   01332 346 088
10 Thornhill Road, Off Albany Road, Derby, DE22 3LX

Little Learners   01332 520 220
Derby College, Prince Charles Avenue, Mackworth,
Derby, DE22 4LR

www.derby-college.ac.uk
12wks-5yrs. 8am-6pm. 50wks. This is the Derby College
nursery that offers places to families outside the college where
they have spaces. Holiday playscheme for children up to 10yrs.

Mulberry Bush Private   01332 344 800
Day Nursery
135 Duffield Road, Derby, DE22 1AF

Playaway Nursery   01332 362 542
352 Uttoxeter New Road, Derby, DE22 3HX

Rydale Children's Centre   01332 521 888
Reigate Drive, Mackworth, Derby, DE22 4EP

Silvertrees Day Nursery   01332 366 663
40 Ashbourne Road, Derby, DE22 3AD

The Cottage Private   01332 346 500
Day Nursery
55, 76 and 78 Bedford Street, Derby, DE22 3PD
www.cottagenurseries.co.uk
2-8yrs. 7.30am-6pm. 50wks.

Woodlands Private Day   01332 346 878
Nursery
194 Duffield Road, Derby, DE22 1BJ
www.thewoodlandsnursery.com
0-8yrs. 7.30am-6pm. 50wks.

DE23

Ace Nursery   01332 774 255
Grange Avenue, Derby, DE23 8DH

La Petite Academy   01332 774 413
10-12 Highfield Road, Littleover, Derby, DE23 1DG

Leapfrog Day Nursery   01332 518 888
Hollybrook Way , Heatherton Village, Littleover,
Derby, DE23 3TZ

Little Scholars   01332 271 608
12 Wellesley Avenue, Littleover, Sunnyhill, Derby,
DE23 1GQ

Little Scholars   01332 760 619
10 Austen Avenue, Littleover, Derby, DE23 3EY

Mary Poppins Day Nursery   01332 510 808
30 Chain Lane, Mickleover, Derby, DE23 5AJ

Yellow Brick Road   01332 600 640
Play Day Nursery
2 Stonehill Road, Derby, DE23 6TJ

DE24

Asquith Creche Derby   01332 372 127
David Lloyd Club, Riverside Way, Pride Park Way,
Derby, DE24 8HX

Carlton Play Day Nursery   01332 766 636
Sinfin Lane, Sinfin Moor, Derby, DE24 9PG

The Caring Nursery
open 51 weeks per year
OPEN 7.30am - 6pm

White House

Qualified mature staff Cosy baby Unit
large gardens   flexible hours
Complete child-care
Warm friendly atmosphere
vouchers accepted

Free child-care for 3-5 year olds

White House Day Nursery 63/65 Nottingham Rd, Spondon, Derby DE21 7NG
Telephone: 01332 666414   Facsimile: 01332 669794
www.whitehousenurseries.co.uk

1907 - 2007 — Celebrating 100 years of Montessori!

DERBY MONTESSORI SCHOOL

REASONS TO CHOOSE MONTESSORI:

A NATURAL APPROACH TO LEARNING THROUGH EXPLORATION & DISCOVERY.
WHERE CHILDREN REALISE THEIR POTENTIAL BY BUILDING THEIR CONFIDENCE, MOTIVATION AND SELF-ESTEEM

Learning for life

CONSISTENCY OF APPROACH
18 MONTHS TO 8 YEARS
EXTENDED CARE AVAILABLE 8.30 –6PM
OPEN UP TO 48 WEEKS
HOLIDAY CLUBS TO 11 YRS
VERY COMPETITIVE PRICES

FOR FURTHER DETAILS CONTACT
296 Uttoxeter New Road, Derby. DE22 3LN
principal@derbymontessori.co.uk
www.derbymontessori.co.uk
Tel: (01332) 346333

Pride Park Day Nursery   **01332 224 288**
2 Royal Scot Road, Pride Park, Derby, DE24 8AJ

Sinfin Community Childcare   **01332 770 167**
Sheridan Street, Sinfin, Derby, DE24 9HG

Woodlands Private Day   **01332 861 731**
Nursery
95 Shardlow Road, Alvaston, Derby, DE24 0JR
www.thewoodlandsnursery.com
6mths-12yrs. 7.30am-6pm. 50wks.

Tiny Tots PDN   **01332 572 387**
The Lodge, 93 Shardlow Road, Alvaston, Derby,
DE24 0JP

DE45
Bakewell Nursery School   **01629 813 888**
Derbyshire House, Matlock Street, Bakewell, DE45 1EE

Scallywags   **01629 813 638**
The Medway Centre, New Street, Bakewell, DE45 1GT

DE55
Busy Bee Play Day Nursery   **01773 580 164**
23 Hilcote Street, South Normanton, Alfreton, DE55 2BQ

Grange Play Day Nursery   **01773 520 347**
Marshall Street, Alfreton, DE55 7BW

Nursery Rhymes Day Nursery   **01773 830 850**
Main Road, Shirland, DE55 6BB

Tiddlers Day Nursery   **01246 251 330**
Main Road, Stretton, Nr. Alfreton, DE55 6ET

Tiny Tots   **01773 862 999**
Gloves Lane, Blackwell, DE55 5JJ

DE56
Alton Manor Private Day Nursery **01773 829 242**
Gregory's Way, Belper, DE56 0HS

Mulberry Bush Day Nursery   **01773 828 813**
33 Wellington Court, Belper, DE56 1UP

Treetops at Castle Garden   **01332 841 844**
King Street, Duffield, Derby, DE56 4EU

Woodlands Private Day   **01773 882 423**
Nursery
1 Gibfield Lane, Belper, DE56 1WA
www.thewoodlandsnursery.com

DE65
Carlton Private Day Nursery   **01283 730 730**
Witham Road, off Eggington Road, Hilton, DE65 5JR

Cherry Tree Day Nursery   **01283 732 297**
1 Cherry Garth, Hilton, Derby, DE65 5FT

Creative Days Nursery   **01283 810 047**
Jubilee Hall, Station Road, Hatton, Derby, DE65 5EL

Happy Days   **01283 732 009**
18 Calder Close, Hilton, Derby, DE65 5HR

Little Jack Horner Nursery   **01283 734 030**
Tynefield Court, Egginton Road, Etwall, Derby,
DE65 6NQ

Old Forge Play Day Nursery   **01283 701 533**
Old Forge, The Green, Findern, Derby, DE65 6AA

DE72
Breaston Manor PDN   **01332 874 544**
90 Wilsthorpe Road, Breaston, Derby, DE72 3EB

Derwent Cottage Day Nursery   **01332 663 443**
162 Nottingham Road, Borrowash, Derby, DE72 3FQ

Little Treasures Daycare Centre **01332 875 000**
44 Derby Road, Draycott, Derby, DE72 3NJ

White House Kids Club   **01332 820 404**
164 Derby Road, Borrowash, Derby, DE72 3HB

DE73
Orchard Day Nursery   **01332 728 545**
129 Derby Road, Chellaston, Derby, DE73 1SB

Orchard Nursery School   **01332 703 204**
92 Derby Road, Chellaston, Derby, DE73 1RF

Scallywags Nursery   **01332 862 188**
Castle Lane, Melbourne, DE73 8JB

DE75
The Cottage Private Day   **01773 715 726**
Nursery
14 Mansfield Road, Heanor, DE75 7AJ
www.cottagenurseries.co.uk
0-8yrs. 7.30am-6pm. 50wks.

Heanor Leisure Centre   **01773 769 711**
Pre School
Hands Road, Heanor, DE75 7HA

Wollaton Village Day Nurseries **01773 531 444**
Wilmott Street, Heanor, DE75 7EF
www.wollatonvillagedaynurseriesltd.co.uk

CHESTERFIELD

S18

Dronfield Nursery   **01246 410 778**
Northfield House, 274 Chesterfield Road, S18 1XJ

Hill Top Tots Day Nursery   **01246 290 063**
51 Highfield Road, Dronfield, S18 1UW

S21

Manor House Nursery   **01246 436 006**
The Manor House, Church Street, Eckington, S21 4BG

S40

Daisy Chain Day Nursery   **01246 558 811**
2 Cobden Road, Chesterfield, S40 4TD

Little Acorns Day Nursery   **01246 557 057**
Ashgate Road, Chesterfield, S40 4AA

Playbox   **01246 550 918**
29 Ashgate Road, Chesterfield, S40 4AG

Promises Day Nursery   **01246 221 184**
Wardgate Way, Holme Hall, Chesterfield, S40 4SL

S41

Easy Tigers   **01246 260 011**
Nurture House, Foxwood Road, Chesterfield, S41 9RF
www.easytigers.co.uk
Easy Tigers Day Nursery is committed to providing high
quality childcare for children aged 4 weeks to 12 years, in a

fun, happy and safe environment. The nursery is open Monday to Sunday 7am till 7pm and offers full time and part time places at competitive rates. Easy Tigers Day Nursery wants your child's day to be filled with lots of opportunities to learn, play, laugh and grow. We would welcome the chance to show you what we can offer you and your child.

Mary Poppins Day Nursery   **01246 555 022**
26 The Green, Hasland, Chesterfield, S41 0LJ

Nursery Rhymes Day Nursery   **01246 450 354**
619 Sheffield Road, Sheepbridge, Chesterfield, S41 9DX

Playbox Day Nursery   **01246 238 826**
Windermere Road, Chesterfield, S41 8DU

S42
Clowns Early Years Centre   **01246 854 841**
Alices View, North Wingfield, S42 5XA

Little Chatterbox Day Nursery   **01246 251 571**
184c Queen Victoria Road, Tupton, New Tupton, Chesterfield, S42 6DU

S43
Fairy Tales Day Nursery   **01246 810 848**
36 Chesterfield Road, Barlborough, S43 4TT

Post House Nursery   **01246 559 990**
15 High Street, Birmington, Chesterfield, S43 1DF
www.posthousenursery.co.uk
Post House Nursery offers a homely, welcome atmosphere, which safeguards and promotes children's welfare. Our planning follows the Early Years Foundation Stage setting the Standards for learning development and care for children from birth to five years. We try to meet diverse needs and work closely in partnership with parents. Our high standards mean that we are able to offer funded sessions for 3- 5 yr olds on application. The meals provided are cooked on the premises with fresh ingredients, our menus are wide ranging and healthy. Always looking for quality improvements we both practice and teach our children the importance of looking after our world, having several environmentally friendly schemes running, including recycling, a real/ terry nappy provision and in the future a forest school availability.

Treasures Neighbourhood   **01246 473 776**
Nursery
23 High Street, Staveley, S43 3UU
www.treasures-nursery.co.uk

Treetops Nursery   **01246 812 444**
Ash Close, Barlborough, Chesterfield, S43 4XL

S44
Breedon House Children's Centre   **01246 563 644**
Dryhurst House, Royal Hospital, Calow, Chesterfield, S44 5BL

Stepping Stones Nursery   **01246 824 041**
Manor Farm, Chesterfield Road, Duckmanton, Chesterfield, S44 5HX
8am-5.30pm. 50wks.

Sunnybank Nursery   **01246 555 952**
Chesterfield Road, Calow, Chesterfield, S44 5UN

Mary Poppins   **01246 555 022**
York House, 26 The Green, Hasland, Chesterfield, S441 0LJ

S45
Ashover Nursery School   **01246 591 769**
Narrowleys Lane, Ashover, Chesterfield, S45 0AU

Clowns Childrens Centre   **01246 250 044**
Stretton Rd, Clay Cross, Chesterfield, S45 9AQ

S60
Oakwood Day Nursery   **01709 836 669**
Oakwood Hall Road, Rotherham District Hospital, Moorgate Road, Rotherham, S60 7AJ

SK13
Glossop Private Day Nurseries   **01457 856567**
27 Kershaw House Nurseries, Glossop, SK13 8NN

Hadfield House Nursery   **01457 858 200**
Hadfield House, 124 Hadfield Road, Hadfield, Glossop, SK13 2DR

Little Beaver Childcare   **01457 869 962**
St. Mary's Hall, St. Mary's Road, Glossop, SK13 8DN

Mersey Bank Day Nursery   **01457 865 577**
21 Chapel Lane, Hadfield, Glossop, SK13 1PG

North View Day Nursery   **01457 857 857**
2 North Road, Glossop, SK13 7AS

South View Day Nursery   **01457 850 999**
26 Derby Street, Glossop, SK13 8LP

Springfield Day Nursery   **01457 860 329**
34 Marple Road, Charlesworth, Glossop, SK13 5DA
0-8yrs. 8am-6pm. 50wks.

Whitfield School Nursery   **01457 857586**
Chadwick St, Glossop, SK13 8EF

Wind In The Willows   **01457 853342**
59 Glossop Road, Glossop, SK13 6JH

SK17
Good News Family Care   **0129 824 761**
Charis House, Hardwick Square East, Buxton, SK17 6PT

Green Lane Nursery   **01298 767 505**
11 Green Lane, Buxton, SK17 9DP

Rhyme and Reason Nursery   **01298 232 612**
15 College Road, Buxton, SK17 9DZ

Willows Private Day Nursery   **0129 879 287**
23 Park Road, Buxton, SK17 6SG

SK22
Springfield Day Nursery   **01663 747 350**
39 Thornsett, Birch Vale, High Peak, SK22 1AZ

SK23
Bridgemont Nursery   **07977 388 225**
Bridgemont Village Hall, Bridgemont, Whaley
Bridge, SK23 7PB

Cheeky Monkeys   **01298 811 731**
Long Lane, Chapel-en-le-Frith, High Peak, SK23 0TQ

Toddbrook Private Day   **01663 719 091**
Nursery School
110a Buxton Road, Whaley Bridge, High Peak,
SK23 7JH

LEICESTERSHIRE
CV13
Market Bosworth Day Nursery   **01455 290 561**
7 Barton Road, Market Bosworth, Nuneaton, CV13 0LQ

DE12
Hill Top Day Nursery   **01530 274 462**
48 Hill Street, Donisthorpe, Swadlincote, DE12 7PL

DE74
Handkerchief Nursery   **01509 670 394**
High Street, Kegworth, DE74 2DA

Jack-in-the-Box   **01332 810 025**
77-77a Station Road, Castle Donington, DE74 2NL

Nightingale Nursery   **01332 811 800**
3 Delven Lane, Castle Donington, DE74 2LJ

LE1
City Nursery   **01162 470 166**
18 Northampton Square, Leicester, LE1 1PA

Holly Bush Nursery   **01162 330 423**
146 Upper New Walk, Leicester, LE1 7QA

Millstone Day Nursery   **01162 512 725**
17 Millstone Lane, Leicester, LE1 5JN

Nippers Nursery   **01162 535 490**
Saxon House, 1 Causeway Lane, Leicester, LE1 4AA

Red Triangle   **01162 556 507**
Leicester YMCA, 7 East Street, Leicester, LE1 6EY

St George's Nursery School   **01162 517 755**
St Georges House, William Street, Leicester, LE1 1RW
www.stgeorgesnursery.com
8mths-5yrs. 7.45am-6pm. 50wks.

Stanhope Day Nursery   **01162 554 277**
114 Regent Road, Leicester, LE1 7LT

The Dolls House   **01162 236 357**
6 New Walk, Leicester, LE1 6TF

LE2
Blossoms Day Nursery   **01162 448 600**
3-5 Stoneygate Road, Stoneygate, Leicester, LE2 2AB

Blueberry Bush Day Nursery   **01162 714 888**
40 London Road, Oadby, Leicester, LE2 5DH

Fairy Tales Day Nursery   **01162 788 782**
Manor Court, The Ford, Glen Parva, Leicester, LE2 9TL

Knighton Day Nursery   **01162 883 030**
559 Welford Road, Leicester, LE2 6FN

Lansdowne Day Nursery   **01162 831 586**
25 Lansdowne Road, Leicester, LE2 8AS

Leicester Montessori Day Nursery   **01162 702 758**
27 St. Johns Road, Leicester, LE2 2BL

Little Acorns Nursery   **01162 705 086**
382 London Road, Stoneygate, Leicester, LE2 2PN

Little Foxes Day Nursery   **01162 718 866**
23 East Street, Oadby, Leicester, LE2 5AF

Little Stars Day Nursery   **01162 839 991**
33 Lutterworth Road, Aylestone, Leicester, LE2 8PH

Pebbles Nursery   **01162 712 215**
Copse Close, Oadby, Leicester, LE2 4FU
7.30am-6pm.

Pebbles Nursery Knighton   **01162 706 916**
205 Knighton Road, Knighton, Leicester, LE2 3TT

Playdays Day Nursery   **01162 440 727**
1-3 Glenhills Boulevard, Leicester, LE2 8UF

River View Day Nursery   **01162 554 666**
Tarragon Road, Leicester, LE2 7ET

Saffron Community Nursery   **01162 838 704**
The Linwood Centre, Linwood Centre, Linwood
Lane, LE2 6QN

Shanklin Day Nursery   **01162 704 603**
443 London Road, Leicester, LE2 3JW

St George's Nursery School   **01162 833 383**
Grace House, 2 Grace Road, Leicester, LE2 8AD
www.stgeorgesnursery.com
0-8yrs. 7.30-6pm. 50wks

St George's Nursery School   **01162 716 161**
33-37 Wigston Road, Oadby, Leicester, LE2 5QF
www.stgeorgesnursery.com
7.30am-6pm. 51wks.

Stoneygate Montessori   **01162 706 662**
Nursery School
279 London Road, Leicester, LE2 3ND

LE3
Allexton Day Nursery   **01162 235 582**
Upper Floor, 63 King Richards Road, Leicester, LE3 5QG

Buttercups Day Nursery   01162 870 562
Flat 27 Staff Residence, Glenfrith Close, Leicester, LE3 9QQ

Cherry Tree Day Nursery   01162 870 092
17 Holmwood Drive, New Parks, Leicester, LE3 9LG

Daneshill Nursery   01162 530 856
1 Daneshill Road, Leicester, LE3 6AN

Lilliput Montessori Day Nursery   01162 321 319
29 Stamford Street, Glenfield, LE3 8DL

Pied Piper Day Nursery   01162 321 312
The Square, Glenfield, Leicester, LE3 8DQ

Westcotes Day Nursery   01162 546 413
35 Braunstone Avenue, Leicester, LE3 0JH

Westleigh Nursery   01162 554 152
10 Westleigh Road, Leicester, LE3 0HH

Wingfield Nursery   01162 541 239
140 Westcotes Drive, Leicester, LE3 0QS

LE4

Abracadabra Pre-School Nursery   01162 223 377
Unit E, Troon Way Business Centre, Humberstone Lane, Leicester, LE4 9HA

Babington Bear Day Nursery   01162 221 616
Strasbourg Drive, Leicester, LE4 0SZ

Belgrave Playhouse   01162 681 423
130-134 Harrison Road, Leicester, LE4 6BS

Birstall Rainbow Nursery   **01162 671 331**
68-74 Wanlip Lane, Birstall, LE4 4GF
www.birstallrainbow.co.uk
6wks-5yrs. 8am-6pm. 52wks.

Charnwood Nursery   01162 696 162
22-24 Lonsdale Road, Thurmaston, Leicester, LE4 8JF

education

Kiddycare 01162 680 258
71 Melton Road, Leicester, LE4 6PN

Leicester Montessori 01162 610 022
Nursery School
137 Loughborough Road, Leicester, LE4 5LQ

Little Peepul Day Nursery 01162 667 673
Belgrave Baheno Peepul Centre, 17 Melrose Street,
Leicester, LE4 6FD

Milky Way Day Nursery 01162 243 584
68 Corporation Road, Leicester, LE4 5PW

Tangent House Day Nursery 01162 640 333
640 Melton Road, Thurmaston Village, Leicester,
LE4 8BB
www.tangenthousenursery.co.uk
2-5yrs. 7.30am-6.30pm. 50wks.

Windsor House Day Nursery 01162 682 550
75 Windsor Avenue, Leicester, LE4 5DU

Woodlands Day Nursery 01162 675 427
1 Park Road, Birstall, Leicester, LE4 3AX

LE5
A1 Evington Nursery 01162 738 830
37 Evington Lane, Leicester, LE5 5PR

Early Learners Nursery School 01162 511 514
Spinney Hill Road, Leicester, LE5 3GH

Hamilton Hilltop Day Nursery 01162 743 090
25 Hilltop Road, Hamilton, Leicester, LE5 1TT
www.hamiltonnursery.co.uk

Humberstone Day Nursery 01162 202 143
11 St. Mary Avenue, Humberstone, Leicester, LE5 1JA

Kids Room Nursery 01162 742 835
The Baptist Church, 78 Uppingham Road,
Leicester, LE5 0QE

Little Poppets Nursery School 01162 434 209
388 Coleman Road, Leicester, LE5 4EF

Parkview Day Nursery 01162 734 237
236 East Park Road, Leicester, LE5 5FD

Sunshine Nursery School 01162 735 561
27 The Common, Evington, Leicester, LE5 6EA

Tiny Gems Nursery 01162 760 504
2 Ambassador Road, Leicester, LE5 4DL

LE6
Mes Enfants 01162 311 507
195 Leicester Road, Groby, Leicester, LE6 0DT

Toddlers Nursery School 01162 321 445
67 Leicester Road, Groby, Leicester, LE6 0DQ

LE7
Glebe Farm Nursery School 01162 596 883
Gaulby Lane, Houghton-on-the-Hill, Leicester, LE7 9HB

Laurels Nursery School 01162 693 858
1514 Melton Road, Queniborough, Leicester, LE7 3FN

Leicester Montessori 01162 607 933
1096 Melton Road, Syston, Leicester, LE7 2HA

Lilliput Montessori Day Nursery 01162 365 353
Latimer Street, Anstey, LE7 7AW

Purple Rocket Nursery 01162 414 686
742 Uppingham Road, Thurnby, Leicester, LE7 9RN

Rothley Park Kindergarten 01162 303 888
Loughborough Road, Rothley, LE7 7NL

LE8
Blackberry Bush Day Nursery 01162 788 744
The Old School House, Leicester Road,
Countesthorpe, LE8 5QU

Daisy Chain Children's Nursery 01162 776 506
Rose Park, Lutterworth Road, Blaby, LE8 4DP

Lilliput Montessori Glenfield 01162 321 319
Stamford Street, Glenfield, Leicester, LE8 8DL

Lilliput Montessori Whetstone 01162 867 761
8 Swan Yard, High Street, Whetstone, LE8 6LQ

Longfield Kindergarten 01162 403 721
Longfield House, Kilby Road, Fleckney, Leicester,
LE8 8BQ

Old School Nursery 01162 796 111
Paget Street, Kibworth, LE8 0HW

Pebbles Nursery 01162 402 971
81 Kilby Road, Fleckney, Leicester, LE8 8BP

Truecare Day Nursery 01162 786 040
170 Lutterworth Road, Blaby, Leicester, LE8 4DP

LE9
Earl Shilton Montessori School 01455 841 951
The Institute, 12-14 Station Road, Earl Shilton,
Leicestershire, LE9 7GA

De Verdun Childrens' Day Nursery 01455 828 853
14 Arnolds Crescent, Newbold Verdon, Leicester,
LE9 9LD

Lynton Childcare 01455 444 180

85 Shilton Road, Barwell, Leicester, LE9 8BP

Teapots Day Nursery 01455 286 688
Elite Court, Main Street, Broughton Astley, LE9 6RE

The Old Rectory Nursery 01455 843 929
93 Shilton Road, Barwell, LE9 8BP

Topsham House Day Nursery 01455 828 885
16 Peckleton Lane, Desford, Leicester, LE9 9JU

LE10
Asquith Nursery Hinckley 01455 234 500
Wheatfield Way, Hinckley, LE10 1YG

Bright Sparks Day Nursery 01455 234 266
31 Hurst Road, Hinckley, LE10 1AB

Orchard End Day Nursery 01455 615 455
129 Leicester Road, Hinckley, LE10 1LR

Priesthills Nursery 01455 614 732
42 Station Road, Hinckley, LE10 1AP

St Bernards Day Nursery 01455 635 456
6 Clarendon Road, Hinckley, LE10 0PL

Stork Day Nursery 01455 635 656
7 Stoke Road, Hinckley, LE10 0EA

LE11
Kingscliffe Day Nursery 01509 263 325
127 Ashby Road, Loughborough, LE11 3AB

Nanpantan Nursery School 01509 239 203
The Old School House, Nanpantan Road,
Nanpantan, Loughborough, LE11 3YD

Nu Nu 01509 217 275
2 Storer Road, Loughborough, LE11 5EQ
www.nunu.co.uk
At Nunu we set our standards very high so that we
continuously exceed expectations. We offer high quality
childcare for children aged 0-5 years. All of our nurseries have
attractive, well-equipped rooms and we provide an all
inclusive service with quality resources. Our Investors in
People award also demonstrates our commitment. We have
full and part-time vacancies available, so please give us a call
or pop in to one of our nurseries at Long Eaton,
Loughborough or Market Harborough, details are listed on
our main advert under Long Eaton. We look forward to
welcoming you! 0-5yrs. 7.30am-6pm. 50wks.

Our Lady's Convent School 01509 263 901
Burton Street, Loughborough, LE11 2DT
www.olcs.leics.sch.uk
In our Early Years and Infants Departments individual
attention is guaranteed in a loving, caring, Christian
environment. Children are helped begin their journey of
discovery into the world of education. Play facilities are
excellent. There is a dedicated computer suite and library.

Parkside Nursery School 01509 213 329
25 Charnwood Road, Loughborough, LE11 2BN

Small World Nursery 01509 262 922
Schofield Centre, Green Close Lane,
Loughborough, LE11 5AS

Gotham Road, East Leake
Loughborough LE12 6JG
Tel: 01509 852666

Watermead Nursery   **01509 239 205**
2 Watermead Lane, Loughborough, LE11 3TN

Westwards Nursery School   **01509 214 551**
8 Burton Street, Loughborough, LE11 2DT

LE12
Charnwood Day Nursery   **01509 508 012**
120 Charnwood Road, Shepshed, Leicester, LE12 9NP

Hind Leys Nursery   **01509 504 511**
Forest Street, Shepshed, Loughborough, LE12 9DB

Honey Bee Day Nursery   **01509 825 666**
20 Gotham Road, East Lake, LE12 6JG

One Lea House Nursery   **01509 620 909**
211 Loughborough Road, Mountsorrel,
Loughborough, LE12 7AR

Quorn Grange Day Nursery   **01509 412 167**
88 Wood Lane, Quorn, Loughborough, LE12 8DB

Sileby Day Nursery   **01509 812 300**
231 Cossington Road, Sileby, Loughborough, LE12 7RR

St Clements   **01509 891 131**
16 Church Hill, Woodhouse Eaves, Loughborough,
LE12 8RT

Steps   **01509 506 878**
St. Bofolph's Old School, 40 Loughborough Road,
Shepshed, Loughborough, LE12 9DN

White House Day Nursery   **01509 505 555**
55 Forest Street, Shepshed, Loughbouough, LE12 9BZ

LE13
Brooksby Melton College   **01664 480 301**
Day Nursery
Asford Road, Melton Mowbray, Leicester, LE13 0HJ

King Edward VII Day Nursery **01664 481 506**
Burton Road, Melton Mowbray, LE13 1DR

Melton Mowbray Nursery School **01664 569 372**
34 Dalby Road, Melton Mowbray, LE13 0BH

LE14

Brunts Farmhouse   01664 822 188
East End, Long Clawson, Melton Mowbray, LE14 4NG

Peapod Day Nursery   0194 981 522
Temples Cottage, Hickling Pastures, Melton Mowbray, LE14 3QG

LE15

Ayston House Day Nursery   01572 821 821
Ayston House, Uppingham, Rutland, LE15 9RL

Knossington Montessori   01664 454 808
Nursery School
The Village Hall, Main Street, Knossington, LE15 8LT

Little Stars Day Nursery   01780 721 676
Rutland College, Barleythorpe Road, Oakham, Rutland, LE15 6QH

The Old Station Nursery   **01572 812 828**
Ashwell Block, RAF Cottesmore, Oakham, Rutland, LE15 7BL
www.theoldstationnursery.co.uk
0-11yrs, 7.30-6pm, 51wks Breakfast and After-school club, holiday club. Provide hot meals and use organic vegetables.

Windmill House School   01572 823 593
22 Stockerston Road, Uppingham, Rutland, LE15 9UD

LE16

Castle Lane Day Nursery   01858 468 006
9 Great Bowden Road, Market Harborough, LE16 7DE

Hanbury Kindergarten   01858 545 788
3 Station Cottages, West Langton, Leicester, LE16 7TQ

Little Angels Day Nursery   01858 469 708
2-4 Angel Row, Angel Street, Market Harborough, LE16 9QG

Little Bowden Pre-School   01858 431 627
St. Nicholas Church Hall, Rectory Lane, Little Bowden, Market Harborough, LE16 8AS

Little Me Nursery   01858 540 042
Bramley House, 25 Main Street, Foxton, Market Harborough, LE16 7RB

Market Harborough Nursery   01858 464 172
75 St. Mary's Road, Market Harborough, LE16 7DT

Market Harborough Nursery   07968 412 135
Coventry Road, Market Harborough, LE16 9QH

Nunu   **01858 431 355**
Torch Way, Off Northampton Road, Market Harborough, LE16 9HL
www.nunu.co.uk
At Nunu we set our standards very high so that we continuously exceed expectations. We offer high quality

childcare for children aged 0-5 years. All of our nurseries have attractive, well-equipped rooms and we provide an all inclusive service with quality resources. Our Investors in People award also demonstrates our commitment. We have full and part-time vacancies available, so please give us a call or pop in to one of our nurseries at Long Eaton, Loughborough or Market Harborough, details are listed on our main advert under Long Eaton. We look forward to welcoming you!

Pebbles Nursery 01858 432 661
88 Northampton Road, Market Harborough, LE16 9HF
0-8yrs. 8am-6pm. 50wks.

Progress House Day Nursery 01162 414 686
96 Northampton Road, Market Harborough, LE16 9HF
8am-6pm. 50wks.

Teddies Nurseries Market 0800 980 3801
Harborough
Bowden Inn Farm, Licester Road, Market
Harborough, LE16 7AU

LE17
Bitteswell Montessori Day Nursery 01455 556 050
Hall Lane, Bitteswell, Lutterworth, LE17 4LN

Lutterworth Day Nursery 01455 556 895
1 Vedonis Works, Leicester Road, Lutterworth,
LE17 4HD

St Mary's Montessori Day Nursery 01455 554 034
The Old Church Hall, Coventry Road, Lutterworth,
LE17 4SH

LE18
First Class Day Nursery 01162 778 829
St. Thomas Road, Wigston, LE18 4TA
0-8yrs. 7.30am-6pm. 51wks.

Gooseberry Bush Nursery 01162 884 046
47 Long Street, Wigston, LE18 2AJ

Leicester Montessori 01162 570 444
Grammar School Nursery
84 Station Road, Wigston, LE18 2DJ

Lighthouse Day Nursery 01162 886 090
The Kings Centre, 56 Bull Head Street, Wigston,
LE18 1PA

Playhouse Day Nursery 01162 812 211
29a Central Avenue, Wigston, LE18 2AB

LE19
Asquith Creche Leicester 01162 631 419
David Lloyd Club, Meridian Leisure Park,
Lubbesthorpe Way, Braunstone, LE19 1JZ

Harlequins 01162 863 045
81 St. John's, Enderby, Leicester, LE19 2BS

Harlequins Private Day Nursery 01162 750 156
1a George Street, Enderby, Leicester, LE19 4NQ

Honey Bees Pre-School Pavilion 07815 549 143
Enderby Cricket Pavilion, Mill Lane, Enderby, LE19 4NW

Leapfrog Day Nursery 01162 865 566
Carlton Park, King Edward Avenue, Leicester, LE19 0LF

Narborough Nursery School 01162 750 973
The Old School House, School Lane, Narborough,
LE19 2GS

Pebbles Nursery 01162 861 992
Copt Oak Court, Narborough, Leicester, LE19 3WY

Smarties Day Nursery 01162 861 407
West Street, Enderby, LE19 4LS

St George's Nursery School 01162 849 700
Unit D1, The Warrens, Warren Park Way, Enderby,
Leicester, LE19 4SA
www.stgeorgesnursery.com
7.45am-6.00pm. 51 wks.

LE65
Ashby Castle Day Nursery 01530 415 541
28 North Street, Ashby-de-la-Zouch, LE65 1HS

LE67
Apple Tree Day Nursery 01530 249 872
27 Church Drive, Markfield, LE67 9UH

Hermitage Day Nursery 01530 814 477
147-149 Hermitage Road, Whitwick, Coalville, LE67 5EL

Holmsdale Manor Nursery School 01530 262 434
150 High Street, Ibstock, LE67 6JP

Lilliput Montessori Coalville 01530 815 888
Railway House, Hotel Street, Coalville, LE67 3EQ
www.lilliputmontessori.co.uk

Markfield Day Nursery 01530 249 789
220 Leicester Road, Markfield, LE67 9RF

Marlborough Day Nursery 01530 814 051
Marlborough Square, Coalville, LE67 3LT

The Old Station Nursery 01522 727 855
Newall House, High Dike, Waddington, Rutland,
LN5 9NJ
www.theoldstationnursery.co.uk
0-5yrs. 7.30am-6pm, 51wks. Pre-school French and yoga.
They also provide hot meals and use organic vegetables.

LINCOLNSHIRE
DN15
Busi Bodies Nursery 01724 868 337
Ferry Road West, Scunthorpe, DN15 8EA

Little Lambs Nursery 01724 277 070
49/51 Oswald Road, Scunthorpe, DN15 7PE

DN16
Wise Owl Private Day Nursery 01724 330 009
62 Old Brumby Street, Scunthorpe, DN16 2AW

DN17

Happy Stars   01724 876 200
46 Glanville Avenue, Scunthorpe, DN17 1DD

The Secret Garden Day Nursery   01724 711 223
307 Wharf Road, Ealand, Scunthorpe, DN17 4JW

Wind In The Willows   01724 840 040
Chapman Avenue, Scunthorpe, DN17 1PL

DN18

Field View Day Nursery   01652 633 500
Falkland Way, Barton-upon-Humber, DN18 5RL

Field View Day Nursery Baby Unit   01652 633 492
72 Pasture Road, Barton-upon-Humber, DN18 5HZ

Rainbow Kindergarten   01652 660 362
15 Bowmandale, Barton-upon-Humber, DN18 5LR

DN20

Rainbow Kindergarten   01652 653 052
Wesley Road, Brigg, DN20 8AF

Southfield Nursery   01652 657 720
Charlotte House, 1 St Clare's Walk, Brigg, DN20 8JS

DN21

Apple Tree Day Nursery   01652 648 011
37 Northcliffe Road, Gainsborough, DN21 4NJ

Corringham Village Nursery   01427 839 353
Corringham Village Hall, 10A Middle Street,
Corringham, Gainsborough, DN21 5QR

Happy Days   01652 648 228
Grove Street, Kirton Lindsey, Gainsborough, DN21 4BY

Little Imps Nursery   01427 617 471
Acland Street, Gainsborough, DN21 2SU

Little Lambs Nursery   01427 615 007
Corringham Road, Gainsborough, DN21 1QH

Ropery Pre-school and Day Nursery 01427 614 278
North Marsh Road, Gainsborough, DN21 2RR

DN32

First Steps   01472 352 524
The Ice House, Victor Street, Grimsby, DN32 7QN

Highfield Day Nursery   01472 509 669
39 Welholme Road, Grimsby, DN32 0DR

St Nicholas Childrens Nursery   01472 347 007
Peaks Lane, Grimsby, DN32 9RP

DN33

Springfield Lodge   01472 874 583
Montessori Day Nursery
Springfield Park, Springfield Road, Grimsby, DN33 3LE

DN34

Franklin First Call   01472 875 025

Franklin College, Chelmsford Avenue, Grimsby,
DN34 5BY

Little Blossoms Day Nursery   01472 350 238
37 Bargate, Grimsby, DN34 4SN

DN35

Ready Teddy Go   01472 601 126
40 Bradford Avenue, Cleethorpes, DN35 0BD

DN36

Busi Bodies Day Nursery   01472 828 060
The Old School, Peppercorn Walk, Holton-le-Clay,
Grimsby, DN36 5DQ

Rainbow Corner Day Nursery   01472 599 009
26 Pinfold Lane, Holton Le Clay, Grimsby, DN36 5DH

DN40

Immingham Day Nursery   01469 571 177
23 Pelham Road, Immingham, DN40 1AA

LN1

Scampton Playmates   01522 731 581
The Playhouse, Gibson Road, Scampton Lincoln,
LN1 2TR

Sunflowers Nursery School   01522 702 155
The Old School House, Saxilby, Lincoln, LN1 2PE

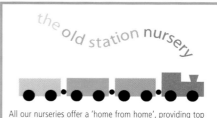

The Old Station Nursery   **01522 511 333**
The Marina, Brayford Pool, Lincoln, LN1 5HQ
www.theoldstationnursery.co.uk

0-5yrs. 8am-6pm, 51wks. Pre-school French and Music with Mummy. They also provide hot meals and use organic vegetables.

LN2

Carlton Day Nursery   **01522 787 070**
The Carlton Centre, Outer Circle Road, Lincoln, LN2 4WA

County Hospital Day Nursery   **01522 573 081**
County Hospital, Sewell Road, Lincoln, LN2 5QY

Heath Farm Day Nursery   **01673 863 140**
The Granary, Heath Road, Dunholme, Lincoln, LN2 3QD

Lincoln Minster Preparatory School   **01522 253 769**
Eastgater, Lincoln, LN2 1QG

St Marys Preparatory School   **01522 524 622**
Pottergate, Lincoln, LN2 1PH

Stepping Stones   **01522 876 226**
Lincoln College, Monks Road, Lincoln, LN2 5HQ

The Old Station nursery   **01522 870 111**
145 Wragby Road, Lincoln, LN2 4PL
www.theoldstationnursery.co.uk
0-11yrs. 8am-6pm, 51wks. Pre-school French, Breakfast and After school club, holiday club, Music with Mummy. They provide hot meals using organic vegetables.

The Old Station Nursery   **01522 876 226**
Sessions House, Monks Road, Lincoln, LN2 5HQ
www.theoldstationnursery.co.uk
0-5yrs. 8am-6pm, 51wks. Pre-school French and Music with Mummy. They also provide hot meals and use organic vegetables.

Young Tots Day Nursery   **01522 568 468**
Limekiln Way, off Greetwell Road, Lincoln, LN2 4US

LN3

Cherry B Day Nursery   **01522 807 081**
37 Church Lane, Cherry Willingham, Lincoln, LN3 4AD

LN4

Branston Community Day Nursery   **01522 880 420**
Branston Community College, Station Road,
Branston, Lincoln, LN4 1LH

Glebe Farm Nursery School   **01522 575 055**
Glebe Farm, Heighington Road, Canwick, Lincoln, LN4 2RJ

Hullabaloo Day Nursery   **01526 323 628**
Lincoln Road, Dunston, Lincoln, LN4 2EX

Kids Corner   **01526 321 388**
45 Sleaford Road, Metheringham, Lincoln, LN4 3DG

RAF Coningsby Nursere Centre   **01526 347 843**
Clinton Park, Tattershall, Lincoln, LN4 4QZ

Teddy Bears Day Nursery   **01522 511 505**
St John's Park, Bracebridge Heath, Lincoln, LN4 2HN

The Mulberry Bush Day Nursery & Kidsclub   **01526 321 094**
High Street, Metheringham, Lincoln, LN4 3EA

LN5

Busy Bees Day Nursery   **01522 575 640**
21-23 Portland Street, Lincoln, LN5 7JZ

Portland Kindergarten   **01522 528 524**
35 Tentercroft Street, Lincoln, LN5 7DB

Rainbow Day Nursery   **01522 722 222**
409 Brant Road, Waddington, Lincoln, LN5 9AL

The Old Station Nursery   **01522 727 855**
Newall House, High Dike, Waddington, Rutland,
LN5 9NJ
www.theoldstationnursery.co.uk
0-5yrs, 7.30am-6pm, 51wks. Pre-school French and yoga. They provide hot meals and use organic vegetables.

The Village Kindergarten   **01400 272 678**
Church Walk, Brant Broughton, LN5 0SN

LN6

Angels Childcare   **01522 705 678**
Kingley Road, Lincoln, LN6 3TA
0-5yrs. 8am-6pm. 51 wks.

Bubbles Day Nursery   **01522 692 000**
98/100 Grange Crescent, Lincoln, LN6 8DA

Nutwood Cottage   **01522 576 716**
553 Newark Road, Lincoln, LN6 8RY

Paper Moon Day Nursery   **01522 681 681**
Jasmin Road, Lincoln, LN6 0QQ
www.papermoondaynursery.co.uk
6wks-5yrs. 8am-6pm. 50wks.

Paper Moon Day Nursery   **01522 560 562**
104 Boultham Park Road, Lincoln, LN6 7TH
www.papermoondaynursery.co.uk
0-5yrs. 8am-6pm. 51wks.

Park School Day Nursery   **01522 681 019**
School Lane, North Hykeham, Lincoln, LN6 9QS

Pinfold Nursery   **01522 691 929**
Woodbank, Skellingthorpe, Lincoln, LN6 5UD

St Nicholas Day Nursery   **01522 812 470**
Runcorn Road, North Hykeham, Lincolm, LN6 3QP

YMCA Woodlands Nursery   **01522 685 499**
Whitethorn Grove, Off Regent Street, Lincoln,
LN6 0PF

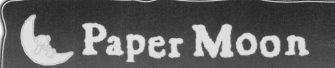

LN7

Abacus Day Nursery 01652 678 631
Keptie, Brigg Road, South Kelsey, Market Rasen, LN7 6PH

LN8

Pegasus Nursery 01673 828 187
Main Street, Osgodby, Market Rasen, LN8 3TA

Town & Country Kiddies 01673 843 228
8 Kilnwell Road, Market Rasen, LN8 3BJ

LN9

Woodlands Nursery 01507 526 755
Horncastle War Memorial Centre, 52 North Street, Horncastle, LN9 5DX

LN10

Kirkby-on-Bain Nursery 01526 352 228
Wharf Lane, Kirkby-on-Bain, Woodhall Spa, LN10 6YW

St Hughs School 01526 351 520
Cromwell avenue, Woodhall Spa, LN10 6TQ

Woodlands Nursery 01526 354 387
Kirkstead Church, Mill Lane, Woodhall Spa, LN10 6QZ

LN11

Busi Bodies Children's Nursery 01507 601 224
68 Keddington Road, Louth, LN11 0BA

Kenwick Leisure Club Nursery 01507 601 852
Kenwick Park hEalth and Leisure Centre, Kenwick Park, Louth, LN11 8NR

Red Hen Childrens Day Nursery 01507 606 845
Manor House Farm, Reston Road, Legbourne, Louth, LN11 8LS

The Limes Play and Learn Nursery 01507 609 199
The Limes, Westgate, Louth, LN11 9YE

Town & Country Kiddies 01507 601 100
48 James Street, Louth, LN11 0JW

LN13

Maypole House School 01507 462 764
Well Vale Hall, Low lane, Well, Alford, LN13 0ET

NG23

Kings Farm Day Nursery 01400 282 662
Winters Lane, Long Bennington, Newark, NG23 5DW

Littlegates for Little People 01636 626 067
Littlegate Farm, Clensey Lane, Dry Doddington, NG23 5HT

NG31

Abacus Day Nursery   01652 678 631
18 North Parade, Grantham, NG31 8AN

Acorn Day Nursery   01476 577 061
Grantham District Hospital, 101 Manthorpe Road,
Grantham, NG31 8DG

Albion House Nursery   01476 562 078
9 Albion Street, Grantham, NG31 8BG

Albion Lodge Day Nursery   01476 592 904
Conduit Lane, Grantham, NG31 6PB

Castlegate Day Nursery   01476 566 555
23a Castlegate, Grantham, NG31 6SW

Dudley House School   01476 400 184
1 Dudley Road, Grantham, NG31 9AA

Headstart Nursery   01476 591 744
The Old School, Dudley Road, Grantham, NG31 9AB

Hill Top Day Nursery   01476 560 622
70 Barrowby Gate, Grantham, NG31 7LT

Hill View Day Nursery   01476 566 031
111 Dysart Road, Grantham, NG31 7DQ

Old St Anne's Schoo   01476 591 744l
/Headstart & Babycare
Dudley Road, Grantham, NG31 9AB

Start Right Nursery   01476 577 115
350 Trent Road, Grantham, NG31 7XQ

Toddle In Day Nursery   01476 577 337
22 Beacon Lane, Grantham, NG31 9DF

Trent Road Nursery   01476 573 188
Trent Road, Grantham, NG31 7XQ
0-8yrs. 7.30am-6pm. 50wks.

NG32

Dappledown House Nursery   01400 250 358
The Old School, Main Street, Honington, NG32 2PG

NG33

Great Wood Farm Early   01476 585 584
Years Centre
Greatwood Farm, Ponton Road, Boothby Pagnell,
Grantham, NG33 4DH

Railway Children's Day Nursery   01780 410 055
Lawn Lane, Creeton, NG33 4QB

NG34

First Steps Nursery   01526 832 518
Meadowbrook, Ruskington, Sleaford, NG34 9FJ

Happy Day Nursery   01529 414 988
Northgate, Sleaford, NG34 7BX

Kidzone   01400 267 826
86C/87 Wellesley Way, RAF Cranwell, Sleaford,
NG34 8HB

Prelude Nursery   01529 455 788
Ensign House, High Street, Osbournby, Sleaford,
NG34 0DG

Redcroft Day Nursery   01529 414 262
Mareham Lane, Sleaford, NG34 7JY

Sleaford Day Nursery   01529 414 464
The Drove, Sleaford, NG34 7AP

Woodside Children's Nursery   01529 307 500
2/4 Hazel Grove, Sleaford, NG34 8BG

PE6

Caterpillar Day Nursery   01778 380 232
The Rundles, 100 Bridge Road, Deeping St James,
PE6 8EH

Headstart Nursery   01778 380 992
26-28 Church Street, Deeping, Deeping St. James,
PE6 8HF

Headstart Nursery (01778 380 992
26/28 Church Street, Deeping St James, Market
Deeping, Peterborough, PE6 8HD

PE9

ABC Day Nursery   01778 343 111
Barholm Road, Tallington, Stamford, PE9 4RJ

Children's Garden Nursery   01780 752 094
1 Silver Lane, Stamford, PE9 2BT

Happy Days Childcare Centre   01780 753 578
60 Queens Street, Stamford, PE9 1QS

Keepers Cottage Day Nursery   01780 721 880
Luffenham Road, Ketton, Stamford, PE9 3UT

Rocking Horse Nursery   01780 757 922
85 Rutland Road, Stamford, PE9 1UP

Stamford YMCA   01780 763 411
13 Radcliffe Road, Stamford, PE9 1AP

The Ark Nursery   01780 482 113
Foundry Road, Stamford, PE9 2PP

PE10

Building Blocks Kindergarten   01778 422 221
Exeter Street, Bourne, PE10 9NS

Daytime Day Nursery   01778 424 244
14 Burghley Street, Bourne, PE10 9NS

Headstart Nursery   01778 393 925
South Road, Bourne, PE10 9LU

Adbolton & Trent Fields Kindergarten

Mission Statement

Encouraging childrens development in a loving, learning, stimulating and homely setting.

Vision

To deliver 'Best Childcare Practices' which we are proud of.

Adbolton Kindergarten
The Lodge, Adbolton Lane, West Bridgford, Nottingham, Nottinghamshire NG2 5AS
Tel: 0115 982 0101

Trent Fields Kindergarten, pre-School & Holiday Club
21, Trent Boulevard, West Bridgford, Nottingham, Nottinghamshire NG2 5BB
Tel: 0115 982 1685

PE11

ABC Day Nursery   01775 724 146
14 Knight Street, Pinchbeck, Spalding, PE11 3RB

Lilliput Day Nursery   01775 766 130
12 High Street, Spalding, PE11 1TW

Puddleducks Day Nursery   01775 769 798
3 Holland Road, Spalding, PE11 1UL

Westfield Farm Day Nursery   01775 640 829
Westfield Farm, West Pinchbeck, Spalding, PE11
3QN

PE12

Twigglets Day Nursery   01406 490 747
Branches Lane, Holbeach, PE12 7BE

PE20

Bramble Hall Day Nursery   01205 460 848
Station Road, Sutterton, Boston, PE20 2JH

Mon-Ami Chilren's Day Nursery   01205 821 244
High Street, Swineshead, Boston, PE20 3LH

PE21

ABC Day Nursery Linc's   01205 311 788
43 Main Ridge East, Boston, PE21 6ST

Conway Nursery School   01205 363 150
Tunnard Street, Boston, PE21 6PL

Mon Ami Children's Nursery   01205 319 499
86 Woodville Road, Boston, PE21 8BB

See Saw Day Nursery   0808 108 0250
Boston West Business Park, Sleaford Road,
Boston, PE21 8EG

PE22

Highgate Nursery   01205 871 038
The Old School House, Leverton, Boston, PE22
0AW

PE25

ABC Day Nursery   01754 760 034
Beresford Avenue, Skegness, PE25 3HY

Peter Pan Day Nursery   01754 764 050
5 Ida Road, Skegness, PE25 2AR

Squirrels Day Nursery   01754 898 100
3 Heath Road, Skegness, PE25 3ST

The Secret Garden   01754 769 695
Children's Day Nursery
Rutland Road, Skegness, PE25 2AX

NOTTINGHAMSHIRE

DN22

All Aboard Day Nursery   01777 702 202
7 Welbeck Road, Ordsall, Retford, DN22 7RP

Claremont House Nursery School   01777 705 742
112 North Road, Retford, DN22 7XN

Shaping Futures   01777 248 554
Dendy Drive, Woodbeck, Retford, DN22 0HW

NG1

Bright Futures Day Nursery 2   0115 912 1633
Within NCN, Bath Street Centre, Bath Street,
Nottingham, NG1 1DA

Learning Works for Children   0115 924 3003
192 Poplar Street, Nottingham, NG1 1GP

Learning Works for Children   0115 915 0115
Day Nursery
Victoria Works, 1 Cairns Street, Nottingham, NG1 3NN

Paper Lace Day Nursery   0115 924 3003
New College Nottingham, 16 Stoney Street,
Nottingham, NG1 1LP

Pretty Windows Day Nursery   0115 988 1429
9-10 Avenue A, Gedling Street, Sneinton Market
Square, Nottingham, NG1 1DS

St Joseph's School   0115 941 8356
33 Derby Road, Nottingham, NG1 5FT

Stepping Stones   0115 910 1162
Day Nursery
Arboretum Street, Nottingham, NG1 4JA
www.steppingstonesltd.com

The Clockhouse   0115 912 1300
Pre-School Centre
229-232 Victoria Centre, Nottingham, NG1 3QP

NG2

Adbolton Kindergarten   0115 982 0101
The Lodge, Adbolton Lane, West Bridgford,
Nottingham, NG2 5AS
www.adboltonkindergarten.com
0-5yrs. 8am-6pm. 50wks.

Busy Bees at Sneinton   0115 950 8148
The Centre for the Child, Edale Road, 144 Sneinton
Dale, Nottingham, NG2 4HT

Castle Meadow Day Nursery   0115 974 0008
The Amenities Building, Inland Revenue, Castle
Meadow Road, NG2 1BE

Children's Corner   0115 981 5649
103 Loughborough Road, West Bridgford,
Nottingham, NG2 7JX
www.childrens-corner.co.uk
6wks-5yrs. 8am-6pm. 50wks.

Greenwood Day Nursery   0115 981 5061
16 Albert Road, West Bridgford, Nottingham, NG2 5GS

Hickory House Day Nursery   0115 914 2222
Hickory House, 66-68 Loughborough Road,
Nottingham, NG2 7JJ
www.hickoryhousedaynursery.co.uk
Hickory House Day Nursery is committed to offering the best possible care to children within a safe, happy and stimulating environment. Parents can feel confident in knowing that their child is valued as an individual with respect for race, culture, religion and language. For babies aged from 6 weeks to children of 5 years. Holiday Club for children aged 4 to 8 years.

Little Friends   0115 981 8040
Adbolton Lane, West Bridgford, NG2 5AS
The Little Friends countryside bungalow is small and friendly, taking only 26 children a day means EARLY booking is essential as places get snapped up extremely quickly. LitFriends has a natural garden with a vegetable patch, from which tasty treats are made, and a wildlife area giving plenty of space to explore. The philosophy of Little Friends isessentially to create a fun filled day for both staff and children. We operate an open door policy feel free to pop in for a chat -with Sarah any time.

Paper Moon Day Nursery   0115 981 1801
The Clock Tower, Compton Acres, West Bridgford,
NG2 7PU
www.papermoonnursery.co.uk
6wks-5yrs.

PROMOTING QUALITY IN EARLY YEARS

NOTTINGHAMSHIRE NDNA MEMBERS

National Day Nurseries Association aims to enhance the development and education of children in their early years, through the provision of support services to members. It seeks to develop, encourage and maintain high standards in education and care for the benefit of children, their families and their local communities.

Acorns Childrens Centre The Old School Room, Church Street

Adbolton Kindergarten Early Years Childcare Group, The Lodge, Adbolton Lane

All Aboard Day Nursery 7 Welbeck Road, Ordsall, Retford

Alphabet House Day Nursery 126 Nottingham Road, Long Eaton

Appleton Day Nursery 73 Appleton Gate

Asquith Nursery Nottingham c/o David Lloyd Club, Aspley Lane

Awsworth Schoolhouse Day Nursery Homestead, 86 Cow Lane, Bramcote

Bingham Day Nursery Early Years Childcare Group, 55 & 59 Long Acre

Brooklyn Day Nursery Forest House, Derby Road, Annesley

Busy Bees at Milford School Milford Primary School, Dungannon Road, Clifton Estate

Busy Bees at Sneinton The Centre for the Child, Edale Road, 144 Sneiton Dale

Carey Days at The Mount Conway Close, Off Woodborough Road

Carrington Day Nursery 315 Mansfield Road, Carrington

Children 1st @ Breedon House Acton Road, 168 Derby Road, Long Eaton

Children 1st @ Breedon House Main Street, 168 Derby Road, Long Eaton

Duncroft Day Nursery 1a Duncroft Avenue, Gedling

East Midlands Development Agency Apex Court, City Link

Fosse Paddock Kindergarten Nottingham Road, Stragglethorpe

Granby House Nursery Lawn Road, Carlton in Lindrick

Greenwood Day Nursery 511 Aspley Lane

Greenwood Day Nursery Limited 16 Albert Road, West Bridgford

Hobby-Horse Nursery School Lane, East Stoke

Leo's Day Nursery 66 St Albans Road, Arnold

Lilliput Day Nursery The Canch c/o Bassetlaw Training Agency, 43 Watson Road

Little Oaks Nursery 92 High Street, Kimberley

Little Stars Day Nursery The Corner House, 18 Strelley Road, Broxtowe

Longdale Nursery School Longdale Lane, Ravenshead

Margaret Mason Briar Lodge, 168 Derby Road, Long Eaton

Millfield Nursery School Tythby Road, Cropwell Butler

Nottingham City Early Years Unit, Education Dept, Sandfield Centre, Sandfield Rd, Lenton

Nottinghamshire EYDCP Nottinghamshire County Council, Education Department, County Hall

Nunu Plc Wilsthorpe Road, Long Eaton

Nurseryworld & Friends Grenfield House, Douglas Road

Old Fire Station Day Nursery Mansfield Road, Blidworth

Papermoon Nurseries The Clocktower, Compton Acres, Wilford

Poplars Nursery School Portland Court, Off Edwards Lane, Sherwood

Radcliffe-on-Trent Day Nursery Downing House, 15 Main Road

Rocking Horse Childcare Centre, Kingsway, Kirkby in Ashfield

Rocking Horse Day Nursery 180 Watnall Road, Hucknall

Rocking Horse Day Nursery 229 Cinderhill Road, Bulwell

Ruddington Day Nursery Grange House, Wilford Road

Scotts Wood II Private Day Nursery 124 126 Radcliffe Road, West Bridgford

Scotts Wood Private Day Nursery 1 Selby Road, West Bridgford

Shaping Futures Day Nurseries 79 Appleton Gate

Station House Childrens Day Nursery 211 Station Road, Beeston

Stepping Stones Day Nursery Arboretum Street

Sunny Days Day Nursery The Summit Centre, Pavilion Road

Sure Start Meadows Drop In, 4 Brideway Centre, The Meadows

The Ark Nursery 1 Vickers Street, Mapperley Park

The Children's House Station Road, Southwell

The Church House Nursery Nether Street, Beeston

The Old Co-operative Day Nursery 7/9 Wallace Street

The Orchard 25 Nether Street, Beeston

The Rocking Horse Day Nursery Station Road

The Secret Garden Private Day Nursery 69 Musters Road, West Bridgford

The Village Nursery 26 Town Street, Bramcote

Tiny Steps 2a The City, Beeston

Tiny World Rock House, Stockhill Lane, Basford

TLC @ Nottingham City Hospital Nottingham City Hospital, Gate 3, Hucknall Road

TLC @ University of Nottingham University of Nottingham, University Park (next to sports ground)

Treetops at Silvertrees Minton Close, Off Swiney Way, Toton

Trent Fields Kindergarten Early Years Childcare Group, 19/21 Trent Boulevard

Valmary's Children's Centre 3 Robinson Road, Mapperley

Westpoint House Day Nursery Homestead, 86 Cow Lane, Bramcote

White House Day Nursery & Out of School Club 41 Bridgford Road

White Post Day Nursery Farnsfield, Newark

Wishing Well Day Nursery 2 Oakfields Road, West Bridgford

Woodthorpe Day Nursery 1 Albemarle Road, Woodthorpe

Rocking Horse Nursery   0115 981 7837
69 Musters Road, West Bridgford, Nottingham,
NG2 7PY

Scotts Wood II Private Day Nursery   0115 981 5281
124-126 Radcliffe Road, West Bridgford,
Nottingham, NG2 5HG

Scotts Wood Private Day Nursery   0115 981 2980
1 Selby Road, West Bridgford, Nottingham, NG2 7BP

Sileby Day Nursery   0115 846 9104
4 Longlands Drive, Nottingham, NG2 6SR

The Gooseberry Bush   0115 982 2220
Day Nursery
Gamston District Centre, Lingsbar Rd, Gamston,
Nottingham, NG2 6PS
The Playroom   0115 981 1168
70 Musters Road, West Bridgford, Nottingham,
NG2 7PR

The Secret Garden   0115 981 7837
Private Day Nursery
69 Munsters Road, Nottingham, NG2 7PU

The White House Day   0115 981 0119
Nursery and Out of School
41 Bridgford Road, West Bridgford, Nottingham,
NG2 6AU

Trent Fields   0115 982 1685
Kindergarten and Pre-School
19/21 Trent Boulevard, West Bridgford,
Nottingham, NG2 5BB
www.adboltonkindergarten.com
2-5yrs. 8am-6pm. 50wks.

Wishing Well Day Nursery   0115 914 2233
2 Oakfields Road, West Bridgford, Nottingham,
NG2 5DN

NG3
Al-Hudaa Nursery   0115 969 0800
Jamia Al Hudaa, Forest House, Berkeley Avenue,
Nottingham, NG3 5TT

Ark Day Nursery   0115 962 4594
1 Vickers Street, Mapperley Park, Nottingham, NG3
4LD

Carey Days Nursery   0115 950 6530
The Mount, Conway Close, Nottingham, NG3 4FS

Forget Me Not Day Nursery   0115 940 4002
9 Parkdale Road, Bakersfield, Nottingham, NG3 7GL

Hillcrest Day Nursery   0115 960 4080
Rowland Avenue, Mapperley, Nottingham, NG3 6BZ

Iona Day Nursery   0115 958 7392
310 Sneinton Dale, Nottingham, NG3 7DN

Valmary's Childrens Centre   0115 960 4259
3 Robinson Road, Nottingham, NG3 6BA
www.ndna.org.uk
1-8yrs. 8am-6pm. 51wks.

Valmary's Childrens Centre   0115 960 4259
145 Woodthorpe Drive, Mapperley, Nottingham,
NG3 5JL
www.ndna.org.uk
1-8yrs. 8am-6pm. 50wks.

NG4
Acorns Children's Centre   0115 931 2745
The Old School Room, Church Street, Lambley,
NG4 4QB

Bright Future Day Nursery   0115 987 3241
64 Vale Road, Colwick, Nottingham, NG4 2ED

Carlton & Gedling Day Nursery   0115 961 7083
37 Gedling Road, Carlton, Nottingham, NG4 3FD

Duncroft Day Nursery   0115 940 4491
1a Duncroft Avenue, Gedling, Nottingham, NG4 3FY

Gedling House Day Nursery   0115 955 2298
Wood Lane, Gedling, NG4 4AD

Good Foundations Day   0115 987 2898
 Nursery

Pentecostal Church 49 Station Road, Carlton, Nottingham, NG4 3AR

Little Bears Day Nursery   **0115 940 4388**
1a First Avenue, Carlton, Nottingham, NG4 1PH

NG5
Academy Day Nursery   **0115 979 7800**
Bestwood Park Drive West, Rise Park, Nottingham, NG5 5EJ

Arnold House Day Nursery   **0115 966 6123**
Mansfield Road, Daybrook, Arnold, NG5 6HW

Carrington Day Nursery   **0115 969 1170**
315 Mansfield Road, Carrington, NG5 2NA

Child's Play Day Nursery   **0115 967 1542**
Elmbridge, Pedmore Valley, Bestwood Park, Nottingham, NG5 5NN

Coteswood House School   **0115 967 6551**
19 Thackerays Lane, Woodthorpe, Nottingham, NG5 4HT

Cuddles Day Nursery   **0115 960 7217**
404 Mansfield Road, Mapperley Park, Nottingham, NG5 2EJ
www.cuddlesdaynursery.com
0-8yrs. 7am-6pm. 51wks.

Educare Day Nursery Two   **0115 969 1700**
16 Pelham Road, Sherwood Rise, Nottingham, NG5 1AP

Hollies Country Park Day Nursery   **0115 920 1826**
11 Woodchurch Road, Bestwood Lodge, Arnold, NG5 8NJ

Hollies Day Nursery   **0115 960 6388**
2 Private Road, Sherwood, Nottingham, NG5 4DB

Leapfrog Day Nursery   **0115 926 4111**
Sir John Robinson Way, Mansfield Road, Daybrook, Nottingham, NG5 6DB

Leo's Day Nursery   **0115 967 3229**
66 St Albans Road, Arnold, Nottingham, NG5 6GS

Pelham Day Nursery   **0115 953 1474**
Pelham Avenue, Nottingham, NG5 1AL

The Poplars Nursery   **0115 967 6051**
Portland Court, Sherwood, Nottingham, NG5 6EX

TLC Day Nursery   **0115 960 5879**
Nottingham City Hospital, Gate 3, Nottingham, NG5 1PB

Tots World   **0115 977 1719**
Southglade Road, Bestwood, Nottingham, NG5 5GF

Woodthorpe Day Nursery   **0115 962 0415**
1 Albemarle Road, Woodthorpe, Nottingham, NG5 3FY

NG6
Angels by Day   **0115 951 9915**
Springfield House, Hucknall Lane, Nottingham, NG6 8AJ

Cherubs Vale View   **0115 979 5994**
362 St Albans Road, Bulwell, Nottingham, NG6 9FS
www.childcareeastmidlands.co.uk
Cherubs Day Nurseries was established by Susan & John Mills in January 1993, who were at that time expecting their first child. There seemed to be a lack of high quality childcare offering: - A friendly, warm and caring environment with professional staff fostering high standards in not only the care but in hygiene, cleanliness and safety, hence Cherubs first Nursery at Executive House opened based on that criteria. We are the only private day nursery in Nottinghamshire and one of only a handful in the Country to achieve the highest grading in every area, this demonstrates our dedication and commitment to providing the best care for each and every child.

Cherubs Executive House   **0115 979 5975**
Executive House, St.Albans Road, Bulwell, Nottingham, NG6 9FT
www.childcareeastmidlands.co.uk
Cherubs Day Nurseries was established by Susan & John Mills in January 1993, who were at that time expecting their first child. There seemed to be a lack of high quality childcare offering: - A friendly, warm and caring environment with professional staff fostering high standards in not only the care but in hygiene, cleanliness and safety, hence Cherubs first Nursery at Executive House opened based on that criteria. We are the only private day nursery in Nottinghamshire and one of only a handful in the Country to achieve the highest grading in every area, this demonstrates our dedication and commitment to providing the best care for each and every child.

Cinders Day Nursery   **0115 916 6331**
Within NCN, Basford Hall, Stockhill Lane, Nottingham, NG6 0NB

Honeypot Day Nursery   **0115 913 6663**
Squires Avenue, Nottingham, NG6 8GL

Rocking Horse Day Nursery   **0115 976 3322**
229 Cinderhill Road, Nottingham, NG6 8SE

Tiny World   **0115 942 2320**
Rock House, Stockhill Lane, Nottingham, NG6 0LJ

Tiny World Arnold Road   **0115 978 2274**
92 Arnold Road, Nottingham, NG6 0DZ

NG7
Angels by Day Nursery   **0115 978 9980**
Hillside House, Derby Road, Lenton, Nottingham, NG7 2DZ

Early Start Day Nursery   **0115 970 6806**

Ortzen Street, Nottingham, NG7 4BN

Edna G Olds Early to Late Club   0115 915 6899
Church Street, Lenton, Nottingham, NG7 1SJ

Educare Day Nursery   0115 962 6226
8 Sherwood Rise, Nottingham, NG7 6JF

Greenfields Day Nursery   0115 941 8441
139 Russel Road, Forest Fields, Nottingham, NG7 6GX

Paper Moon Day Nursery   **0115 942 4800**
Faraday Road, Lenton, Nottingham, NG7 2DU
www.papermoondaynursery.co.uk

Pehla Qadam Day Nursery   0115 979 1864
412/414 Radford Road, Radford, Nottingham, NG7 7NP

Sandfield Day Nursery   0115 979 2424
Ashburnham Avenue, Lenton, Nottingham, NG7 1QD

Small World Day Nursery   0115 955 3703
Berridge Centre, Stanley Road, Forest Fields,
Nottingham, NG7 6HW

Tardis Day Nursery   0115 911 7368
65-67 Radford Road, Hyson Green, NG7 5DR

TLC @ University of Nottingham   0115 922 9117
University of Nottingham, Nottingham, NG7 2RD

University Hospital   **0115 942 0978**
Day Nursery
Queens Medical Centre, South Road, Nottingham,
NG7 2UH

University of Nottingham   0115 951 5222
Day Nursery
University of Nottingham, Nottingham, NG7 2RD

Young Ones Day Nursery   0115 979 0988
Derby Road, Lenton, NG7 2EB

NG8

Asquith Creche Nottingham   0115 929 8035
David Lloyd Club, Aspley Lane, Nottingham, NG8 5AR
www.asquithcourt.co.uk
3mths-5yrs. 8am-6pm. 51wks

First Steps Day Nursery   0115 975 0003
139 Frinton Road, Broxtowe, Nottingham, NG8 6GR

Greenwood Day Nursery   0115 929 3300
511 Aspley Lane, Aspley, Nottingham, NG8 5RW

Leapfrog Day Nursery   0115 928 0508
Bramcote Lane, Wollaton, Nottingham, NG8 2NG

My Start Nursery   0115 970 5152
Minver Crescent, Nottingham, NG8 5PN

Robins Wood Day Nursery   0115 929 6655
Nottingham West District Land Registry, Chalfont Drive, Aspley, NG8 3LT

Wollaton House Day Nursery   0115 928 1181
5 Bridge Road, Wollaton, Nottingham, NG8 2DG

Wollaton Village Day Nursery   0115 928 2239
Wollaton Road, Wollaton Village, NG8 2AN
www.wollatonvillagenurseriesltd.co.uk
2-5yrs. 9.15-11.45am & 12.40-3.10pm.

NG9

Alphabet house Day Nursery   0115 943 6220
10 Chilwell Road, Beeston, Nottingham, NG9 1EJ

Arthur Mee Centre Day Nursery   0115 917 5414
Church Street, Stapleford, Nottingham, NG9 8GH

Bizzy Kidz   0115 946 6814 / 0115 925 7735
Village Hotel, Brainsfield Way, Chilwell, Nottingham, NG9 6DL
www.bizzy-kidz.co.uk
0-5yrs. 6am-11pm 7 days a week. Wrap around childcare from all local schools (including pick up and drop off).

Bramcote Village Nursery & Pre-school   0115 943 0053
26 Town Street, Bramcote, Nottingham, NG9 3HA
www.bramcotevillagenursery.co.uk
6wks-5yrs. 7.30am-6pm. 51wks.

Brookhill House Day Nursery   0115 849 2304
19 Brookhill Street, Stapleford, Nottingham, NG9 7BQ

Cared 4 Nottingham   0115 849 2304
19 Brookhill Street, Stapleford, Nottingham, NG9 7BG

Children 1st @ Breedon House   0115 972 1113
5 Banks Road, Toton, NG9 6HE
0-8yrs. 7.30am-6pm. 50wks.

Church House Day Nursery 0115 967 7684
Nether Street, Beeston, NG9 2AT

Family First Day Nursery 0115 925 8113
Sure Start Children's Centre, Chilwell, Nottingham,
NG9 4HQ

Silvertrees Day Nursery 0115 973 2311
Minton Close, Toton, Nottingham, NG9 6PZ

Station House Day Nursery 0115 967 7677
211 Station Road, Beeston, Nottingham, NG9 2AB

Stepping Stones 0115 922 3144
42/44 Attenborough Lane, Beeston, NG9 5JW

The Church House Nursery 0115 967 7684
25 Nether Street, Beeston, Nottingham, NG9 2AT

The Orchard 0115 983 0003
25 Nether Street, Nottingham, NG9 1HX

The Village Nursery 0115 925 4027
26 Town Street, Bramcote, Nottingham, NG9 3HA

Tiny Steps Private Day Nursery 0115 925 9111
2a The City, Beeston, Nottingham, NG9 2ED
3-4yrs. 8am-6pm. 50wks.

Treetops at Silvertrees 0115 973 2311
Minton Close, Chilwell, Beeston, Nottingham, NG9 6PZ

Wollaton Village Day Nursery 0115 922 2454
Chapel Street, Bramcote Village, Nottingham, NG9 3HB
www.wollatonvillagenurseriesltd.co.uk

Young Rascals Day Nursery 0115 943 0053
5 City Road, Beeston, Nottingham, NG9 2LQ

NG10

Alphabet House Day Nursery 0115 941 8356
126 Nottingham Road, Long Eaton,
Nottingham,NG10 2BZ

Breedon House Children's Centre 0115 972 1113
5 Banks Road, Toton, Nottingham, NG10 4BJ

Children 1st @ Breedon House 0115 972 0888
146 Derby Road, Long Eaton, NG10 4AX
2-14yrs. 7.30am-6pm. 50wks.

Children 1st @ Breedon House 0115 946 8732
18a Main Street, Long Eaton, NG10 1GR

Clowns Private Day Nursery 0115 939 0105
69 Derby Road, Sandiacre, Nottingham, NG10 5HY
www.clowns-nursery.co.uk

Nightingale Nursery 0115 973 1414
545 Tamworth Road, Sawley, Nottingham, NG10 3FB

Places now available at....
Edwalton Day Nursery

About Edwalton

The nursery has seven main playrooms for individual age groups with an additional messy play area. Outside is a fully enclosed, attractively laid out garden. Two fields and a playground are part of the nursery ensuring that the children have access to a variety of outdoor stimulation with an opportunity to explore, learn and play.

Our 3-5 year old children are visited by a French teacher to support further learning in a different language. Children join in with games, songs and activities with a French theme. Other age groups benefit from a music teacher and Tots in Sport activities.

- For children age 6 weeks to 5 years
- Open from 8.00am and 6.00pm, 52 weeks a year (except Public Holidays)
- 80 places on a full or sessional basis
- Seven main play and teaching rooms
- Fully equipped outdoor play area with superb garden

Location

Edwalton is located in a leafy suburb of Nottingham, approximately 3 miles from the city centre. There is easy access to the M1.

Edwalton Day Nursery, 227 Melton Road, Edwalton, Nottingham, Notts NG12 4DB
Telephone 0115 9452741

CHILD BASE Nurseries

Montessori
Schools Association
Working for the Montessori movement across the UK

Here is a list of the Montessori Schools that are registered with the MSA in the East Midlands area.

Children's Garden Nursery
1 Silver Lane, Stamford, Lincolnshire, PE9 2BT
Telephone:01780 752 094

Children's House
Station Road, Stallingborough, Lincolnshire, DN41 8AJ
Telephone:01472 886 000

Derby Montessori School
296 Uttoxeter New Road, Derby, Derbyshire, DE22 3LN
Telephone:01332 346 333
Website:www.derbymontessori.co.uk

Earl Shilton Montessori School
12-14 Station Road, Earl Shilton, Leicester, Leicestershire, LE9 7GA
Telephone:01455 841 951

Lilliput Montessori Anstey
Latimer Street, Leicester, Leicestershire, LE7 7AW
Telephone:0116 236 5353
Website:www.lilliput-anstey.co.uk

Lilliput Montessori Coalville
Railway House, Hotel Street, Coalville, Leicestershire, LE67 3EQ
Telephone:01530 815 888
Website:www.lilliputmontessori.co.uk

Lilliput Montessori Glenfield
Stamford Street, Glenfield, Leicester, Leicestershire, LE8 8DL
Telephone:0116 232 1319

Lilliput Montessori Whetstone
8 Swan Yard, High Street, Whetstone, Leicestershire, LE8 6LQ
Telephone:01162 867 761

Maidford Montessori Nursery School
Rectory Farm, Maidford, Towcester, Northants, NN12 8HG
Telephone:01327 860 666

Manor Farm Montessori School
Branston, Grantham, Lincolnshire, NG32 1RU
Telephone:01476 879 320

Market Harborough Nursery School
Coventry Road, Market Harborough, Leicestershire, LE16 9QH
Telephone:07968 121 135

Springfield Lodge Montessori Day Nursery
Springfield Park, Springfield Road, Grimsby, Lincolnshire, DN33 3LE
Telephone:01472 874 583

Staunton Montessori Nursery School
Staunton-in-the-Vale, Nr.Orston, Nottingham, Nottinghamshire, NG13 9PE
Telephone:01400 282 860
Website:www.staunton-montessori.com

To join the MSA please call Caroline Harraway on 0207 493 8300 or go online to www.montessori.org.uk/msa membership is free

Changing times...

"Many of my works were written about at the beginning of my endeavours, and they often refer to scientific theories and experiments that were popular then or to situations that were familiar in those days. Times have changed and science has made great progress, and so must our work."

Maria
Montessori
1870 - 1952

STAUNTON MONTESSORI NURSERY SCHOOL & TUTORIAL

Honorary Patron:
Dr Miriam Stoppard MB MD MRCP DSc
Fellow of the Royal College of
Physicians

Montessori Centenary Celebration at Staunton Montessori School
Attended by Celebrity Honorary Patron Dr Miriam Stoppard and
Hosted by Headteacher Mr Robert Staunton

To celebrate the 100th Anniversary of the Montessori Movement and the beginning of the National Montessori Week, Staunton Montessori School hosted a Garden Party on 9th June attended by the school's Honorary Patron Dr. Miriam Stoppard and her son, actor Ed Stoppard. Dr Stoppard, a television presenter, Mirror columnist and celebrity doctor, is one of the world's greatest champions of the Montessori cause.

Gorgeous weather greeted the school's honorary patron as children's entertainer Geoffrey Jumper generated much laughter and happiness with his singing and magic show. Music from 'Jazz Café' played throughout the day, which gave the event a carnival atmosphere. After the family picnic in the school grounds, there were speeches from Headteacher Mr Robert Staunton and Dr Stoppard.

Mr Staunton said in his Centenary speech,
"The centenary of Montessori is really significant globally and for us in England. There are 22,000 Montessori schools worldwide and 750 across the UK. The first Montessori school, called the *Casa dei Bambini*, started in January 1907 in the San Lorenzo district of Rome and it changed a whole community - lifting its morale. Within six months royalty had visited the school. What followed was a rapid international expansion. And now here we are in rural Nottinghamshire celebrating Montessori and childhood."
Mr Staunton went on to compare Dr Miriam Stoppard with Dr Maria Montessori, saying that they are both revolutionaries in their fields.
"Dr Miriam has revolutionised the public's understanding of the miraculous process of pregnancy, childbirth and early childhood. Dr Maria has revolutionised our attitude to children and pioneered child-centred learning."
Mr Staunton also compared Dr Maria and Dr Miriam in terms of their incredible scholarship, their talent for having reached so many people and indeed their genuine love of children. Dr Miriam has sold over 20 million books worldwide.

Dr Miriam Stoppard said, speaking about Staunton Montessori School,
"I'd lie across the threshold to get my children into this school. Local parents are very lucky to have a school like this."
Dr Stoppard also cited scientific evidence that shows the effectiveness of the Montessori Method in nursery age children. She discussed the importance of following the child's lead in both parenting and in education, and continued to advocate Montessori and child-centred schooling.

The event was attended by about 100 people and was widely covered in the local press. Dr Stoppard, who stayed on to attend the Christening of Robert & Adrienne Staunton's children, wrote saying:
"Thank you for the time of my life. It is a great honour to be involved with Montessori and particularly with Staunton Montessori. You give me hope for the future."
Ed Stoppard left his stay with the Stauntons directly to join the cast of the forthcoming period drama movie adaptation of 'Brideshead Revisited', in which he co-stars with Emma Thompson. Ed said that he loved his visit to Staunton Montessori and hoped that the Montessori Movement would thrive for many centuries to come.

Mr Staunton said,
"The late Dr Maria Montessori lives on in her 22,000 schools and most importantly in the children, who continue to flourish."

Director:
Mr Robert Staunton MA
(Hons) PGCE
RSA CTEFLA

MONTESSORI
Full Member: M.S.A.
(Montessori Schools Association)

Directress:
Mrs Adrienne
Staunton

Nunu   **0115 946 3003**
Wilsthorpe Road, Long Eaton, Nottingham, NG10 3RX
www.nunu.co.uk
At Nunu we set our standards very high so that we
continuously exceed expectations. We offer high quality
childcare for children aged 0-5 years. All of our nurseries have
attractive, well-equipped rooms and we provide an all
inclusive service with quality resources. Our Investors in
People award also demonstrates our commitment. We have
full and part-time vacancies available, so please give us a call
or pop in to one of our nurseries at Long Eaton,
Loughborough or Market Harborough, details are listed on
our main advert under Long Eaton. We look forward to
welcoming you!

NG11

Busy Bees at Milford School   **0115 984 7882**
Dungannon Road, Nottingham, NG11 9BT
www.busybees.com
8mths-3yrs. 7.30am-6.30pm. 50wks.

Old Co-operative Day Nursery   **0115 983 0003**
7-9 Wallace Street, Gorham, NG11 0HJ
0-8yrs. 7.30am-6.30pm. 50wks.

Ruddington Day Nursery   **0115 984 8125**
Grange House, Wilford Road, Ruddington, NG11 6NA
8am-6pm. 50wks.

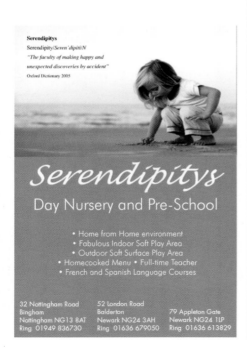

Serendipitys
Serendipity/Seren´dipiti/N
"The faculty of making happy and
unexpected discoveries by accident"
Oxford Dictionary 2005

Serendipitys
Day Nursery and Pre-School

- Home from Home environment
- Fabulous Indoor Soft Play Area
- Outdoor Soft Surface Play Area
- Homecooked Menu • Full-time Teacher
- French and Spanish Language Courses

32 Nottingham Road	52 London Road	79 Appleton Gate
Bingham	Balderton	Newark NG24 1LP
Nottingham NG13 8AT	Newark NG24 3AH	Ring 01636 613829
Ring 01949 836730	Ring 01636 679050	

The Gatehouse Day Nursery   **0115 984 7432**
163 Loughborough Road, Ruddington, Nottingham,
NG11 6LQ

NG12

Edwalton Day Nursery   **0115 945 2741**
227 Melton Road, Edwalton, NG12 4DB
www.childbase.com
Edwalton Day Nursery is a full day care setting of the highest
quality catering for children aged 6 weeks to 5 years. The
nursery benefits from a beautiful building set in wonderful
surroundings. The nursery is a converted house that has
retained original features with a homely feel, which many find
appealing. There are eight playrooms for different age groups
including specialist areas for babies. The landscaped, fully
enclosed gardens are divided into a variety of safe and
secure play and interest area. 6wks-5yrs. 7.30am-6.30pm.
50wks.

Fosse Paddock Kindergarten   **0115 989 4226**
Fosse Paddock, Nottingham Road, Nottingham,
NG12 2JU
www.fossepaddock.co.uk
6wks-5yrs. 8am-6pm. 52wks.

Grosvenor School   **0115 923 1184**
218 Melton Road, Edwalton, Nottingham, NG12 4BS

Holly Court Nursery   **0115 984 5496**
Landmere Lane, Edwalton, NG12 4DG

Millfield Nursery School   **0115 933 4085**
Millfield House, Tithby Road, Cropwell Butler,
Nottingham, NG12 3AJ
www.millfieldnurseryschool.co.uk

Radcliffe-on-Trent Day Nursery   **0115 933 3133**
15 Main Road, Radcliffe-on-Trent, Nottingham,
NG12 2FD

Rocking Horse Nursery   **0115 937 4755**
Station Road, Plumtree, Nottingham, NG12 5NA

NG13

Bingham Day Nursery   **0194 983 9242**
55 Long Acre, Bingham, Nottingham, NG13 8AG

www.earlyyearschildcaregroup.co.uk

Serendipitys Day Nursery   **0194 983 6730**
32 Nottingham Road, Bingham, NG13 8AT
www.serendipitysdaynursery.co.uk
With 5 children their own Serendipitys proprietors Kelly and
Matt Alls know too well the importance of quality childcare.
Everything at Serendipitys is designed to provide the absolute
highest quality childcare. Serendipitys home from home
environment is of great importance to parents who leave their
children in their care. Serendipitys really have thought of
everything from a strict recruitment process, in depth policies
and procedures, parent involvement and forums, healthy
homemade meals incorporating the 5 day (fruit and
vegetables) guideline, fabulous equipment, staff training,

Applegarth Day Nursery
For the apple of your eye

FREEPHONE 0800 028 65 44

Ideal for Sherwood Business Park, MI,
Linby, Papplewick, Ravenshead &
North Nottingham to Nottingham City Centre
Robey Close, Linby Nottingham NG15 8AA
Email: enquiries@applegarthdaynurseries.co.uk

Applegarth Day Nursery provides
Exceptional Quality Childcare, Play Facilities & Early Years Education
in a richly stimulating and exciting environment.
Seeing is believing! Come and visit this amazing Nursery in it's trendy, modern
building with beautiful grounds and outdoor provision

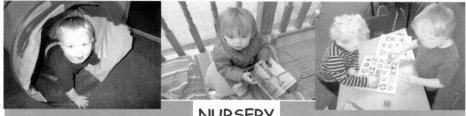

NURSERY

- **WEBCAM — A FIRST FOR THE EAST MIDLANDS** - use your home or work Computer to see your child at Nursery through secure webcam facility.
- **BABY UNIT** is thoughtfully organised, beautifully equipped with designated areas to enable babies & toddlers to grow and develop in a safe and colourful environment.
- **BABY UNIT** has a tranquil sleeps room filled with music, a creative activity area, dining area and milk kitchen.
- **PAMPERS NAPPIES** Johnson's Baby Wipes and Formula of choice are provided.
- **BABY UNIT** Fully qualified experienced mature staff.
- **MOVERS & SHAKERS** for children 1 to 2 years and **EXPLORERS & ADVENTURERS** for children 2 to 3 years are units for the children to progress at their individual pace & developmental stage.
- **EARLY YEARS SPECIALIST** for **SCHOLARS** in the Foundation Stage. Oxford Reading Scheme for pre-school children.
- **NURSERY EDUCATION FUNDING** Sessions provided for all 3 & 4 year olds. FREE 2.5 hours available.
- **DANCE TEACHER** provides a morning session of fun music & movement.
- **SWIMMING LESSONS** for Scholars at the local Leisure Centre weekly.
- **NUTRITIONALLY BALANCED MEALS** cooked daily on the premises from fresh local produce. All dietary needs catered for.
- **HOURS OF OPENING** 7.15am—6.15pm Monday to Friday. 51 weeks per year excluding Bank Holidays.
- **CHILDCARE VOUCHERS** —ALL Employers subsidised childcare vouchers welcome.

THE ZONE
Dedicated Outstanding Out Of School facility
For children of 4 years to 14 years
Providing quality, accessible, inclusive affordable childcare
Before School After School & Holiday Club
Take & Pick up from ALL local schools showing a
commitment to partnership working in the community
FUN, FRIENDLY, FAB FOOD, LOVE THE CRAFT ROOM, CHILL WITH YOUR FRIENDS
Quotes from the children!

regular meetings with local schools and obviously the highest quality care and early years education. Come and see what your child can discover at Serendipitys.

Staunton Montessori Nursery School 0140 028 2860
Staunton-in-the-Vale, Orston, Nottingham, NG13 9PE

NG14
Alphabet House Day Nursery 0115 966 4556
Gunthorpe Road, Lowdham, NG14 7EN

Daisies Day Nursery 0159 966 5282
63 Main Street, Lowdham, Nottingham, NG14 7BD

Homestead Day Nursery 0115 965 2540
9 Mews Lane, Calverton, Nottingham, NG14 6JW

Honey Pot Day Nursery 0115 931 4411
2 Nottingham Road, Burton Joyce, Nottingham, NG14 5AE

Top Spinney Nursery School 0115 926 2096
Barn Farm, Nottingham Road, Nottingham, NG14 6EH

NG15
Applegarth Day Nursery 0800 028 6544
Robey Close Linby, Lindby, NG15 8AA
6wks-14yrs. 7.30am-7.15pm. 51wks.

Brooklyn Day Nursery 0162 375 2092
Forest House, Derby Road, Annesley, Nottingham, NG15 0AQ

Hucknall Day Nursery 0115 968 0797
100 Nottingham Road, Hucknall, Nottingham, NG15 7QE

Lee Mills Pre-School 0115 964 2725
The Old Church, Carlingford Road, Hucknall, NG15 7AE

Longdale Nursery School & Childrens Centre 0162 349 1919
Longdale Lane, Ravenshead, NG15 9AH
www.childcareeastmidlands.co.uk
Cherubs Day Nurseries was established by Susan & John Mills in January 1993, who were at that time expecting their first child. There seemed to be a lack of high quality childcare offering: - A friendly, warm and caring environment with professional staff fostering high standards in not only the care but in hygiene, cleanliness and safety, hence Cherubs first Nursery at Executive House opened based on that criteria. We are the only private day nursery in Nottinghamshire and one of only a handful in the Country to achieve the highest grading in every area, this demonstrates our dedication and commitment to providing the best care for each and every child.

Nottingham Montessori School Baby Unit & Nursery 0115 964 0001
2 Connery, Hucknall, Nottingham, NG15 7AH

Rocking Horse Day Nursery 0115 963 2923
180 Watnall Road, Hucknall, Nottingham, NG15 6FB

Sunshine Corner Day Nursery 0115 840 2073
Portland Road, Hucknall, Nottingham, NG15 7SN

NG16
Awsworth School House Day Nursery 0115 944 4114
The Lane, Awsworth, Nottingham, NG16 2QQ
www.awsworthschoolhousedaynursery.co.uk
0-11yrs. 7am-6.30pm. 51wks.

Cherubs Kimberley 0115 938 9090
The High Street, Kimberley, Nottingham, NG16 2PD
www.childcareeastmidlands.co.uk
Cherubs Day Nurseries was established by Susan & John Mills in January 1993, who were at that time expecting their first child. There seemed to be a lack of high quality childcare offering: - A friendly, warm and caring environment with professional staff fostering high standards in not only the care but in hygiene, cleanliness and safety, hence Cherubs first Nursery at Executive House opened based on that criteria. We are the only private day nursery in Nottinghamshire and one of only a handful in the Country to achieve the highest grading in every area, this demonstrates our dedication and commitment to providing the best care for each and every child.

Discovery Childcare 0115 938 4805
83-85 Smithurst Road, Giltbrook, Nottingham, NG16 2UD
www.discoverychild.co.uk

Little Oaks Nursery 0115 938 2022
92 High Street, Kimberley, NG16 2PD

Wollaton Village Day Nursery 0177 371 1721
52 Church Street, Eastwood, Nottingham, NG16 3HS
www.wollatonvillagenurseriesltd.co.uk
0-8yrs.

Wollaton Village Day Nursery 0115 922 2454
Chapel Street, Bramcote Village, NG16 3HS
www.wollatonvillagenurseriesltd.co.uk
0-5yrs. 8am-6.30pm. 50wks.

NG17
Learning Tree Day Nursery 01623 512 324
10 Alfreton Road, Sutton-on-Ashfield, NG17 1FW

Learning Tree Nursery 01623 552 144
200 Kirkby Road, Sutton-in-Ashfield, NG17 1GP

Little Chicks Day Nursery 01623 438 909
84-86 Outram Street, Sutton-in-Ashfield, Mansfield, NG17 4FS

Little Millers Day Nursery 01623 622 515
Mansfield Road, Sutton-in-Ashfield, NG17 4JL

Nurseryworld and Friends Nursery   01623 440 624
Grenfield House, Douglas Road, Sutton-in-Ashfield, NG17 2EE
www.nurseryworldandfriends.co.uk

Paper Moon Day Nursery   01623 440 011
Mansfield Road, Sutton-in-Ashfield, NG17 4HW
www.papermoonnursery.co.uk

Rocking Horse Nursery   01623 408 330
Kingsway Primary School, Kingsway, Kirkby-in-Ashford, NG17 7FH

Sunny Days Day Nursery   01623 723 232
The Summit Centre, Kirkby-in-Ashford, NG17 7LL

NG18

Bright Sparks Day Nursery   01623 652 220
Derby Road, Mansfield, NG18 5BN

Butterflies Day Nursery   01623 413 015
Derby Road, Mansfield, NG18 5BH

Mulberry Bush Day Nursery   01623 429 555
Littleworth, Mansfield, NG18 2RT

Shaping Futures   01623 600 638
Mansfield 1 Centre, Hamilton Way, Mansfield, NG18 5BR

Smarties Private Day Nursery   01623 636 100
205 Nottingham Road, Mansfield, NG18 4AA

Tiny World Mansfield   01623 420 600
Layton Avenue, Mansfield, NG18 5PJ

NG19

Cherubs Childcare Centre   01623 420 940
Walbeck Road, Mansfield Woodhouse, Nottingham, NG19 9LA
www.childcareeastmidlands.co.uk
Cherubs Day Nurseries was established by Susan & John Mills in January 1993, who were at that time expecting their first child. There seemed to be a lack of high quality childcare offering: - A friendly, warm and caring environment with professional staff fostering high standards in not only the care but in hygiene, cleanliness and safety, hence Cherubs first Nursery at Executive House opened based on that criteria. We are the only private day nursery in Nottinghamshire and one of only a handful in the Country to achieve the highest grading in every area, this demonstrates our dedication and commitment to providing the best care for each and every child.

Chesterfield Road Day Nursery   01623 627 191
Chesterfield Road South, Mansfield, NG19 7BB

Safe Haven Day Nursery   01623 480 554
61a High Street, Mansfield Woodhouse, Mansfield, NG19 8BB

Springfield Nursery   01623 819 829
Chesterfield Road North, Pleasley, Mansfield, NG19 7SP

NG20

Shaping Futures   01623 845 359
Church Street, Warsop, Mansfield, NG20 0AQ

NG21

Bright Beginnings Day Nursery   01623 822 440
17 Mansfield Road, Edwinstowe, Mansfield, NG21 9NL

Old Fire Station Day Nursery   01623 490 222
Mansfield Road, Blidworth, Mansfield, NG21 0PN

Vicar Water Day Nursery   01623 660 555
123-125 Mansfield Road, Clipstone, NG21 9AA

NG22

Bumble Bees   01623 836 880
Fountain Court, Darwin Drive, Sherwood Energy Centre, New Ollerton, NG22 9GS

Hand in Hand   0115 960 7217
404 Mansfield Road, Sherwood, Nottingham, NG22 9TD

White Post Day Nursery   0162 388 3114
Mansfield Road, Farnsfield, Newark, NG22 8HL
www.whitepostdaynursery.co.uk
The White Post Day Nursery at Farnsfield is a family run and staffed by caring professionals priding itself on providing the highest possible standard of education and care for babies and children up to the age of eight years. All meals are

NURSERY and Friends WORLD

Est. 1990

Nursery and Pre-School

Member of

NDNA

national day
nurseries association

PRE SCHOOL

LEARNING
ALLIANCE

An independent & owner managed Day
Nursery catering for children from
six weeks to five years

Registered for 37 children

Excellent OFSTED report

Mature and experienced staff
(qualified to level 3 or above)

Children cared for in small groups with
a maximum of six babies in baby room

ANY INSPECTION WELCOME

Tel 01623 44 06 24

Grenfield House, Douglas Road,
Sutton-in-Ashfield, Notts. NG17 2EE
www.nurseryworldandfriends.co.uk

Working in partnership
with Nottinghamshire Early
Years Development and
Childcare Partnership

SureStart

Neighbourhood Nurseries Initiative

New Opportunities Fund
LOTTERY FUNDED

prepared and cooked on the premises using fresh produce. The nursery is situated alongside the White Post Farm Centre and children have access to the farm as an additional learning resource. The Nursery accepts all nursery vouchers and offers nursery grants.

NG23

Cherubs Newark   **0163 670 6525**
Bathley Lane, North Muskham, Newark, NG23 6HN
www.childcareeastmidlands.co.uk
Cherubs Day Nurseries was established by Susan & John Mills in January 1993, who were at that time expecting their first child. There seemed to be a lack of high quality childcare offering: - A friendly, warm and caring environment with professional staff fostering high standards in not only the care but in hygiene, cleanliness and safety, hence Cherubs first Nursery at Executive House opened based on that criteria. We are the only private day nursery in Nottinghamshire and one of only a handful in the Country to achieve the highest grading in every area, this demonstrates our dedication and commitment to providing the best care for each and every child. 6wks-8yrs. 7.30am-6pm. 50wks.

Hobby-Horse Nursery   **0163 652 5012**
and Kids Club
School Lane, East Stoke, NG23 5QL

Poppies Child Centre   **0163 662 6260**
Old School, School Lane, Claypole, Newark, NG23 5BQ

NG24

Appleton Day Nursery   **0163 661 3833**
73 Appleton Gate, Newark, NG24 1LN

Balderton Village Day Nursery   **0163 670 4708**
173 London Road, New Balderton, Newark, NG24 3BW

Beacon Hill Day Nursery   **0163 670 4823**
29 Beacon Hill Road, Newark, NG24 2JH

Children 1st @ Breedon   **01636 671 805**
House
Muskham Road, Newark, NG24 1DP

Children 1st@ Breedon House   **0163 661 1914**
Torridon House, Muskham Road, Newark, NG24 1NP
7.30am-6pm. 50wks.

Mother Hens Day Nursery   **0163 661 1603**
Old Station Masters House, Great North Road, Newark, NG24 1BW

Serendipitys Day Nursery   **01636 613 829**
79 Appleton Gate, Newark, NG24 1LP
www.serendipitysdaynursery.co.uk
With 5 children their own Serendipitys proprietors Kelly and Matt Alls know too well the importance of quality childcare. Everything at Serendipitys is designed to provide the absolute highest quality childcare. Serendipitys home from home environment is of great importance to parents who leave their children in their care. Serendipitys really have thought of

everything from a strict recruitment process, in depth policies and procedures, parent involvement and forums, healthy homemade meals incorporating the 5 day (fruit and vegetables) guideline, fabulous equipment, staff training, regular meetings with local schools and obviously the highest quality care and early years education. Come and see what your child can discover at Serendipitys.

Serendipitys Day   **01636 679 050**
Nursery and Pre-school
52 London Road, New Balderton, Newark, NG24 3AH
www.serendipitysdaynursery.co.uk
With 5 children their own Serendipitys proprietors Kelly and Matt Alls know too well the importance of quality childcare. Everything at Serendipitys is designed to provide the absolute highest quality childcare. Serendipitys home from home environment is of great importance to parents who leave their children in their care. Serendipitys really have thought of everything from a strict recruitment process, in depth policies and procedures, parent involvement and forums, healthy homemade meals incorporating the 5 day (fruit and vegetables) guideline, fabulous equipment, staff training, regular meetings with local schools and obviously the highest quality care and early years education. Come and see what your child can discover at Serendipitys.

The Old Station Nursery   **0163 670 6043**
Newark College, Friary Street, Newark, NG24 1PB
www.theoldstationnursery.co.uk
2-8yrs. 8am-6pm. 51wks. Breakfast and After-school club, holiday club. Provide hot meals and use organic vegetables.

NG25
Children's House Day Nursery   **0163 681 4738**
Station Road, Southwell, NG25 0ET

Southwell Day Nursery   **0163 681 6606**
17 Allenby Road, Southwell, NG25 0NL

S80
Earlybirds Day Nursery   **01909 723 947**
Gypsy Lane, Worksop, S80 4JD

Lilliput Day Nursery   **01909 531 271**
The Canch, Worksop, S80 2HX

Westbourne House Nursery School   **01909 470 330**
7 Newcastle Street, Worksop, S80 2AS

S81
Granby House Nursery   **01909 733 833**
Lawn Road, Carlton-in-Lindrick, Worksop, S81 9LB

Rainbow Day Nursery   **01909 730 249**
Parish Centre, Church Lane, Carlton-in-Lindrick, S81 9GE

Treetops Nursery   **01909 479 342**
Celtic Point, Worksop, S81 7AZ

schools

Abbotsholme School   **01889 590 217**
Roster, Uttoxeter, Derbyshire, ST14 5BS

Arley House PNEU School   **01509 852 229**
8 Station Road, East Leake, Loughborough,
Leicestershire, LE12 6LQ
www.arley-pneu.eastleake.sch.uk
Co-ed 3-11yrs.

Attenborough   **01159 436 725**
Preparatory School
The Strand, Attenborough, Nottingham,
Nottinghamshire, NG9 6AU

Ayscoughfee Hall School   **01775 724 733**
Welland Hall, London Road, Spalding,
Lincolnshire, PE11 2TE

Barlborough Hall School   **01246 810 511**
Barlborough, Chesterfield, Derbyshire, S43 4TJ
www.barlboroughhallschool.com
Co-ed 3-11yrs.

Bicker Preparatory School   **01775 821 786**
School Lane, Bicker, Boston, Lincolnshire, PE203DW

Bramcote Lorne Preparatory School   **01777 838 636**
Rectory Lane, Gamston, Retford, Nottinghamshire,
DN22 0QQ

Brooke Priory School   **01572 724 778**
Station Approach, Oakham, Rutland, LE15 6QW

Colston Bassett School   **0115 933 6700**
School Lane, Cropwell, NG12 3FD
www.colstonbassettschool.com
(see advert on right)

Conway School   **01205 363 150**
Tunnard Street, Boston, Lincolnshire, PE21 6PL

Copthill Nursery and   **01780 757 506**
Preparatory School
Uffington, Stamford, Lincolnshire, PE9 4TD

Coteswood House School   **0115 967 6551**
19 Thackerays Lane, Woodthorpe, Nottingham,
Nottinghamshire, NG5 4HT

Dagfa House School   **0115 913 8330**
57 Broadgate, Beeston, Nottingham,
Nottinghamshire, NG9 2FU
www.dagfahouse.notts.sch.uk
Girls and boys from 3-16yrs. 8.40am-3.30pm. 36wks.

Dame Catherine Harpur's School   **01332 862 792**
Rose Lane, Ticknall, Derbyshire, DE73 1JW

Derby Grammar School for Boys   **01332 523 027**
Rykneld Hall, Rykneld Road, Littleover, Derby,
Derbyshire, DE23 4BX

Derby High School   **01322 514 267**
Hillsway, Littleover, Derby, Derbyshire, DE23 3DT

Dixie Grammar School   **01455 292 244**
Market Bosworth, Nuneaton, Leicestershire, CV15
0LE

Dudley House School   **01476 400 184**
1 Dudley Road, Grantham, Lincolnshire, NG31 9AA

Emaneulle House Christian School   **01332 340 505**
Juniper Lodge, 43 Kedleston Road, Derby,
Derbyshire, DE22 1FP

Fairfield Preparatory School   **01509 215 172**
Leicester Road, Loughborough, Leicestershire,
LE11 2AE

Fen School   **01529 460 966**
Side Bar Lane, Heckington Fen, Sleaford,
Lincolnshire, NG34 9LY

Foremarke Hall   **01283 703 269**
(Repton Prep School)
Milton, Derby, Derbyshire, DE65 6EJ

Gateway Christian School   **01159 440 609**
Moor Lane, Dale Abbey, Ilkeston, Derbyshire, DE7 4PL

Grace Dieu Manor School   **01530 222 276**
Thringstone, Coalville, Leicestershire, LE67 5UG
www.gracedieu.com
A flourishing Catholic Independent Day School for boys and
girls aged 3 – 13 of all denominations

Greenholme School   **01159 787 329**
392 Derby Road, Nottingham, Nottinghamshire,
NG7 2DX

Grosvenor School   **01159 231 184**
218 Melton Road, Edwalton, Nottinghamshire,
NG12 4BS
www.grosvenorschool.co.uk
The Year 8 leavers from Grosvenor School again had 100%
success for entry to their first school of choice; They, along
with Year 6 leavers, will move on to either Nottingham High
Schools, Loughborough Grammar, Trent College or Ratcliffe
College. Grosvenor School offers a wide ranging curriculum,
with specialist teaching for children aged 4 to 13 years in a
family environment. We would welcome the opportunity to
show you what we can offer your child. School may be
viewed during our monthly open sessions or by individual
appointment. Please call 0115 9231184 or visit our website
at www.grosvenorschool.co.uk

Handel House   **01427 612 426**
Preparatory School
The Northolme, Gainsborough, Lincolnshire, DN21 2JB

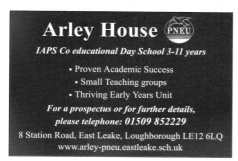

Hollygirt
SCHOOL

Independent day school for girls aged 3-16

Happy children,
small classes,
excellent results...

call us on 0115 958 0596 or
email info@hollygirt.co.uk
Elm Avenue, Nottingham NG3 4GF
www.hollygirt.co.uk

Hazel Hurst Preparatory School   0115 960 6759
400 Westdale Lane, Mapperley, Nottingham, Nottinghamshire, NG3 6DG

Highfields School   01636 704 103
London Road, Newark, Nottinghamshire, NG24 3AL

Hollygirt School   01159 580 596
Elm Avenue, Nottingham, Nottinghamshire, NG3 4GF
www.hollygirt.co.uk
Hollygirt School is an independent day school for girls aged 13 to 16 conveniently situated on a tree-lined pedestrian avenue in the heart of Nottingham. The school provides a warm, friendly and supportive environment where girls can perform to the best of their ability in small classes. Examination results are excellent and high expectations promote respect for each other. Entrance is usually at age 3,4 or 11 although a few places exist in other years. Entrance from age 7 upwards is by entrance examination. Academic and music scholarships are available from age 11.

Iona School Association   0115 941 5295
310 Sneiton Dale, Sneiton, Nottingham, Nottinghamshire, NG3 7DN

Kirkstone House School   01778 560 350
Main Street, Peterborough, Lincolnshire, PE6 9PA

Lammas School   01623 516 879
Lammas Road, Sutton-in-Ashfield, Nottinghamshire, NG17 2AD

Leicester Grammar Junior School   01162 101 299
Evington Hall, Spencefield Lane, Evington, Leicester, Leicestershire, LE5 6HN

Leicester High School for Girls   01162 705 338
454 London Road, Leicester, Leicestershire, LE2 2PP
www.leicesterhigh.co.uk

Lincoln Minster Preparatory School   01522 523 769
Eastgate, Lincoln, Lincolnshire, LN2 1QG

Lincoln Minster School   01522 551 300
Prior Building, Upper Lindum Street, Lincoln, Lincolnshire, LN2 5RW

Nottingham High School For Girls

"...The school is a happy, secure, multi-cultural community where all pupils feel valued..."

Inspection 2005

For further details, or an appointment to visit telephone: 0115 941 7663
s.webb-bowen@not.gdst.net
www.gdst.net/nottinghamgirlshigh

Girls' Day School Trust

Lovell House   **0115 845 2232**
13 Waverley Street, Nottingham, Nottinghamshire, NG7 4DX
www.nottinghamhigh.co.uk/lovell-house
Independent Day School for boys and girls aged 3-11 yrs.

Manor House School   **01530 412 932**
South Street, Ashby-de-la-Zouch, Leicestershire, LE65 1BR
www.manorhouseashby.co.uk
Co-ed 4-16yrs, 9am-4pm. 36wks.

Mansfield Preparatory School   **0162 342 0940**
Welbeck Road, Mansfield Woodhouse, Nottingham, NG19 9LA
www.childcareeastmidlands.co.uk

Maypole House School   **01507 462 764**
Well Vale Hall, Low Lane, Well, Alford, Lincolnshire, LN13 0ET

Michael House- Rudolf Steiner School   **01773 718 050**
The Field Shipley, Langley Mill, Derbyshire, DE75 7JH

Morley Hall Preparatory School   **01332 674 501**
Hill House, Morley Road, Chaddesden, Derby, Derbyshire, DE21 4QZ

Mount St Mary's College   **01246 433 388**
Spinkhill, Sheffield, Derbyshire, S21 3YL
www.msmcollege.com

Mountford House School   **01159 605 676**
373 Mansfield Road, Nottingham, Nottinghamshire, NG5 2DA
www.mountfordhouse.nottingham.sch.uk
2-11yrs 8.30am-3.30pm. Term time.

Nottingham High School   **0115 978 6056**
Waverley Mount, Nottingham, Nottinghamshire, NG7 4ED
www.nottinghamhigh.co.uk
Independent Day School for boys aged 11-18.

Nottingham High Junior School   **0115 845 2214**
Waverly Mount, Nottingham, Nottinghamshire, NG7 4ED
www.nottinghamhigh.co.uk
Independent day school for boys aged 4-11

Lovel House (Nottingham High School)   **0115 978 3230**
13 Waverley Street, Nottingham, NG7 4DX
www.nottinghamhigh.co.uk
Independent day school for boys aged 4-7

Nottingham High School for Girls   **01159 417 663**
9 Arboretum Street, Nottingham, Nottinghamshire, NG1 4JB
www.gdst.net/nottinghamgirlshigh.co.uk
Girls 4-18yrs, 8.30am-3.40pm. 35wks.

Ockbrook School   **01332 673 532**
The Settlement, Ockbrook, Derbyshire, DE72 3RJ
www.ockbrookprimary.co.uk
Co-ed 3-18yrs.

Our Lady's Convent School **01509 263 901**
Burton Street, Loughborough, Leicestershire, LE11 2DT
www.olcs.leics.sch.uk
The individual is highly valued at Our Lady's Convent School. There is a happy, caring Christian environment. Pupils are continually helped and encouraged to develop their full potential. Academic achievement is high. A wide range of subjects are offered. Facilities available to students are continually being enhanced.

Plumtree School **01159 375 859**
Church Hill, Plumtree, Nottingham, Nottinghamshire, NG12 5ND

Ranby House School **01777 703 138**
Ranby, Retford, Nottinghamshire, DN22 8HX
www.ranbyhouseschool.co.uk
Co-ed 3-13yrs.

Ratcliffe College **01509 817 000**
Fosse Way, Ratcliffe on the Wreake, Leicestershire, LE7 4SG

Rutland House School for Parents **0115 985 8178**
Elm Bank, Mapperley, Nottingham, NG3 5AJ
School for parents. Pre-school for children with a major difficulty. We teach parents to facilitate their children in their development.

Salterford House School **01159 652 127**
Salterford Lane, Calverton, Nottinghamshire, NG14 6NZ
www.salterfordhouseschool.co.uk
Salterford House School is an independent preparatory school situated in rural Nottinghamshire taking children from 2?-11yrs. They also offer half-term and holiday play schemes to children from outside the school where spaces are available. 2½-4½yrs. 34wks.

Saville House School **01623 625 068**
11 Church Street, Mansfield Woodhouse, Nottingham, Nottinghamshire, NG19 8AH

St Anselm's Preparatory School **01629 812 734**
Stanedge Road, Bakewell, Derbyshire, DE45 1DP

St Crispin's School **01162 707 648**
6 St. Mary's Road, Leicester, Leicestershire, LE2 1XA

St Hugh's School **01526 352 169**
Cromwell Avenue, Woodhall Spa, Lincolnshire, LN10 6TQ

St Joseph's Convent School **01246 232 392**
42-44 Newbold Road, Chesterfield, Derbyshire, S41 7PL

St Joseph's School   **01159 418 356**
33 Derby Road, Nottingham, Nottinghamshire, NG1 5AW
www.st-josephs.nottingham.sch.uk
From an early age, St Joseph's School encourages a happy
and hard working environment, helping young people to
reach their full potential, to be adaptable for the future,
encouraging each child's sense of individual worth. The
Christian ethos of the school and the dedication of its staff
ensure that all pupils are given every opportunity to find
success. St. Joseph's takes children from the age of
eighteen months up to eleven years. Its city centre location
and before and after school clubs mean that parents who live
or work in the city can have their children safe and happy at a
school nearby.

St Wystan's School

INDEPENDENT DAY SCHOOL AND NURSERY
FOR GIRLS AND BOYS FROM 2 TO 11 YEARS

High Street, Repton, Derbyshire, DE65 6GE
tel: 01283 703258 **email:** head@stwystans.org.uk
website: www.stwystans.org.uk

Open: 7.30am to 6.30pm during term time.
Holiday Club also available.

Please contact us to experience the unique St Wystan's
atmosphere and to meet our dedicated staff and children.

Registered Charity No: 527181

WELLOW HOUSE SCHOOL

- Set in 20 acres on the edge of Sherwood Forest
  with a tradition of academic, artistic, sporting and
  musical excellence
- Boy and girls 3-13 years
- Exciting new pre-prep department
- Morning collection from Southwell, Newark and
  Mansfield
- Co-educational Preparatory day and weekly boarding
- Scholarships and Bursaries available

email: wellowhouse@btinternet.com
Web: www.wellowhouse.notts.sch.uk
Tel: (01623) 861054
Fax: (01623) 836665
Wellow, Newark, Nottinghamshire, NG22 0EA

Reg Charity no 538234

St Mary's Preparatory School   **01522 524 622**
5 Pottergate, Lincoln, Lincolnshire, LN2 1PH

St Peter's & St Paul's School   **01246 278 522**
Brambling House, Hady Hill, Chesterfield,
Derbyshire, S41 0EF

St Wystan's School   **01283 703 258**
11a High Street, Repton, Derby, Derbyshire, DE65
6GE
www.stwystans.org.uk
Co-ed 2$_{1/2}$-11yrs.

Stamford Junior School   **01780 484 400**
Kettering Road, Stamford, Lincolnshire, PE9 2LR

Stoneygate College   **01162 707 414**
2 Albert Road, Stoneygate, Leicester,
Leicestershire, LE2 2AA

The Elms   **01158 494 942**
Junior School to Trent College, Derby Road, Long
Eaton, Nottinghamshire, NG10 4AD

The Grantham Prep School   **01476 593 293**
Gorse Lane, Grantham, Lincolnshire, NG31 7UF

The Viking School   **01754 765 749**
140 Church Road North, Skegness, Lincolnshire,
PE25 2QJ

Twycross House Prep School   **01827 880 725**
The Hollies, The Green, Twycross, Leicestershire,
CV9 3PQ

Wellow House School   **01623 861 054**
Wellow, Newark, Nottinghamshire, NG22 0EA
www.wellowhouse.notts.sch.uk
Co-ed 3-13yrs. Wellow House is the leading independent
co-educational school in Nottinghamshire and is a member of
IAPS.

Witham Hall   **01778 590 222**
Witham on the Hill, Bourne, Lincolnshire, PE10 0JJ

Worksop College   **0115 978 3230**
Sparken Hill, Worksop, Nottinghamshire, S80 3AP

GROSVENOR SCHOOL
Edwalton, Nottingham
Boys and Girls, ages 4 - 13

A successful, forward-thinking, friendly, family school
with a long history and traditional values.
If you are interested in the above please call Mrs Dexter
on 0115 9231184 or e-mail: office@grosvenorschool.co.uk

shopping

Your favourite pastime is about to skyrocket to new levels.
That burgeoning bump will require a new wardrobe for a start. Next, you'll be stockpiling bottles, breast pumps, sterilising units, nappies and lotions and potions, not to mention the baby carrier, the buggy, the car seat, the cot and the new linen. Then comes the fun bit – dear little outfits for babies, toddlers and tweenies, as well as dressing-up gear, swimwear and toys. Not sure where to find all this? Here we guide you to the best shops, mail-order catalogues and websites in the country. Plus you'll find creative ways to announce baby's arrival to the world, as well as sources of pretty presents and a stash of portrait artists and photographers to capture you and your offspring for posterity.

Items	Buy from...	Borrow from...	Gift from...
For the nursery			
☐ cot and mattress			
☐ moses basket/crib			
☐ linen (sheets, blankets, etc)			
☐ changing mat/table			
☐ wardrobe			
☐ chest of drawers			
☐ playmat			
Clothing			
☐ 6 cotton sleepsuits			
☐ 3 sleeping bags			
☐ 4 cotton vests			
☐ 1-2 two-piece outfits			
☐ 2-4 cardigans			
☐ 4-6 pairs socks/bootees			
☐ 1 pair gloves/mittens (for winter)			
☐ 1 snowsuit (for winter)			
☐ muslin cloths/ bibs			
☐ 1 hat			
Essential supplies			
☐ disposable or washable nappies			
☐ baby wipes, cotton wool			
☐ nappy bags			
☐ barrier cream, Vaseline			
☐ breast pump			
☐ bottles			
☐ sterilizer			
For travelling			
☐ pram/pushchair			
☐ rain cover and Buggysnuggle			
☐ car seat			
☐ baby carrier/sling			
☐ travel and changing bag			
☐ travel cot			

baby accessories

These suppliers have designed unique and stylish products that offer something practical with a great sense of style.

The Gooseberry Bush   **0115 922 8866**
80 High Street, Beeston, Nottingham, NG9 2LF
www.thegooseberrybushltd.co.uk
Organic cotton babywear, soft toys and a good range of organic skincare is available from this Nottingham maternity and baby store.

JoJo Maman Bébé   **0870 241 0560**
www.jojomamanbebe.co.uk
JoJo Maman Bébé is a one-stop shop for pregnancy and beyond, offering fashionable maternity wear for every occasion, quirky children's clothing and adorable babywear. The company also provides an extensive range of practical products, toys and gifts for your baby, nursery and family home. Free P&P on all UK mainland orders.

Mummy and Me Hampers   **01530 263 350**
www.mummyandmehampers.co.uk
Mummy & Me Hamper Co offer an exclusive collection of treats for Mum & Baby, including best loved brands; Burts Bees, Kissy Kissy, Mama Mio, Funky Feet and Steiff.

birth announcements

Happyhands   **0845 466 0171**
www.happyhands.co.uk
Your baby's hand and foot prints on cards. Ingenious ink-free kit provided

book shops

Pegasus Children's Books   **01522 525 557**
3 Central Market, Sincil Street, Lincoln, LN5 7ET
Lovely children's book shop where you'll receive a warm welcome and lots of useful advice.

book reviews

Jo Frost's   **020 7240 3444**
Complete Baby Care
www.orionbooks.co.uk
Jo Frost has become a household name for practical parenting advice and in this, her first baby book, she brings her wealth of knowledge and experience as the UK's most trusted nanny to help parents and carers feel confident in all aspects of baby's first year. Published by Orion Books £12.99 paperback.

www.babydirectory.com

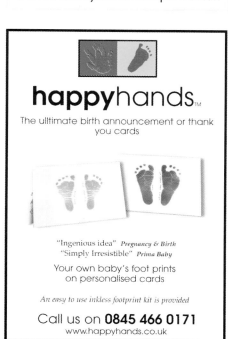

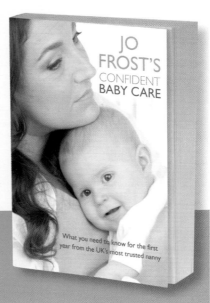

JO FROST'S CONFIDENT BABY CARE

The UK's most trusted nanny with you every step of the way

JO FROST'S CONFIDENT BABY CARE

What you need to know for the first year from the UK's most trusted nanny

bras

Bras 4 Mums   **0845 373 3875**
www.bras4mums.co.uk
Bras4mums helps you to find attractive, affordable maternity and breastfeeding lingerie and swimwear to meet YOUR exact needs. As well as providing telephone and online help and advice they stock a superb range of products on their website www.bras4mums.co.uk.

breast pumps

Breast pumps allow you to express and store milk, which can then be bottle-fed to your baby. You can either select a hand-operated model or an electric/battery model. The manual models are quieter, lighter and easier to travel with – but can be slow and tiring. Electronic pumps are faster and generally more effective.

Amber Medical   **01823 336 362**
www.ambermedical.co.uk
Rent a Ameda dual electric breast pump directly from Amber Medical who are now the exclusive distributor of the Ameda brand of products which include electric and manual breast pumps as well as a comprehensive range of breastfeeding accessories. We are the first choice for Health Care Professionals. Order at www.ameda.com or by telephone 01823 336 362.

Medela   **0161 776 0400**
www.medela.co.uk
Medela manufacture a range of manual, battery and electric breast pumps. They also have a small travel set which can be used effectively for mums who go back to work but want to continue feeding breast milk full time and a set of pumps if you are breastfeeding twins. They can also be hired.

NUK **0845 300 2467**
www.nuk.de
NUK make a manual and battery-operated model. The
manual model has an adjustable strength swivel handle for
left- or right-handed mothers, plus a soft silicone cushion
which massages as you express.

castings

Happyhands **0845 466 0171**
www.happyhands.co.uk
Colourful hand and foot prints preserved on ceramic tiles and
mugs. An ingenious ink-free kit is provided to make it really
easy and not at all messy.

Little Impressions **01455 611 881**
Jamesbrook, Burbage, LE10 2JH
www.little-impressions.com
Tried DIY casting kits? Happy with the results? When it
comes to capturing the unique detail of your children's hand
and feet, don't leave it to chance. At Little Impressions we
create highly detailed 3-dimensional casts of hands and feet.
Hand crafted, professionally finished and framed. Don't be
tempted by imitations, for little more than the cost of some
DIY kits you can invest in your own Little Impression, quality
casts which you will be proud to hang on your wall, the
perfect timeless keepsake and gift idea.

John Lewis **0115 941 8282**
Victoria Centre, Nottingham, NG1 3QA
www.johnlewis.com
Imprints at John Lewis. Simply ring to arrange and
appointment.

PitaPata Lifecastings **0115 984 3519**
27 Maythorn Close, West Bridgford, Nottingham,
NG2 7TE
nwalters@ntlworld.com
A fabulous way to capture tiny toes and fingers in a cast that
lasts forever. You can also call on 0797 084 8939 [see
advert overleaf].

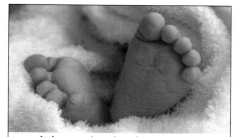

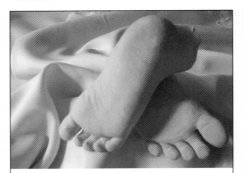

PitaPata Lifecastings

*A fabulous way to capture
tiny toes and fingers in a cast
that lasts forever*

Natasha Dorey
Telephone 0115 984 3519
Mobile 0797 084 8939
e-mail: nwalters@ntlworld.com

happyhands™

The Perfect Christening Gift

*A beautiful
mahogany memories
box with the baby's
own prints on an
inlaid ceramic tile*

£5 off
for Baby
Directory
Readers Quote
BDS11

Call us on **0845 466 0171**
www.happyhands.co.uk

**Militia
Immaculatae
Trust**

Take time to browse through the
range of Communion and Christening
gowns as well as other accessories.

35 New Bond Street, Leicester,
LE1 4RQ
0116 251 3477
www.mitrust.org

Smallprint
www.smallp.co.uk
An exciting and new product looks set to take East Midlands
by storm. Looking for a unique personal gift for someone
special? Then look no further than Smallprint. Smallprint
makes beautiful pieces of handcrafted jewellery that capture
your baby or child's fingerprint in polished silver. Just think, in
years to come you will still be able to treasure their tiny
fingerprint on a unique piece of jewellery! We offer charm
bracelets, pendants, cufflinks and keyrings in a variety of
shapes. So, for a wonderful and unique gift for yourself or
your family, call Smallprint and capture those precious
moments! Contact your nearest Smallprint franchisee to
arrange a home visit [see ad for details].

christening gifts

John Lewis　　　　　　　**0115 941 8282**
Victoria Centre, Nottingham, NG1 3QA
www.johnlewis.com
A full range of clothes and gifts available.

Happyhands　　　　　　　**0845 466 0171**
www.happyhands.co.uk
Colourful hand and foot prints preserved on ceramic tiles and
mugs. An ingenious ink-free kit is provided to make it really
easy and not at all messy. The gift comes in a smart red box
with a white ribbon.

christening gowns

Balloons Childrenswear　　**01159 455 829**
52 Rectory Road, West Bridgford, Nottingham, NG2 6BU
www.balloonsweb.co.uk
Balloons provides high quality designer children's clothing
and baby clothes through our store in West Bridgford and e-
commerce on our website. With over 15 years experience in
the children's designer clothing business, Balloons is proud
to offer a range of leading brands including: Catimini, Jean
Bourget and Pampolina. Balloons' designer children's clothes
are available for all ages from newborn to 16 years for boys
and girls. Balloons aims to complement their high quality
designer children's clothes with excellent service.

County Mouse　　　　　　**01530 411 844**
11 Mill Lane Mews, Ashby de la Zouch, LE65 1HP
www.countrymousechildrenswear.co.uk
Designer children's clothes shop from 0-10 years. Including
Christening wear for boys and girls. Great collection of bears,
dolls and wooden toys.

Militia Immaculatae Trust　　**0116 251 3477**
35 New Bond Street, Leicester, LE1 4RQ
www.mitrust.org
Take time to browse through the range of Communion and
Christening gowns as well as other accessories. They also
sell a range of baby roseries, religious Christmas cards and
children's bibles and prayer books.

Expert advice, absolutely free

Trust John Lewis to help you welcome a little one into the world

Meeting up with a John Lewis Nursery advisor is a great way to prepare for your new arrival. Fully trained to guide you through the Nursery department, your advisor will explain the latest safety information and product styles. The service is completely free and the generous 2–hour appointment mean there's more than enough time to make the most of some expert, impartial advice that's tailored to your needs.

Find everything you need in one place

At John Lewis, you'll find everything you need to set up the nursery and enjoy life with a new arrival. We have a lovely collection of nursery furniture, specially chosen to give you a choice of styles at a range of prices. And your little one will be able to eat, sleep and live John Lewis with our choice of bottles and nursing aids, cosy bedding plus gorgeous babywear and fun toys. And when

it comes to getting out and about, the right travel equipment makes all the difference. Your advisor will be able to explain the ins and outs of car seat safety – including the latest Isofix styles – and buggies, prams or travel systems. Together you'll find the kit that will suit you and your baby best.

Make shopping simple with a Nursery List

At the end of your appointment, your advisor can help you compile

a Nursery List. You'll be able to buy from it at any John Lewis shop, online or by phone. It'll be easy for friends and family to choose gifts if you choose to share your list with them. We'll keep everything together and deliver it all in one go, at a convenient time.

Book your appointment

To find out more and book an appointment, call John Lewis Nottingham on **0115 941 8282** or head to **johnlewis.com/nottingham**

John Lewis
johnlewis.com

Piccolo   **01623 824 000**
16 High Street, Edwinstowe, NG21 9QS
Visit our store to view our extensive christening range including victorian family heirlooms, which can be pased down through the generations; smart suits for boys and delicate trimmed dresses for a little girl's winter christening. We also have a wide range of beautiful shawls and accessories. We offer a personal and friendly service, please call and ask for either Julie or Sally. We also have a large range of designer clothing including Timberland, Elle, Ollie Chipie and many many more.

Pitta Patter   **01777 719 432**
13 Bridgegate, Retford, DN22 6AE
A wonderful range of children's designer wear, including Sarah Louise, Lego and Quicksilver. Also a selection of Christening wear and shoes. They also offer home visit parties.

clothing shops: fashion

DERBYSHIRE
Ekko   **01246 272 004**
23 Knifesmithgate, Chesterfield, S40 1DL
Large range of designer brands including Timberlands, Elle and DKNY for 0-14 year olds. Easy parking just outside the shop.

Ekko   **01332 224 434**
2 Cheapside, Derby, DE14 1BE

Ekko   **01332 541 129**
502 Duffield Road, Allestree, Derby, DE22 2DL

Evolution   **01773 744 553**
42 Oxford Street, Ripley, DE5 3AP
www.designerclothes4kids.co.uk
Top designer brands for newborns-16yrs; including Ted Baker, Diesel, DKNY, Elle, Lacoste and Timberland. Shoe also available.

Junior B by Bridgens   **01332 202 373**
54 Sadler Gate, Derby, DE1 3NQ
Designer children's wear including Burberry, Kenzo and DKNY. Also stocks Christening Wear.

Moop   **01246 271 118**
413 Chatsworth Road, Brampton, Chesterfield, S40 3AD
www.moop-kids.co.uk
Beautiful gifts and a large range of designer clothing for children from 0 to 12 years including Ted Baker, Jean Bourjet, Diesel and many more.

Polarn O Pyret   **01332 200 796**
South Mall, Westfields Centre, Derby
www.polarnopyret.com
Come rain, snow or shine, Sweden's leading childrenswear brand has everything you could possibly need to dress your babies, toddlers and children up to eleven years for all weather. Water repellent and windproof fleece suits, rain hats, wellington boots, ski goggles, snow-board gear, waterproof suits, UVF swimwear and polarising baby sunglasses - the list of highly functional garments and

accessories from Sweden is extensive. Swedes have a saying 'there is no such thing as bad weather - just bad clothes!' - PO.P in to see for yourself.

Puddle Jumpers   **01629 552 224**
3 Snitterton Road, Matlock, DE4 3LU
www.puddlejumpers.co.uk

Sazoo   **01332 381 158**
34ab Eagle Centre Market, Derby, DE1 2AZ
www.sazoo.co.uk
For party wear, or clothing for weddings, christenings and holy communions. Whatever the special occasion they stock quality fashion clothing for boys and girls from 0-16 years.

Young and Funky   **01332 553 595**
15 Park Farm Centre, Allestree, DE22 2QQ

LEICESTERSHIRE
Clafoutis   **0116 262 7027**
25 Loseby Lane, Leicester, LE1 5DR
Exclusive children's designer shop including Dior, Kookai and DKNY. They also stock shoes and provide a mail order service.

Country Mouse   **01530 411 844**
11 Mill Lane Mews, Ashby de la Zouch, LE65 1HP
www.countrymousechildrenswear.co.uk
Designer children's clothes shop from 0-10 years. Including Christening wear for boys and girls. Great collection of bears, dolls and wooden toys.

The Clothes Horse   **01530 415 055**
8 Elford Street, Ashby de la Zouch, LE65 1HH
High street brand labels at discounted prices.

The Stork   **01664 564 215**
12 The Bell Centre, Melton Mowbray, LE13 1PJ
Established for 21 years this shop stocks baby wear,
children's wear and school uniforms from 0-16yrs. On the
high street with a coffee shop to relax in three doors down,
this shop with a lot of room for pushchairs could be the
answer to stressful high street shopping. Open Mon-Sat
9am-5pm.

TickTock Childrenswear 01509 211 944
1-2 Swan Street, Loughborough, LE11 5BJ
www.ticktockchildrenswear.com
Ticktockchildrenswear is an on-line store for designer
children's clothes. They also have two retail stores in Oakham
and Loughborough. Choose from a wide range of brands
such as, Timberland, Noa Noa, Pampolina and many more to
fit children from birth up to 16 years.

Toffs 01572 724 133
2 The Maltings, Mill Street, Rutland, LE15 6EA
www.toffschildrenswear.com
Designer casual children's wear including French labels such
as Jeanbourget, Catimini and Pampolina. Open Mon-Fri
10am -5.45 .Sat 10am-5pm.

LINCOLNSHIRE

Betty McKenzie's 01472 697 150
17 Market Street, Cleethorpes, DN35 8LY
www.bettymckenzie.co.uk
A friendly family run business by the seaside in Cleethorpes.
Specialists in designer children's wear including Pampolina
and Elle for boys and girls from birth all the way up to 18
years. Open 9.30am-5pm Mon-Sat.

Betzee Bugz 01522 787 424
29-31 Mint Street, Lincoln, LN1 1UB
Bright, bold and fun designer clothes for your kids including
Cakewalk, Oilily and Jeep. There is a playroom for the
children to enjoy whilst you browse.

isobel&henry
clothes for growing up in

We stock small, independent brands, many of which are new
and exclusive to this area, but all of which share our passion
to let children be children. With all of our brands being very
affordable we believe that even climbing trees can be an
opportunity to look stylish!
Brands stocked: Joules, Minymo, Uttam, Me Too, Infancy,
ilovegorgeous, Their Nibs, Albetta, Toby Tiger
and accessories by Lollipop. For children aged 0-12.

We look forward to welcoming you soon, and don't be afraid
to bring the kids! - we have a dedicated kids' corner with a
TV, books and wooden toys so that our most important
customers are happy.

15 Union Street, Bingham, Nottinghamshire,
NG13 8AD   Tel 01949 836 767
Mon-Fri - 9.30 -5.00
Wed - 9.30 -12.30
Sat - 9.30 -4.00

Boomerang 01476 578 581
25 Watergate, Grantham, NG31 6NS
www.boomerangkids.co.uk
The only independent Childrenswear shop in Grantham, this
attractive ground floor boutique with its old fashioned
frontage is just off the high street and stocks clothes for all
ages from premature babies up to 10 years old. Larger sizes
are available where applicable and subject to availability.
Designer brands include Chipie, Elle and Timberland. They
also have christening and occasion wear and boys 3 piece
suits available from 2 years-15 years in 7 different cloths.
They stock some occasion shoes as well as fun and funky
leather shoes for boys and girls. Open 9.30-4.30 Mon to Sat.
Out of hours appointments are available on request.

Bumps 'N' Boos 01529 414 445
16 Westgate, Sleaford, NG34 7PN

Harlies 01522 511 549
6 Lambeth House, Woodhall Drive, Lincoln, LN2 2AD

Portobello 01522 544 662
Cathedral Quarter, 68 Bailgate, Lincoln, LN1 3AR

NOTTINGHAMSHIRE

Ambience 01623 404 420
1 Lucknow Drive, Coxmoor Road, Sutton-in-
Ashfield, NG17 4LY
www.ambiencekidswear.co.uk
This modern childrenswear shop is just 5 minutes from
Kingsmill Hospital and stocks an electric range from Stone
Island Jnr, Burberry and Diesel amongst others. They also
have shoes including brands such as Replay and Diesel as
well as accessories and new baby gifts. Open 9.30am-
5.3pm Mon-Sat and by appointment on Sundays.

Balloons Childrenswear 01159 455 829
52 Rectory Road, West Bridgford, NG2 6BU
www.balloonsweb.co.uk
Balloons provides high quality designer children's clothing
and baby clothes through our store in West Bridgford and e-
commerce on our website. With over 15 years experience in
the children's designer clothing business, Balloons is proud
to offer a range of leading brands including: Catimini, Jean
Bourget and Pampolina. Balloons' designer children's clothes
are available for all ages from newborn to 16 years for boys
and girls. Balloons aims to complement their high quality
designer children's clothes with excellent service.

Cashe Designer Childrenswear 0115 941 1617
42 Pelham Street, Nottingham, NG1 2EG
In its new city centre location this treasure trove of designer
labels contains three floors of designer childrenswear 0-16 years.
Stockists for Burberry, Armani and D & G and lots more.

Isobel and Henry 01949 836 767
15 Union Street, Bingham, NG13 8AD
This smart, sophisticated and modern boutique in Bingham
offers delightful designer children's clothes that you can't find
anywhere else in the area. The shop has a strong community
focus, listening to customers and offering them something
different. It's a great little shop and the perfect place to buy a
present for a little one.

ambience

Sutton-in-Ashfield

Designer Kidswear & Shoes **0-16yrs**

QUOTE ABSOLUTE GUIDE TO RECEIVE INSTORE DISCOUNT

Kenzo	CP Company
Paul Smith	DKNY
Fake-London-Genius	Evisu
Moschino	Stone Island
Replay	Burberry
Diesel	and many more

1 Lucknow Drive
Coxmoor Road
Sutton-in-Ashfield
NG17 4LY

Tel: **01623 404420**
www.ambiencekidswear.co.uk

Mon - Sat: 9.30am - 5.30pm
Sunday by appointment only
2 MINS FROM KINGSMILL HOSPITAL
FREE CAR PARKING

www.ambiencekidswear.co.uk

DESIGNER CHILDRENSWEAR FROM NEWBORN TO 16 YEARS

Catimini · Kenzo
Jean Bourget · Pampolina
Chipie · Miniman · Replay
Miss Sixty · Timberland
Ted Baker · Quiksilver
O'Neill · Absorba
Emile et Rose

Baby Gifts and
Christening Wear
available

balloons
DESIGNER CHILDRENSWEAR

Telephone 0115 945 5829
52 Rectory Road · West Bridgford · Nottingham
Order online at www.balloonsweb.co.uk

Obi   **0115 988 1515**
King John's Arcade, Bridlesmith Gate, Nottingham, NG1 2GR

Our Little Angels   **0115 928 8122**
154 Russell Drive, Wollaton, NG8 2BE
www.ourlittleangels.co.uk
This light and airy shop sells designer clothes for boys and girls from 0-5yrs including Noppies, Esprit, Joules and BFC. They also stock newborn and christening gifts and a great selection of traditional wooden toys. Baby massage classes and photography sessions can be arranged. Open 9am-5pm Mon, Tues, Sat and Sun; 9am-5.30 Wed and 9am-1pm Thurs. Free parking.

pcZ Designer wear for Kids   **0115 967 0818**
159/161 Nottingham Road, Arnold, Nottingham, NG5 6JN
www.pczdesignerwear.com

Pitta Patter   **01777 719 432**
13 Bridgegate, Retford, Nottinghamshire, DN22 6AE
A wonderful range of children's designer wear, including Sarah Louise, Lego and Quicksilver. Also a selection of Christening wear and shoes. They also offer home visit parties.

The Clothes Horse   **01530 415 055**
8 Elford Street, Ashby de la Zouch, LE65 1HH
High street brand labels at discounted prices.

clothing shops: high street

Adams Childrenswear   **0500 330 040**
www.adams.co.uk
Stock up on all your basics from pajamas to Wellington boots. Good selection of dressing up costumes as well as gifts. Collect Nectar points. Recently launched a user-friendly online store offering good deals such as '3 for the price of 2' East Midlands branches in: Beaumont Leys, Boston, Chesterfield, Derby, Grantham, Hinckley, Ilkeston, Lincoln, Loughborough, Mansfield, Nottingham (Broadmarsh and Victoria Centre,) Skegness and Stamford.

John Lewis   **0115 941 8282**
Victoria Centre, Nottingham, NG1 3QA
www.johnlewis.com
The John Lewis stores offer a practical range of clothing, shoes, nursery equipment and toiletries as well as a good selection of prams, pushchairs, car seats, highchairs and nursery furniture, many of which are on display so you can test them out. Open 10am-9pm Mon-Fri. 9am-8pm Sat. 11am-5pm Sun. Or shop online.

Matalan   **01695 554 423**
www.matalan.co.uk
Catwalk-inspired family fashion at fantastic prices with easy parking facilities. You can also look at a small collection of seasonal ideas on the website, but you can't buy online. East Midlands branches in: Boston, Chesterfield, Derby, Grimsby, Leicester, Lincoln and Nottingham.

Monsoon Baby   **0870 155 3553**
www.monsoon.co.uk
Beautiful clothes for newborn-10 years. Charming accessories including hats, socks and booties. Several stores across the East Midlands.

Piccolo   **01623 824 000**
16 High Street, Edwinstowe, NG21 9QS
They have a large range of designer clothing including Timberland, Elle, Ollie Chipie and many many more.

Primark   **01189 606 300**
www.primark.co.uk
If you want your little ones to follow seasonal trends without it costing a fortune, then this is the place to shop. Website offers limited information. East Midlands branches in: Chesterfield, Leicester, Loughborough, Lincoln, Nottingham.

Pumpkin Patch   **0800 458 8914**
www.pumpkinpatch.co.uk
The Patch store provides one-stop shopping - every parent's dream. The coordinated collections offer quality, affordable kid's wear that's the junior version of current looks with a fresh, young twist. There's also a must-see comprehensive maternity wear collection that mums-to-be will adore. Shop with ease, there's plenty of room for strollers and a TV area for the kids. And remember to visit regularly as there are new styles arriving all the time.Open: Mon-Fri 9.30am-6.00pm, Wed 9.30am-8.00pm Sat 9.00am-6.00pm, Sun 11.00am-5.00pm. East Midlands branches in: Derby, Nottingham and Leicester.

TK Maxx
www.tkmaxx.com
Designer labels at discounted prices but in odd sizes! Website offers little information. East Midlands branches in: Boston, Grantham, Leicester, Lincoln, Loughborough, Mansfield, Newark, Nottingham (Broadmarsh and Chilwell) and Scunthorpe.

Country Mouse   **01530 411 844**
11 Mill Lane Mews, Ashby de la Zouch, LE65 1HP
www.countrymousechildrenswear.co.uk
Designer children's clothes shop from 0-10 years. Including Christening wear for boys and girls. Great collection of bears, dolls and wooden toys.

JoJo Maman Bebe   **0870 241 0560**
www.jojomamanbebe.co.uk
JoJo Maman Bébé is a one-stop shop for pregnancy and beyond, offering fashionable maternity wear for every occasion, quirky children's clothing and adorable babywear. The company also provides an extensive range of practical products, toys and gifts for your baby, nursery and family home. Free P&P on all UK mainland orders.

cots and cribs

BedNest   **01249 783 768**
www.bednest.com
Award winning baby crib designed for closeness and security within arm's reach without the risk associated with bed-sharing (see advert pg 44).

department stores

Department stores are useful places, especially when it's bucketing outside. And with the recent changes at Selfridges, and refurbishment at Peter Jones, they're good for a quick nappy trip, major purchase or just a fun day out.

Debenhams   **08445 616 161**
www.debenhams.com
One stop shopping for all your needs. Designer clothing from birth (J Junior and Little Rocha): educational toys at in-store ELC shops, shoes, dressing up clothes. Child-friendly restaurant has Organix baby food, bottle warmers, highchairs and even baby wipes! Stores are open 7 days a week. Collect nectar points. East Midlands branches in: Derby, Leicester, Lincoln, Mansfield and Nottingham.

Kids at Christopher Scotney's   0116 2556942
132 London Road, Leicester, LE2 1EB
www.christopherscotney.co.uk
A well known site on the main high street of Leicester, Scotney's has been a well established independent store for over 30 years. The Kids Department is on the ground floor so easily accessible for mums with pushchairs and offers a wealth of designer labels for 0-16yrs. The department also offers a play area for children, baby changing and tea and coffee for frazzled parents. The great advantage of this shop is that it extends over 7 floors and so whilst there is great shopping for your little ones there is also fabulous shopping for yourself. Open Mon-Sat 9am-6pm.

John Lewis   0115 941 8282
Victoria Centre, Nottingham, NG1 3QA
www.johnlewis.com
John Lewis caters for a complete range of needs and requirements that you will have as a parent; from castings to maternity wear, toys to pushchairs. Reliable and experienced we know exactly the things parents need and offer them guidance. You'll have a lot of questions as a first time parent. At John Lewis we can provide you with many of the answers you need.

food: ready made

Little London Herbal Store   01159 476 569
4 Kings Walk, Nottingham, NG1 2AE
www.all-ages-vitamins.co.uk

Tiny Olive   0115 974 8522
www.tinyolive.co.uk
This is a brand new range of freshly made to order organic baby and toddler food. Specialising in homemade to order organic weaning purees for babies aged from four months and organic meals, organic sauces and organic desserts for babies and toddlers aged from six months for home delivery throughout Nottinghamshire. For home deliveries to Derbyshire and Leicestershire please call in advance.

gifts: ideas

A Little Star   01476 576 141
The George Centre, Grantham, NG31 6LH
www.alittlestar.co.uk
A Little Star specialises in providing customers with an exclusive range of baby gifts and accessories such as stunning baby wear bouquets by The Flower Stork and gorgeous cuddly animals by Jelly Cats. It also provides Gift List Hosting, Bespoke Gift Packages, Gift Vouchers and much more.

Daisy Daisy   0115 982 7005
91a Melton Road, West Bridgford, NG2 6EN
www.daisydaisy.me.uk
They've even provided a colouring table to occupy the children while you browse and baby changing facilities should the need arise. So why not pop along to 91a Melton Road and have a look around yourself!

Heydiddlediddle   01623 405 022
www.babygiftstore.co.uk
This is a beautifully designed, family-run online baby toys and gifts website based in Nottinghamshire. All of the products are hand-picked from overseas suppliers and are hard to find in the UK, therefore making excellent and original gifts. With speedy delivery and personal customer services you can shop with confidence.

Maminka   01509 218 735
29 Biggin Street, Loughborough, LE11 1UA
www.maminka.co.uk
Luxury and contemporary gift shop for family and home including toys, t-shirt making kits, babywear and jewellery.

Mummy and Me Hamper   01530 263 350
www.mummyandmehampers.co.uk
Mummy & Me Hamper Co offer an exclusive collection of treats for Mum & Baby, including best loved brands; Burts Bees, Kissy Kissy, Mama Mio, Funky Feet and Steiff.

RT Design   07906 547 911
www.r-t-designs.co.uk
Interior Designer Rachel England and Illustrator Tina Wardle started RT Designs in 2006. Designed and handmade by the sisters, they can create affordable, inspirational, personalised artwork and bespoke arts and crafts for babies and children, ideal for that special gift.

Smallprint
www.smallp.co.uk
An exciting and new product looks set to take East Midlands by storm. Looking for a unique personal gift for someone special? Then look no further than Smallprint. Smallprint makes beautiful pieces of handcrafted jewellery that capture your baby or child's fingerprint in polished silver. Just think, in years to come you will still be able to treasure their tiny fingerprint on a unique piece of jewellery! We offer charm bracelets, pendants, cufflinks and keyrings in a variety of shapes [see ad for details].

Solutions   01858 463 621
Manor Walk, Market Harborough, LE16 9BP
Surrounded by cafes and coffee shops this enticing shop stocks all sorts of gifts for the ages of newborn and up as well as a range of toys. Open Mon-Sat 9.30am-5.30am.

Casual wear

Work wear

Evening dress

Bridal maternity

Gifts

Lingerie

17 Churchgate
Loughborough
Leicestershire

01509 238300

www.gracematernity.co.uk

lotions and potions

If you are looking for something a little more special than the supermarket standards, all these suppliers offer an organic, additive- and SLS- free alternative.

Barefoot Botanicals   0870 220 2273
www.barefootuk.com
Good-quality natural skincare including an SOS Skin Rescue Bath Oil with lavender, neroli and chamomile.

Bodywise (UK) Natracare   01179 823 492
www.natracare.com
Organic and natural baby toiletries and tampons.

thegreenboxshop.co.uk
0115 974 7096

the green box shop
NATURAL PRODUCTS TO YOUR DOOR

E45 Junior
www.e45.com
Dermatologist- and paediatrician-approved. Developed for children with dry, sensitive skin or eczema. Available from all leading supermarkets and pharmacies.

Earth Friendly Baby   0845 310 4411
www.earthfriendlybaby.co.uk
This is a range of high-quality products that use natural plant-based ingredients with no artificial colouring or synthetic fragrances. Available from Sainsburys, Green Baby and other health shops across the UK - or online at their own website.

Green Baby   020 7359 7037
www.greenbabyco.com
Natural baby toiletries and baby massage oils.

Green People   0870 240 1444
www.greenpeople.co.uk
Organic range of products developed for children with sensitive skins.

Verde   020 7720 1100
www.verde.co.uk
Mother and baby range. 16 products including Extra Rich Stretch Mark Oil, Chamomile Baby Body Balm, Bizzy Kids Bathtime, Soother, lice repel lotion. Organic and pure plant preparations.

www.babydirectory.com

mail order: general

The Green Box Shop   0115 974 7096
www.thegreenboxshop.co.uk
The Green Box Shop offers a fantastic range of natural and Eco friendly household and baby products. The online shop and home delivery service was set up two years ago by a local mother of three, Michelle Darkin-Price. With a family history of Asthma, allergies and Eczema and a growing concern for the environment, she recognised the importance of switching from chemical to natural products and wanted others to do the same. She has spent the last 8 years trying new products and offers her choice of 'best' based on purity, effectiveness and cost. For more details or to place your order visit www.thegreenboxshop.co.uk or call 0115 974 7096.

Smilechild   01242 269 635
www.smilechild.co.uk
Earth Friendly Baby, Badger, Faith in Nature brands offered as well as natural toothbrushes and sponges (includes natural lice products).

Tummy Tubs   01635 255 725
www.tummy-tub.co.uk
This is a new concept for bathing babies from newborn up to 6 months. Babies assume the foetal position in the tub and are immersed in the water up to their shoulders, ensuring they remain warmer for longer.

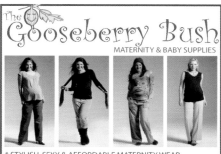
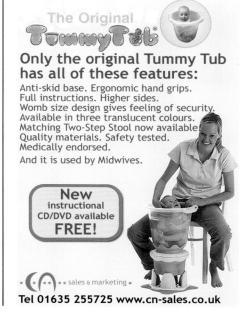

maternity shops

H&M Mama
www.hm.com
Leicester 0116 251 7454 Nottingham 0115 852 3760. High
fashion at affordable prices with H&M Mama maternity
section. Stocks casual wear, special occasions, sportswear
and work wear. Sizes: S-XL.

JoJo Maman Bébé   0870 241 0560
www.jojomamanbebe.co.uk
JoJo Maman Bébé is a one-stop shop for pregnancy and
beyond, offering fashionable maternity wear for every
occasion, quirky children's clothing and adorable babywear.
The company also provides an extensive range of practical
products, toys and gifts for your baby, nursery and family
home. Free P&P on all UK mainland orders.

Mamaway   020 8741 8297
www.mamaway.co.uk
Stylish mothers' choice for nursing wear. Mamaway
is dedicated to making nursing mothers look and
feel their best! Products include nursing tops,
dresses, bras, nightwear as well as baby slings and
carry bags.

DERBYSHIRE
Polarn O Pyret   01332 200 796
South Mall, Westfields Centre, Derby
www.polarnopyret.com
PO.P- Sweeden's award winning leading maternity,
baby and childrenswear brand is no available in
Derby! Swedes rave about this functional and
playful brand that offers mums-to-be and babies
and children up to 6 years high quility Swedish style
at sensible prices.

LEICESTERSHIRE
Crave Maternity   0870 240 5476
1st floor Manor House, 14 Market St, Lutterworth,
LE17 4EH
www.cravematernity.co.uk
Maternity clothes for those who wish to maintain their style
and fashion sense throughout their pregnancy. Smart and
casual clothing as well as office wear and party wear.

Grace Maternity   01509 238 300
17 Churchgate, Loughborough, LE11 1UD
www.gracematernity.com
This contemporary maternity and bridal maternity wear shop
stocks a good range of labels including Vida Vita, Noppies
and Mamas & Papas. They also sell maternity lingerie, gifts,
changing bags and evening/special occasion wear. The
collection has new items in every week, including non-
pregnancy fashion that fits well with bump-accommodating
brands. Open 10am-5pm Tues-Sat.

The Clothes Horse   01530 415 055
8 Elford Street, Ashby de la Zouch, LE65 1HH

LINCOLNSHIRE

Bumps N Boos   **01529 414 445**
Westgate, Sleaford
Good selection of maternity wear including Melba and Pas de Deux. Open 10am-3pm Mon-Sat (closed Tues).

Does My Tum Look Big in This   **01522 568 378**
21 Exley Square, Lincoln, LN2 4WP
www.doesmytumlookbiginthis.com
Fabulous range of designer maternity wear and maternity evening wear hire. The UK's largest collection of maternity wedding dresses and bridesmaid dresses. Pregnancy skincare products. Maternity lingerie and accessories. Gift vouchers also available.

Mummy and Little Me   **01522 548 811**
13 Garmston Street, Lincoln, LN2 1HZ
www.mummyandlittleme.co.uk
Stylish maternity clothes with brands including Noppies, Valja and Melba Maternity. Lingerie by the wonderful Amoralia and Bravado. Also sell baby clothes for 0-2yrs by No Added Sugar, Bob & Blossom and Bonnie Baby as well as selected gifts and accessories. Open 9.30am-5.30pm Mon-Sat and by appointment in the evenings or on Sundays. Online shop also.

NOTTINGHAMSHIRE

Formes   **0115 958 5550**
12 Exchange Archade, Nottingham
www.formes.com
Internationally renowned French designer maternity clothes. Day wear, casual, smart and evening gowns. Open Mon- Sat 9.30am-5.30pm Sun 11am-4pm.

John Lewis   **0115 941 8282**
Victoria Centre, Nottingham, NG1 3QA
www.johnlewis.com
Free Lingerie advice service. Guidance on choosing the right size and type of bra throughout your pregnancy and advice on Nursing bras.

Swells Maternity Wear   **0115 947 0408**
204 Drury Walk, Broadmarsh Shopping Centre,
Bridlesmith Gate Entrance, Nottingham
www.swells.co.uk

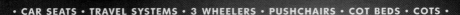

Swells stock the best maternity fashion collections available from Europe and beyond. Items include stretch jeans, hipster and over-the-bump trousers, skirts, business clothing, evening and wedding outfits, bridalwear, pre-natal and feeding bras, thongs, briefs and swimwear. Fashion and underwear styles are designed to last right through pregnancy and beyond, so there is no need to buy bigger sizes every month! Sizes from 8-28.

The Gooseberry Bush   0115 922 8866
80 High Street, Beeston, Nottingham, NG9 2LF
www.thegooseberrybushltd.co.uk
Affordable and stylish maternity wear plus Emma Jane underwear and maternity nightwear. Eco birthing pools, tummy tubs, tushies disposable nappies and natural skincare for mother and baby.

maternity wear: online

Isabella Oliver   0870 240 7612
www.isabellaoliver.com
Isabella Oliver is adored in Hollywood and London for sexy, soft, stylish looks that celebrate your curves. Gorgeously gift wrapped at www.IsabellaOliver.com or call 0870 240 7612, anytime.

Mamaway   020 8741 8297
www.mamaway.co.uk
Stylish mothers' choice for nursing wear. Mamaway is dedicated to making nursing mothers look and feel their best! Products include nursing tops, dresses, bras, nightwear as well as baby slings and carry bags.

Jo Jo Maman Bebe   0870 241 0560
www.jojomamanbebe.co.uk
Extremely stylish maternity wear at reasonable prices, plus underwear, nursery goods and children's clothing.

SJM Baby Products   01673 843 142
Ambleside, Gallamore Lane, Middle Rasen, Market Rasen, LN8 3UB
www.wjmbabyproducts.co.uk
Revolutionary swimming support for pregnant women. The patented design of the Swimlite® Aqua Mum can relieve backache and tension in the neck without placing any pressure on your 'bump'. It provides buoyancy to allow the wearer to float and swim with confidence.

murals

Murals by Tess   01773 599 079
Willoughby
www.tesswilloughby.com

name tapes

Easy2Name   01635 298 326
www.easy2name.com
Easy2name are suppliers of dishwasher proof stickers and iron-on tapes. We like the white transfer nametapes which are perfect for dark coloured socks.

Courtyard Arts presents..
Murals for YOU!!
Perfect for nurseries, bedrooms, schools, clubs & much more!
Bright! Bold! Designed just for you!
Contact Tess for more details
tesswilloughby@yahoo.co.uk
The Courtyard, 8 Market Place, Belper, De56 IFZ
As seen at The Heights of Abraham and Chucklebutties!

nappies: cloth

There is now a huge range of cotton nappies available and many websites helping you select the most suitable design for your baby and lifestyle.

Angel Tots   01530 456 717
46 Charnwood Street, Coalville, LE67 3DG
www.angeltots.co.uk
We supply and offer tailored advice on a wide range of real cloth nappies, slings, eco-friendly menstrual products, and accessories for mum and baby, all with sustainability, quality, comfort, and practicality in mind. Nappy Demo's are available in and around North West Leicestershire, and Nappuchino's are held once a month in Coalville. We pride ourselves on excellent customer service, value and speedy delivery.

Nature Babies Real Nappies 01509 621 879
Unit 17-18, Clear View Farm, Quorn, LE12 8DU
www.naturebabies.co.uk
Creating a cleaner future for your baby, whether washing at home, or using our laundry wash service. Whatever your circumstances/ budget we will find a leak proof, hassle free system to suit you.

nearly new

Sues Nearly Nues   01159 396 737
52 Station Road, Sandiacre, Nottingham,
Nottinghamshire, NG10 5AS
www.suesnearlynues.com
My name is Sue and I have been in the business for 20 years.
I am a mum and grandma so I have plenty of experience to
advise and guide on the purchase of suitable products for
you and your baby's needs. Don't be fooled by the name! As
our name implies we do sell quality nearly new nursery goods
which are fully checked, cleaned and around 12 months old.
All of which comply to the current British standards and
legislation. We also sell a wide range of as new children's
outfits from top high street chains- Next, GAP, Pumpkin
Patch, Mothercare etc. Again all of these are laundered,
pressed and checked for any damage or wear marks. We do
however stock a complete range of quality value for money
new equipment and accessories, which these days makes up
for the majority of our sales. As for the name, having traded
under Sues Nearly Nues for 20 years it has become well
known in the local area.

nursery furniture and interiors

John Lewis   0115 941 8282
Victoria Centre, Nottingham, NG1 3QA
www.johnlewis.com
Expert advice, absolutely free. Make an appointment with our
Nursery Advisor for all your nursery needs. Nursery catalogue
available. Free delivery and Customer Collection Point.

nursery goods: online

Snuggle N Snooze   0777 905 7950
www.snugglensnooze.co.uk
For baby slings; carriers that are not only functional, but
ergonomically comfortable, stylish and safe. You will be able
to hold baby close and continue to meet the challenges of
everyday life.

Babyworld   01491 821 877
www.babyworld.co.uk
The UK's most efficient and well set-out online store, with
customer reviews and articles to help you choose which are
the most relevant products for your needs. Good delivery
and stock levels. Full range of nursery furniture, prams,
pushchairs, accessories etc.

nursery shops

DERBYSHIRE
Babies Galore   01909 487788
Unit 10 Shireoaks Network Centre, Worksop
www.babiesgalore.co.uk
A one stop Nursery Shop stocking everything you could
imagine you need for a newborn. Babies Galore is a extensive
shop slightly out of the way of the main centre which offers a
relaxed environment to contemplate all those important

decisions form crib size to furniture needs. Light and airy, stocking all major brands and offering a very efficient free delivery service. Open Tues-Sat 9am-5pm and Sun.

Babies R Us   0115 985 1185
www.toysrus.co.uk
The Babies R Us chain offers just about everything you need from a complete set of nursery furniture to a packet of disposables. It's a similar range that you might find in Mothercare, but the products are generally less expensive. Worth visiting to try out the products if you live nearby. They have a catalogue and website which offers an even greater range than can be found in store. East Midlands branches in;Derby, Leicester, Lincoln, Nottingham and Scunthorpe.

BabyCare   01246 454 498
Brimington Road North, Whittington Moor, Chesterfield, S41 9AP

Children's Choice   01773 825 865
17 Bridge Street, Belper, DE56 1AX
Specialists in school wear. Official scout's and guide's shop and children's fashions from newborn to teens. Nursery equipment. Everything you need for your baby! Suppliers of nursery equipment direct to nurseries and schools. Open from 9am-5pm Mon-Sat.

Early Times   01332 541561
8 Blenheim Parade, Allestree, DE22 2GP
Stocking a wide range of baby accessories such as stair gates, baby locks and car seat covers, this shop is situated in a village shopping precinct with excellent parking facilities. They also offer a popular hire service for nursery equipment, which is very useful in accommodating holidays, family visits or friends visiting from abroad. A delivery service is available on Saturdays. Open Mon-Fri 9am-4.30pm.

Giraffe Nursery Stores   1246 277 088
247 Chatsworth Road, Chesterfield, Derbyshire, S40 2BL
www.giraffenurserystores.co.uk
For parents who want to invest in something different-without the restriction of high prices, Giraffe stocks the very best of new, unique and international products ranging from the traditional to the contemporary. With a wide range of baby equipment and just about everything from car seats to cotton nappies including all the major brands (Bugaboo, Musty, Petite Star) they offer a like for like purchase policy where they will guarantee to match any price found elsewhere in the UK.

Mothercare   01332 280 570
Wyvern Retail Park, Chaddesden Sidings, Derby, Derbyshire, DE2 6NZ
www.mothercare.com
In larger stores you will find everything you need from the smallest babygrow through to a travel system. If you prefer online shopping check out their website or catalogue. Baby changing facilities are available in stores.

Stork Talk   0115 930 6700
Birkdale Close, Manners Industrial Estate, Ilkeston, Derbyshire, DE7 8YA
www.chiccomailorder.co.uk
Stock a wide range of prams, cots, strollers, car seats, highchairs and bouncy chairs. Located minutes from Junction 25 of the M1 motorway but if you are too far away to visit they have a mail order service.

Thorpes of Ilkeston   0115 932 7834
38-44 South Street, Ilkeston, Derbyshire, DE7 5QJ
www.pramshops.co.uk
Stocks nursery furniture, rocking horses, highchairs, prams and car seats in all the leading brands, Graco, Maclaren, Chicco. Mail order service available.

LEICESTERSHIRE
Babes 2 Tots   01530 564 446
The Courtyard, 52 Market Street, Ashby de la Zouch, LE65 1AN
Baby and nursery equipment retailers with stocklists for; Bugaboo, Mamas and Papas and Recaro.

Baby Love   0116 283 2170
225-227 Saffron Lane, Leicester, LE2 6UD
www.babyloveleicester.com

Baby Planet   0116 255 6222
36 Western Road, Leicester, LE3 0GA
www.babyplanet.biz
(See advert on page 136)

Kinder Garden   **01509 234 532**
48-49 Church Gate, Loughbborough, LE11 1UE
www.kinder-garden.co.uk
Just off the main high Street this light airy shop is all on one floor with large aisles for maneuvering down with push chairs. Stockists of all the major brands; Mclarens, Mama & Papa's etc it offers many of the nursery and baby goods that you could find yourself in want of. Open 10am-5pm Mon-Fri, 9am-5pm Sat; Closed Wed and Sun.

Mothercare   **0116 262 0768**
Unit 14, The Shires Shopping Centre, Leicester, LE1 4FQ
www.mothercare.com
In larger stores you will find everything you need from the smallest babygrow through to a travel system. If you prefer online shopping check out their website or catalogue. Baby changing facilities are available in stores. Other Leicestershire branches: St Georges Retail Park, Leicester tel- 0152 252 1825.

Peek-a-Boo Baby   **0845 603 7713**
3 Churchgate Mews, Loughborough, LE11 1TL
www.peek-a-boobaby.co.uk
Baby gifts, soft toys and high quality baby nursery furniture; just some of the wonderful baby items that are available from peek-a-boo. Both the website and shop offer parents, family and friends a superb service and gift selection. The range includes everything for baby and nursery from bedtime to playtime.

Diddyland

For Beautiful Beginnings

Diddyland

Are a family run business established for over 25 years, offering a friendly & professional service from our fully trained staff, all of whom are mothers & grand mothers themselves giving you the chance to benefit from their years of experience & knowledge at this new and exciting time.

Main Stockists of

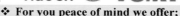

❖ **For you peace of mind we offer;**
- Large choice of quality prams & pushchairs
- Large choice of cots & cot beds
- Great selection of nursery linens
- Competitive prices on brand names
- In store car seat fitting service
- In store repair centre
- Deposit system available
- Goods laid away until babies arrival

Visit our NEW furniture showroom

Opening Hours
Monday to Saturday
9.15 - 5.00
Sunday
11.00 - 3.00

906 Woodborough rd
Mapperley
Nottingham
NG3 5QR
TEL; 0115 9623000

Website; www.diddyland.co.uk
Email; info@diddyland.co.uk

Prams 'N' Things   **0800 389 8074**
108 St Mary's Road, Market Harborough, LE16 7DX
Established in 1989, this nursery shop has stood the test of
time and continues to offer special services such as after
hours appointments and pick up times to customers. An
excessively well stocked two story shop with goods ranging
from bedding to prams, cradles to potties, Silver Cross to
Bebe Car. Open Tues-Sat 9.30am- 5.15pm.

Whizzy Wheels   **01162 702 888**
69 Queens Road, Clarendon Park, Leicester, LE2
1TT
www.whizzywheels.co.uk
Owned by Angelique, a former Midwife and Neo-Natal nurse,
Whizzy Wheels has a wide range of brands including Stokke,
Jané and Out N About. Stocks products for every pocket
and promises all customers the same standard of service no
matter what the size of their budget. Open 9am- 5.30 Tue-
Sat, 9am- 7pm on Tuesdays and Sundays 11am- 3pm.

LINCOLNSHIRE

Alison Baby Carriages   **01406 426 007**
The Homestead, Washway Road, Holbeach,
Spalding, PE12 7PP
Stock a range of prams and pushchairs.

Babies R Us   **01522 568 787**
1 The Sidings, Lincoln, LN6 7TP
The Babies R Us chain offers just about everything you need
from a complete set of nursery furniture to a packet of

disposables. It's a similar range that you might find in
Mothercare, but the products are generally less expensive.
Worth visiting to try out the products if you live nearby. They
have a catalogue and website which offers an even greater
range than can be found in store.

Baby Grows   **01754 765 301**
112 Roman Bank, Skegness, PE25 2SP
www.baby-grows.com
Well established family run business. Also sell christening
wear as well as online.

Baby Occasion   **01522 540 692**
13b Garmston Street, Lincoln, LN2 1HZ
www.emmas4baby.co.uk
Small shop selling prams and christening wear by Little
Darlings. Open 10am-5pm Mon-Sat.

Bambinos   **01472 600 599**
196 Grimsby Road, Cleethorpes, DN35 7EZ
www.bambinoscleethorpes.co.uk
Stocking a wide range of nursery goods including high chairs,
prams, pushchairs and cots and bedding from Italy.
Excellent service, shop in store or order from their website.

Eden & Eve   **01427 629 990**
16 Morton Road, Laughton, Gainsborough, DN21
3PS
www.edenandeve.co.uk
Anything and everything you and your baby want or need can
be found here. Day, night, mealtime, bath time and playtime
they have it covered. Car seat fitting service is offered.

Growing Pains   **01522 544 956**
276 Wragby Road, Lincoln, LN2 4PX

Little Angels   **01522 575 575**
41 Steep Hill, Lincoln, LN2 1LU

Little Rascals Baby Centre   **01427 811 404**
Trinity Street, Gainsborough, DN21 1HS

Lullabys   **01724 276 104**
19 Robert Street, Scunthorpe, DN15 6LU

Moisers   **01472 342 334**
252-256 Freeman Street, Grimsby, DN32 9DR
www.moisers.co.uk
This family business run by John and Mike Moiser, great-
grandsons of the founder, boasts over 25 years experience of
selling baby and nursery equipment. With excellent product
knowledge and a first class after sales service, they stock all
the major brands including Mamas & Papas, Bugaboo and
Tippi Toes.

Mothercare   **01522 521 825**
Unit 7, St Marks East, Lincoln, LN5 7DB
In larger stores you will find everything you need from the
smallest babygrow through to a travel system. If you prefer
online shopping check out their website or catalogue. Baby
changing facilities are available in stores. Branches are: 15
Friargate, Grimsby tel- 0147 235 2793; St Mark's East,
Lincoln 01522, 521, 825.

Nicola's Nursery World   01754 762 858
12 High Street, Skegness, PE25 3NW
Independent retailer of baby goods including pushchairs,
prams, cots, car seats and all other nursery and baby related
products. They have an online store. Stocklists for Out and
About, Prince Lionheart and Quicksmart Quinny among
others. One of few UK stores to be a Maclaren 1st class
retailer. Open 7 days a week 9am - 5pm Mon-Sat & 11am -
5pm Sunday.

Ramsden Nursery Store   01472 315 270
361 Cleethorpes Road, Grimsby, DN31 3BP

Tiny Togs   01476 590 207
14 Westgate, Grantham, NG31 6LT

NOTTINGHAMSHIRE

Bambino Baby and Nursery   0115 914 1434
Goods
52 Rectory Road, West Bridgford, NG2 6BU
www.bambino.org.uk
Bambino Baby & Nursery Goods is a small but perfectly
formed independent store with a wide range of individually
chosen nursery goods, pushchairs, car seats, cots, bedding
and much more. If you are looking for something specific we
will see if we can locate it for you from our wide range of
suppliers. With friendly staff who are parents themselves, we
are here to help and advise you at this very happy and special
time and with Bambino's price match policy you can't go
wrong.

Bristol's Early Days   01623 554 227
61 Outram Street, Sutton in Ashfield, NG17 4BG
www.bristolsearlydays.co.uk
Good range of high quality nursery goods and furniture from
all leading manufacturers including Silver Cross, Maclaren
and Britax at competitive prices. This is also
Nottinghamshire's only Mamas & Papas platinum stockists.
Located only 10 minutes from the M1 junction 28. Open
9am-5.30pm Mon-Sat.

Diddyland   0115 962 3000
906 Woodborough Road, Mapperley, NG3 5QR
www.diddyland.co.uk
Diddyland has been a family run business for well over 25
years, with a team of staff who are friendly, welcoming and
have years of experience and knowledge behind them. With
their consultative approach, they pride themselves on being
on hand to help advise and assist you. The shop is fully
stocked with everything you could ever need from new born
to toddlers including pushchairs, car seats, beds, nursery
furniture, high chairs, traditional toys, safety and accessories.
Diddyland stock all the big names including Mutsy, Maclaren,
Grobag, East Coast, Bébé Confort, Silver Cross, Jane,
Noukie's, Britax, Maxi-Cosi, Out 'n' About, Hauck, Tomy and
Clair de lune and are Mamas & Papas.

John Lewis   0115 941 8282
Victoria Centre, Nottingham, NG1 3QA
www.johnlewis.com
Make a free appointment with their Nursery Adviser for all your
nursery needs. Free delivery and customer collection point..

Mothercare   0162 362 5403
BHS, 32-34 Westgate, Mansfield, NG18 1RS
www.mothercare.com
In larger stores you will find everything you need from the
smallest babygrow through to a travel system. Baby
changing facilities are available in stores. Other
Nottinghamshire branches: Castle Bridge Road, Nottingham
tel- 0115 240 870, 32 Middlegate, Newark tel- 0163 670
1695, 14 Bridge Place, Worksop tel- 0190 947 4370.

Nursery Rhymes   01777 711 332
5 West Street, Retford, DN22 6ES

Serendipitys   01949 831707
35A Long Acre, Bingham
Serendipitys Baby Goods. Serendipitys, situated in Bingham
only 6 miles from Nottingham is the one stop shop for all your
baby needs. Travel systems, car seats, cots, highchairs,
bedding, clothing, accessories and bouncers, basically
everything you will ever need all under one roof. The store was
opened with the aim of providing quality equipment at
affordable prices with that all important personal service.
Serendipitys carries a large stock of all major brands (saving
that trip into town) and is also a recognised car seat specialist.
Serendipitys prides itself on its choice of stockists from market
leaders to continental new designers and manufacturers
ensuring that degree of exclusivity for its clients.

The Gooseberry Bush 0115 922 8866
www.thegooseberrybushltd.co.uk
Organic cotton babywear, soft toys and a good range of organic skincare is available from this Nottingham maternity and baby store.

photography

Amazing Photography 01773 513220
4 Chapel Street, Ripley, DE5 3DL
www.amazingphotography.co.uk

Montage 0115 933 4280
45 Queens Road, Radcliffe-on-Trent, NG12 1DL
www.montageworks.co.uk

Phunky Fotos 0115 978 8888
The Maltings, Nottingham, NG7 7EA
www.phunkyfotos.co.uk
At Phunky Fotos we don't do traditional portraits rather every picture we take tells a story. We take photographs that capture emotions and occasions and give you special memorable pictures that you will love With Phunky Fotos, there are no dreary portrait sittings instead we want you to jump, wrestle, cuddle, kick a football around but above all, have fun! At very affordable prices, there's no pressure to buy they're your Fotos, so you decide.

Pixi Foto 0115 924 1025
Mothercare, Castle Meadow Retail Park, Castle Bridge Road, Nottingham, NG7 1GX
www.pixifoto.co.uk

Venture 01332 227 790
5 Queen Street, Derby, DE1 3DL
www.thisisventure.co.uk

Wow Shots 0800 321 3733
14 Hayes Close, West Hallam, DE7 6PB
www.wowshots.co.uk

Family Portrait special offer
session & framed print for just £25.00
(normally £70.00, save £45.00).

Amazing Photography
Tel: 01773 513220 www.amazingphotography.co.uk

every **venture** tells a story

POPPY, SCARLET AND THEIR 'METRO' FROM THE NEW VENTURE 07 COLLECTION

WHAT WILL YOURS SAY? In a one hour studio session, our talented Venture photographers will bring your story to life. We'll then create a contemporary piece of art that will transform your home. Whatever it is that makes you who you are, a Venture New Generation Portrait will reveal it. For more information call your local studio or visit **thisisventure.co.uk**

Derby : 01332 227790
Leicester : 0116 270 0995
Nottingham : 0115 959 9999

venture
NEW GENERATION PORTRAITS

shoes: online

Starchild Shoes   **01509 817 601**
www.starchildshoes.co.uk
Handmade soft leather shoes that stay on. Wonderful
designs for boys and girls (0-4yrs).

Hippychick   **01278 434 440**
www.hippychick.com
Hippychick import the brand Shoo Shoos from South Africa.
Sizes from 0-24 months.

Papillon Shoes   **020 7834 1504**
www.papillon4children.com
Children's moccasins and loafers in all sizes.

shoes: shops

Good quality, correctly fitted shoes are vital for the health
of growing feet. Children's shoes come in 8 width fittings
so make sure you have them measured and fitted by a
professional. The following are approved Start-rite or
Clarks fitters and stockists, unless otherwise stated.

DERBYSHIRE
EKKO   **01332 541 129**
Duffield Road, Allestree, Derby, DE22 2DL

Luv Shoes   **01246 239 907**
21 Old Road, Bramton, Chesterfield, S40 2RE

The Clarks Shop   **01332 382 180**
34 Cornmarket, Derby, DE1 2DG
Quality shoes for the whole family. Other Derbyshire
branches in; Buxton tel- 01298 28579, High Street,
Chesterfield tel- 01246 231 326, The Pavements,
Chesterfield tel- 01246 274 466, Mothercare World, Derby
tel- 01332 281 761, 3 Crown Walk tel- 01332 362 996,
Ilkeston tel- 0115 944 2767.

Wigleys   **01335 342 884**
18-20 St John Street, Ashbourne, DE6 1GH

LEICESTERSHIRE
Ammonite Shoes   **01530 563 500**
6 Bath Street, Ashby-De-La-Zouch, LE65 2FH

Christians Shoes   **01858 465 466**
10 High Street, Market Harborough, LE16 7NJ
Well established shop with good range of children's shoes
including Buckle My Shoe, Petasil and Ricosta. Do not stock
Start-rite. Open 9am-5.30pm Mon-Sat.

Fitter Shoes   **01509 235 200**
60 Wards End, Loughborough, LE11 3HB

Grahame Gardner   **0116 255 6326**
Stamford Buildings, Stamford Street, Leicester, LE1 6NJ

H2   **01572 821 933**
2 Stockerton Road, Uppingham, Oakham, LE15 6EA
www.h2clothingandfootwear.co.uk
H2 Kids provide a comprehensive range of continental
brands of clothing from 0-8yrs enhanced with a wide range of
hosiery and accessories, including primary school colours.
The staff are all fully trained Start-rite fitters ensuring the best
footwear for children from 0 to teens. They also stock Ecco,
Kickers with fringe brands. Free parking outside the shop.

Jellyrolls Footwear   **0116 242 5222**
10 St Martins Square, Leicester, LE1 5DE
www.jellyrollskidswear.com

The Clarks Shop   **0116 262 6990**
2 Humberstone Gate, Leicester, LE1 3PH
www.clarks.co.uk
Quality shoes for the whole family. Other Leicestershire
branches in; Coalville tel- 01530 832 361, Hinckley tel-
01455 633 439, Mothercare World, Leicester tel- 0116 262
9537, Fletcher Mall, Leicester tel- 0116 236 4925,
Loughborough tel- 01509 215 883, Market Harborough tel-
01858 462 037, Melton Mowbray tel- 01664 500 808.

LINCOLNSHIRE
Crumbsnatchers   **01673 885 794**
Ashview, 1 Snelland Rd, Wickenby, Lincoln, LN3 5AH
www.crumbsnatchers.co.uk
Footwear for all at fantastic prices: boy's shoes, girl's shoes
and school shoes.

My New Shoes   **01472 267 565**
1 Osbourne Street, Grimsby, DN31 1EY
www.mynewshoes.co.uk

North's Shoes   **01778 422 886**
18 North Street, Bourne, PE10 9AB

Piggy's Footwear   **01780 763 758**
14 St Mary's Hill, Stamford, PE9 2DP
www.piggys-shoes.co.uk

Poynton's Shoes   **01507 522 582**
18 High Street, Horncastle, LN9 5BL

Radley Footwear   **01529 302 413**
9 Southgate, Sleaford, NG34 7SU

Revills Shoes   **01775 768 504**
4 Francis Street, Spalding, PE11 1SH

The Clarks Shop   **01724 840 802**
10 Jubilee Way, The Parishes, Scunthorpe, DN15 6RB
www.clarks.co.uk
Quality shoes for the whole family. Other Lincolnshire
branches in; Boston tel- 01205 362 094, Cleethorpes tel-
01472 694 352, Grantham tel- 01476 563 244, Grimsby tel-
01472 343 766, Lincoln tel- 01522 512 689, Skegness tel-
01754 765 900, Stamford tel- 01780 762 548.

W A Clarke   **01652 632 443**
106-108 High Street, Barton-on-Humber, DN18
5PU
www.waclarke.co.uk

Kids' shoes without queues

Why spend time waiting in line, when Footling can do the legwork for you?

Our trained shoe fitters will visit you in your home, measure your children's feet, and provide a range of high quality school shoes, toddler shoes and trainers from leading brands such as Hush Puppies, Ricosta, Buckle My Shoe, Skechers and Merrell.

Visit **www.footling.co.uk** to find out more and book an appointment.

Or call us on 08707 200555.

Feet come first

NOTTINGHAMSHIRE

Footling   08707 200 555
www.footling.co.uk
Children's shoes, professionally fitted, at your home or toddler group, anywhere in and around Nottingham or London. Footling makes it easy for parents to look after their children's feet. They provide a wide range of high quality shoes and their fitters are professionally trained. Children can have their feet measured and can choose the shoes they like at a time and place convenient to everyone.

Jessop and Son   0115 941 8282
Victoria Centre, NG1 3QA

John Lewis   **0115 941 8282**
Victoria Centre, Nottingham, NG1 3QA
www.johnlewis.com
Full shoe fitting service available.

Morleys   0115 9258046
116 - 118 Bramcote Avenue, Chilwell, NG9 4DR

The Clarks Shop   0115 941 0797
Victoria Centre, Nottingham, NG1 3QG
www.clarks.co.uk
Quality shoes for the whole family. Other Nottinghamshire branches in; Mansfield tel- 01623 624 563, Newark tel- 01636 703 614, Mothercare World, Nottingham tel- 0115 920 4089, Long Row, Nottingham tel- 0115 947 2690, Weelergate, Nottingham tel- 0115 941 9158, Retford tel- 01777 707 446

toy shops

DERBYSHIRE
Early Learning Centre   0870 535 2352
www.elc.co.uk
All singing all dancing toy shop which offers value for money without compromising on quality. Whether you want a cuddly toy, jigsaw puzzle, blackboard or a sandpit you're bound to find it here. Look out for the '3 for the price of 2' deals and craft activities in store. Well laid out website makes online shopping easy. Catalogue makes interesting reading for children and adults alike- use it for cut and paste activities when you've finished with it! East Midlands Branches in: Derby tel- 01332 242 018, Burton-on-Trent tel- 01283 510 822, Chesterfield tel- 01246 208 708, Grimsby tel- 01472 353428, Lincoln, tel- 01522 545216, Mansfield tel- 01623 645 217, Kettering tel- Leicester tel- 0116 262 5092, Nottingham Victoria Centre tel- 0115 947 4203 Exchange walk tel- 0115 941 0431.

Toys R Us
www.toysrus.co.uk
Warehouse style toy shopping. Whatever you need you'll find it here from rattles to bicycles. Wide aisles and easy parking. Catalogue and website which offers even more variety and better discounts than in store. East Midlands branches in: Wyvern Way, Chaddesden, Derby tel- 01332 678 181. St Georges Way, Leicester tel- LE1 1SG. The Sidings, Lincoln tel 01522 568 787. Queens Drive, Nottingham tel 0115 985 1185. Doncaster Road, Scunthorpe tel 01724 847 800.

TOYS, TOYS, TOYS

From Bob The Builder and Barbie, to Playmobil and Fisher Price our extensive range of toys will excite children of all ages!

OUTDOOR FUN

kites, climbing frames, water pistols, paddling pools... we have all you need to create an adventure playground in your own back garden.

MODELS & KITS

Trains, planes and automobiles galore! From radio controlled cars to construction kits, we stock all well known brands including Airfix, Corgi, Hornby, K'nex, Meccano, Scalextric and Lego.

ARTS & CRAFTS

We have the largest choice of professional arts and crafts materials in Leicestershire, including ranges by Windsor & Newton and Daler Rowney.

COLLECTABLES

Whether you are a dollhouse collector or a lover of Beanie Babies and Steiff teddy bears, our range of high quality toys and games include many collectable favourites.

GAMES & PUZZLES

Puzzled? You will be with our fantastic selection of jigsaws. And with all your favourite board games to choose from even the brightest minds will be tested.

VALUE & SERVICE

our helpful staff provide specialist advice and a personal service that has been our trademark since 1983.

DISCOUNTS

available for preschools, playgroups, children's activity groups - call for details

The Midland's favourite toy shop: four floors, fifteen departments, more choice than ever

DOMINOES

High Street Leicester • Tel 0116 253 3363 • www.dominoestoys.co.uk

About Dominoes Toys

The Dominoes store at 66 High Street Leicester spans over four heavily laden floors and has many specialist departments. Read on below for an insight into this most memorable store.

Train lovers will appreciate the fantastic collection of Hornby & Bachmann trains, whilst aspiring engineers will love the construction room for Lego, K'nex, Mega Bloks, Meccano and Geomag.

Looking for action? There's plenty in our action figures department, Actionman, Superman, Transformers and many more favourites.

We have pocket money toys galore, all sorts of marbles and plenty of activity toys for some outdoor fun!

For the youngest members of the family we have a comprehensive range of pre-school and educational toys and with all your favourite board games in our games room we promise you won't be bored!

Puzzled? You will be, with our fantastic selection of jigsaws!

For those who love teddy bears our dollhouse and collectables department is a must. Feeling crafty? We have a marvellous collection of craft ideas and a comprehensive art department which caters for the novice and enthusiast alike!

Visit Crumblin Cookie tea and coffee lounge on the first floor. We also have L.C.F.C. (selling merchandise and match-day tickets) and Jellyrolls concessions on the ground floor If you're in the area why not come in and see for yourself? We have so much choice in store for all the family!

Dominoes Toys - The UK's largest independent retailers of toys, models, arts & crafts

Dominoes is a family run business established since 1983 delighting customers both young and old with our huge range of traditional and modern toys and so much more. We are now the UK's largest independent retailer of toys, models, arts & crafts.

If you don't know your way here, have a quick look at the map to the right:

Children's Choice   **01773 825 865**
14 Bridge Street, Belper, DE56 1AX
www.childrenschoice.co.uk
Children's Choice is a treasure trove for parents, children and mums to be. A family business which opened back in 1990 we have just celebrated our first birthday at our new spacious premises. Spring 2008 will see the launch of a new website www.childrenschoice.co.uk where customers will be able to purchase both NURSERY GOODS including travel systems, pushchairs, car seats and accessories and TOYS from brands such as Orchard, Galt, Great Gizmos, Playmobil, Sylvanian Families and Siku, to name but a few. We also specialise in School Uniforms and both embroider and print in Store. We sell FASHIONS from newborn to TEENS and christening wear and are also an Official

LEICESTERSHIRE

Cots n' Togs   **01858 468 568**
Market Harborough, LE11 2PZ
A welcoming family Business for over 40 years, with other shops in both Coalville and Tamworth, this is a shop that stocks all ranges and all toys you could possibly want, from Chicco to Fisherprice, Tony to Lego. There is also a large wooden train set to distract the children from other pressies they may spy, leaving you to buy for Father Christmas or Birthdays without little beady eyes watching. Open Mon-Fri 9am-5.30pm, Sat 9am-5pm.

Dominoes   **0116 253 3363**
66 High Street, Leicester, LE1 5YP
www.dominoestoys.co.uk
Dominoes is a family run independent retailer of toys, models, arts & crafts. They stock a huge range of traditional and modern toys in their store which spans over four heavily laden floors and has many specialist departments. There is more choice than ever before at unbeatable value! Toys, Construction Toys, Games, Puzzles, Action Figures, Dolls, Dolls Houses, Soft Toys, Outdoor Toys, Models, Plastic Kits, shop. Open Mon-Sat 9am-5pm.

LINCOLNSHIRE

Baby and You   **01780 755 996**
14 St Mary's Street, Stamford, PE9 2DF
Traditional toy shop with lovely wooden and soft toys. Brands include Manhattan Toys, Pin. Also sell designer children swear.

Beecroft's Toys   **01522 778 885**
Swinderby Road, North Scarle, Lincoln, LN6 9EU
www.beecroftstoys.co.uk
Well established (since 1840!) family-run toy shop. Their specialty is agricultural toys by Bruder and Britains, so if you're after a tractor or stables this is the place to come. They also stock Thomas and Friends.

Fun Junction   **01775 719 304**
62 Swan Street, Spalding, PE11 1BT
www.funjunctiononline.com
Stockists of toys from birth to 12 years; Playmobil, Lego, Hama and K'Kids. Open Mon - Sat 9.00am - 5.00pm, and Sundays 11.30-3.30pm.

Kidz Toys   **01522 801 226**
31c Redwood Drive, Waddington, Lincoln, LN5 9BN

Little Acorns   **01529 462 037**
1 Main Road, Little Hale, Sleaford, NG34 9BB
For inspirational and unusual gifts for kids of all ages. Visit the store or shop on-line in minutes for birthday presents, Christmas gifts, party favours and all manner of toys, games and surprises for children of any age to enjoy.

Rand Farm Park   **01673 858 904**
Rand, Lincoln, LN8 5NJ
www.randfarmpark.co.uk
Well stocked toy- shop located at this popular working farm (see Days Out). You don't have to visit the farm to shop here. Brands include Playmobil, Orchard Toys and Tollo. Also stock the Kidorable range of children's wet weather clothing and Wellingtons.

Wood & Toys   **01522 512 958**
10 The Strait, Lincoln, LN2 1JD
Retailer of traditional, educational toys, games, puzzles and ragdolls this boutique shop is about the size of a garage and a treasure trove of interest both for your children and you, close to the market place there are lots of other children stockists around this shop. Open 9.30am-5pm Monday to Friday and 9.30am-4pm on a Thursday.

NOTTINGHAMSHIRE

Amuse Me Toys   **01636 672 652**
12 Queens Head Court, Newark, NG24 1EL
www.amusemetoys.co.uk
We offer imaginative soft toys, traditional, educational wooden toys, pedal cars and children's bedroom accessories. All our toys and gifts are high quality and offer outstanding value for money as well as excellent play and educational value.

Geoff's Toys   **01509 216 966**
30 High Street, Coalville, LE11 2PZ
A welcoming family Business for over 40 years with other shops in both market Harborough and Tamworth this is a shop that stocks all ranges and all toys you could possibly want, from Chicco to Fisherprice, Tony to Lego. There is also a large wooden train set to distract the children from other pressies they may spy, leaving you to buy for Father Christmas or Birthdays without little beady eyes watching. Open Mon-Fri 9am-5.30pm, Sat 9am-5pm

Shellbrook Toys   **01530 412 185**
1a Market Street, Ashby De La Zouch, LE6 51AF
Just at the start of the main street, this quaint old fashioned toy shop is the place to go for traditional quality toys, such as beautifully made wooden rocking horses. Established since 1932 there is plenty upon the shelves to capture the interest of your children as you browse. Open Mon-Sat 9.30am-5pm except Wed 9.30am-1pm.

Toymaster   **01530 832 795**
30 High Street, Coalville, LE67 3ED
Under Construction
This spacious store has a beautiful display floor on its second storey. Set in the middle of the town Centre and going for two generations this offers every toy imaginable for the 0-5 age range.

John Lewis   0115 941 8282
Victoria Centre, Nottingham, NG1 3QA
www.johnlewis.com
Full range available for all ages, plus outdoor equipment. .
Also worth visiting their website to look at the latest toys, new
releases and reviews.

The Entertainer   0870 905 5125
302b Victoria Centre, Nottingham, NG1 3QN
www.theentertainer.com
Open 9.30am-5.30pm Mon-Sat. Until 8pm on Thurs. Closed Sun.

Wood & Toys   01636 613 131
6 Chain Lane, Newark, NG24 1AU
Retailer of traditional, educational toys, games, puzzles and
ragdolls this boutique shop is about the size of a garage and
a treasure trove of interest both for your children and you,
close to the market place there are lots of other children
stockists around this shop. Open 9.30am-5pm Monday to
Friday and 9.30am-4pm on a Thursday..

toys/gifts: delivered in 2 days

Babyworld   01491 821 877
www.babyworld.co.uk
Babyworld stocks a massive range of cot, soft, wooden, ride-
on and rocking toys. Order online for delivery within two
working days.

Two Monkeys   07824 666 639
29 Rolleston drive, Arnold, NG5 7JA
www.twomonkeys.uk.com
Never enough time? Want more for your money? Two
Monkeys, the company for busy families, is the answer. It's
an exceptional new members club for busy families to save
time and £££££s on everyday and luxury things. Members
also get an online activity calendar, e-newsletters, free
monthly gifts and a whole host of information for VIP
treatment. Register now (no commitment) by emailing
info@twomonkeysuk.com and qualify for Founder
Membership rates at £75 for a year (50% off the standard
cost). Still not sure? Don't forget the money back guarantee.
Life's too short so make the most of it.

toys: garden

Kiddie Barn Activity   **01335 330 681**
Toy Centre
The Park, Ashbourne, DE6 2DT
www.kiddiesbarn.co.uk
Built within a large field 3 miles outside of Ashbourne this
shop offers a try before you buy faciliity with its outdoor
stowroom such as Tepee activity toys. With eight frames set
up at any time, the equipment ranges from trampolines, to
climbing frames, goalposts to swings. Very rarely can you
combine the fresh air with shopping and even less rarely are
children encouraged to run around, climb on everything and
let off steam as you browse, so make the most of the
opportunity. Delivery available. Open 7 days a week but call in
advan.

toys: online

Hawkin's Bazaar   **0870 429 4000**
www.hawkin.co.uk
Best selection of stocking fillers, tricks, educational and
science-based toys from £1 up.

Little Acorns   **01529 462 037**
www.giftsforkids.co.uk
Sleaford-based online shop that also offers a buy at home
service. High quality creative and educational toys for 0-12yrs.
TP Activity Toy stockist with free delivery to NG34 postcodes.
Also visit shows like the Lincoln Show. See website for details.

Loddon Valley Garden Toys   **0845 644 1546**
www.lvgt.co.uk

Satellite Toy Shop   **01509 211 300**
www.satellitetoyshop.co.uk

Win Green Company   **01622 746 516**
www.wingreen.co.uk
Little Gretels will be the envy of their pals with Win Green's
Gingerbread Play House, made from appliquéd and embroidered
cotton, with lace curtains. Perfect for bedrooms and playrooms,
and can move outside for the summer. Many more designs.

Wonderful Wooden Toys   **0115 944 2007**
www.wonderfulwoodentoys.co.uk
Welcome to the world of Wonderful Wooden Toys where you
will find a vast array of handfinished and traditional wooden
toys. When you explore their online shop you can choose
from games, educational products, dolls houses, ride-alongs,
wooden bikes and cars, musical and much, much more.

twins

Twins Things   **01600 715 146**
www.twinsthings.co.uk
This is an excellent website with a great range of innovative
and practical products for parents of twins or multiples. They
also have a number of beautiful gift ideas as well as useful
information and links to other twin and multiple websites.

our name says it all!

Only wood from reforested sources is used,
decorated with lead-free paint and we make
a point of using environmentally friendly
packaging wherever possible.

www.wonderfulwoodentoys.co.uk
0115 944 2007

TwinsThings ™
An Emphasis on Things for Twins!

A large range of innovative & practical baby
products, unique & beautiful gifts, and our own
exclusive range of Things4Twins™ gift sets
many with an emphasis on,

but not just
for Twins!

For all your Things for Twins!
01600 715146
info@twinsthings.co.uk

www.twinsthings.co.uk

travel

Some parents swear that travel abroad and babies do not mix. They may well be right or they may be missing out. Here we offer ideas for both the adventurous and the stay-at-homes, featuring family-orientated hotels in the UK and overseas travel companies for those wanting to venture further afield. Bon voyage!

Image © jojomamabebe

family hotels and holidays

The following hotels offer special facilities for children and babies, ranging from crèches and child-listening to playgrounds and pools.

AVON

The Bath Spa Hotel   01225 444 424
Sydney Road, Bath
www.bathspa-hotel.co.uk

CHANNEL ISLANDS

Stocks Island Hotel   01481 832 001
Manor Valley, Sark
www.stockshotel.com

CORNWALL

Bedruthan Steps Hotel   01637 860 555
Mawgan Porth, Cornwall, TR8 4BU
www.bedruthan.com/index-pleasure.html
Great indoor soft play area including separate toddler section with ride on toys. Themed art and craft workshops supervised by trained nursery assistants. Good outdoor activities including a shallow paddling/learners' swimming pool and activity playground. Baby listening in the evenings with children's tea between 4.30pm to 6.15pm.

Fowey Hall   01726 833 866
Hanson Drive, Fowey, Cornwall, PL23 1ET
www.luxuryfamilyhotels.com
Part of the Luxury Family Hotels Group – unique, elegant country house hotels with fantastic facilities for families including ofsted registered crèches and babysitting, spa treatments & fabulous food – a luxury break for the whole family.

Tredethy House Country Hotel   01208 841 262
Helland Bridge, Bodmin
www.tredethyhouse.co.uk

Watergate Bay Hotel   01637 860 543
Watergate Bay, Newquay, Cornwall, TR8 4AA
www.watergate.co.uk
Great indoor playroom, which is supervised during mealtimes so parents can enjoy a meal on their own. There is also an outdoor playground, a warm paddling pool, sandpits and trampolines. A children's tea is between 5-6pm and a free baby listening service in the evenings.

CUMBRIA

Armathwaite Hall Hotel   01768 776 551
Bassenthwaite, Keswick, Cumbria, CA12 4RE
www.armathwaite-hall.com
This Luxury 4 star Lake District Country House Hotel is privately owned by the resident Graves family. They have many excellent facilities for families including an indoor

swimming pool (and Spa), their own animal farm next door and children's summer holiday activities. They offer baby listening if you are dining in the hotel, or they can arrange for a baby sitter to come in if you are going out.

Castle Inn Hotel   01768 776 401
Bassenthwaite, Keswick
www.corushotels.com/castleinn

Cumbria Allerdale Court Hotel   01900 823 654
Market Place, Cockermouth
www.allerdalecourthotel.co.uk

Hilton Keswick Lodore   01768 777 285
Borrowdale Road, Keswick

DEVON

Langstone Cliff Hotel   01626 868 000
Mount Pleasant Road, Dawlish Warren, Dawlish
www.langstone-hotel.co.uk
19 acres of woodland, children's suppers, indoor and outdoor pools, tennis, therapy rooms, go-karts.

Thurlestone Hotel   01548 560 382
Thurlestone, Nr Kingsbridge, TQ7 3NN
Thurlestone luxury hotel is situated in a stunning coastal location near Salcombe in South Devon. They have a free Danny the Dolphin Club which plans a number of children's activities throughout the week. They also have indoor and outdoor swimming and paddling pools, climbing frame, family tennis courts and offer a children's tea time menu. All family rooms have baby listening and they can provide cots, linen, highchairs, and pre-bookable baby sitting service.

DORSET

Knoll House   01929 450450
Studland Bay, Dorset, BH19 3AQ
www.knollhouse.co.uk
Gardens, pools, tennis, golf, health spa, playroom, children's restaurant, adventure playground

Moonfleet Manor   01305 786 948
Fleet Road, Weymouth, Dorset, DT3 4ED
www.luxuryfamilyhotels.com
Part of the Luxury Family Hotels Group – unique, elegant country house hotels with fantastic facilities for families including ofsted registered crèches and babysitting, spa treatments & fabulous food – a luxury break for the whole family.

Sandbanks Hotel   01202 707 377
15 Banks Road, Sandbanks, Poole
Child-orientated hotel with direct access to the gorgeous sandy beach.

GLOUCESTERSHIRE

Calcot Manor   01666 890 391
Tetbury, Gloucestershire, GL8 8YJ
www.calcotmanor.co.uk
The charming country house hotel, set in peaceful gardens, is renowned for the excellence of its restaurant and the informality of its gumstool Inn. It offers 30 beautifully furnished bedrooms, a fantasitc creche facility, dedicated accomadation for families and a superb health and beauty spa- the perfect cotswold retreat.

HERTFORDSHIRE

The Grove   01923 807 807
Chandler's Cross, Rickmansworth, WD3 4TG
www.thegrove.co.uk
Fabulous designer hotel in stately home and grounds with state-of-the-art spa and golf course. Anouska's crèche and play area will occupy your children all day if required.

INVERNESS

Polmaily House Hotel   01456 450 343
Drumnadrochit, Loch Ness
www.polmaily.co.uk
Polmaily House Hotel is a comfortable and informal 14 bedroom country house hotel, set in 20 acres of wooded gardens, with a heated indoor swimming pool, tennis court, lawns and woodland paths. All rooms are specially equipped for families with a supervised playroom, outdoor toys and activities, as well as a kids high tea.

ISLE OF WIGHT

The Clarendon Hotel and   01983 730 431
Wight Mouse Inn
Newport Road, Chale
Family-friendly hotel/inn on the picturesque south coast.

Priory Bay Hotel   01983 613 146
Eddington Road, St. Helens
www.priorybay.co.uk
Beautifully decorated, friendly country house hotel with private beach, outdoor pool, pretty grounds and tennis courts.

JERSEY

Longueville Manor Hotel   01534 725 501
St Saviour, Jersey, JE2 7WF
www.longuevillemanor.com
Lovingly restored 13C Norman manor house, with log fires and bedrooms with four-posters. Owners Malcolm and Patricia Lewis have two young children and so welcome children warmly. Their service Little Needs for Babies and Toddlers allows you to order in advance anything from a bed guard to baby wipes. Lovely grounds, pool, fresh garden produce.

The Club Hotel and Spa   01534 876 500
Green Street, St. Helier, Jersey, JE2 4UH
www.theclubjersey.com
Chic townhouse hotel with marine-based spa and Michelin-starred Bohemia restaurant to pamper mum and dad, but youngsters welcome too - an Avent Naturally Baby Must-Haves pack (baby body and hair wash, massage gel, talc, etc) and appropriate books from the hotel's library are placed on baby's bed. Flat screen TVs, DVDs, CDs - plus nearby sandy beaches.

www.babydirectory.com

OXFORDSHIRE

Le Manoir aux Quat'Saisons 01844 278 881
Church Road, Great Milton, OX44 7PD
www.manoir.co.uk
Cot and baby listening services provided at no additional
charge. Private babysitting can be arranged at £5 per hr. No
separate playroom, although toys are provided. Highchairs in
the main restaurant with children's menu.

SCOTLAND

Polmaily House Hotel   01456 450 343
Drumnadrochit, Loch Ness, Inverness-Shire, IV63 6XT
www.polmaily.co.uk
Polmaily House Hotel is a comfortable and informal 14
bedroom country house hotel, set in 20 acres of wooded
gardens, with a heated indoor swimming pool, tennis court,
lawns and woodland paths. All rooms are specially equipped
for families with a supervised playroom, outdoor toys and
activities, as well as a kids high tea.

SOMERSET

Babington House   01373 812 266
Babington, Frome, Somerset, BA11 3RW
www.babingtonhouse.co.uk
This is a small boutique hotel with 28 bedrooms, located in
the Main House, Coach House, Stable Block and Lodge. The
family bedrooms are really mini-apartments with adjoining
bedrooms, ensuite bathrooms and equipped with the latest
technology from plasma screens and DVD players to wireless
internet access. They provide a free creche service in The
Little House from 1yr+ where entertainment, games and other
activities are provided for all ages. An indoor and outdoor
swimming pool provides special children's sessions 12
months of the year.

SUFFOLK

Ickworth House   01284 735 350
Bury St Edmonds, Suffolk, IP29 5QE
www.luxuryfamilyhotels.com
Part of the Luxury Family Hotels Group – unique, elegant
country house hotels with fantastic facilities for families
including ofsted registered crèches and babysitting, spa
treatments & fabulous food – a luxury break for the
whole family.

WARWICKSHIRE

Lea Marston Hotel   01675 470 468
Haunch Lane, Lea Marston

WILTSHIRE

Woolley Grange Hotel   01225 864 705
Woolley Green, Bradford on Avon
www.luxuryfamilyhotels.co.uk
Part of the Luxury Family Hotels Group - unique, elegant
country house hotels with fantastic facilities for families
including Ofsted registered crèches and babysitting, spa
treatments and fabulous food - a luxury break for the
whole family.

WORCESTERSHIRE

The Elms   01299 896 666
Stockton Road, Abberley, Worcester, WR6 6AT
www.luxuryfamilyhotels.com
Part of the Luxury Family Hotels Group - unique, elegant
country house hotels with fantastic facilities for families
including ofsted registered crèches and babysitting, spa
treatments & fabulous food - a luxury break for the whole

resorts

Center Parcs   0870 520 0300
www.centerparcs.co.uk
Centres at Longleat, Elveden and Sherwood Forest with more
centres across Europe. Great outdoor activities and huge
indoor pools with

Club Med UK   0843 676767
www.clubmed.co.uk
All inclusive holiday villages located all over the world. A
number of them offer childcare facilities for babies and young
children during the day with good family discount packages.

Mark Warner   0870 770 4227/4228
www.markwarner.co.uk
Winter Ski and Summer sun for children from 4mths+ with no
additional childcare costs from 2-7yrs. Locations are Turkey,
Greece and

Siblu   0870 242 6666
www.sibluholidays.com
Siblu specialise in holidays for babies and toddlers. They
have 24 parcs across France, Spain and Italy with fantastic
entertainment for all ages including exciting clubs, a full range
of supervised activities and superb water complexes. They
also provide a baby pack hire so you don't have to travel with
cots, buggies, high chairs, sterilizers and baby baths.   Prices
start from under £200 per week for the whole family.

Sunsail Clubs   023 9222 2266
www.sunsail.co.uk
Parents can relax knowing their little ones are well cared for at
Sunsail Clubs' activity and watersports resorts. Tots to teens
have great fun in the all day Kids' Clubs, which provide a daily
programme of exciting activities. Please call 0870 427 0083
or visit www.sunsail.co.uk/sebaby

ski companies

Classic Travel –   0870 411 900
The Lapland Specialists
www.santavisits.co.uk
This is a Lapland holiday specliast for those in search of
Father Christmas. They offer day trips, 1-5 night stays in a
choice of log cabin, apartment, bungalow, hotel or even an
igloo!

www.babydirectory.com

Chilly Powder   020 7289 6958
www.chillypowder.com
The Chilly Powder chalet is situated opposite the main cable car linking Morzine and Avoriaz in the Portes du Soleil ski area on the French/Swiss border. Their team of in-house nannies can look after children from 2 months. The crèche has 2 zones for under 2s and over 2s and a separate

Esprit Holidays   01252 618 300
www.ski-esprit.co.uk
Esprit has holidays in France, Italy and Austria. Their Classic Childcare options cater for children from 4mths-3yrs in a nursery setting, and the Spritelets Ski School from 3yrs-5yrs (max 6 in a class). A Snow Club in the afternoon keeps the non-skiing 3-5yr olds well entertained. The nannies are all English-speaking and are offered on a strict ratio of nannies to children. Care is available 6 days per week from 8.30am-5pm. Prices are £150 for nanny care and £125 for Spritelets.

Meriski   01285 648 518
www.meriski.co.uk
If you have your heart set on Meribel, then Meriski provides either in-chalet nannies or crèche facilities (maximum of 8 places) from 9am-5pm Mon-Sat. Cots and highchairs are provided in the chalets, as well as kids meals cooked separately by your chef. From 3yrs+ children can ski with Les Petits Loups, a ski school run by Ecole de Ski Francais, accompanied by an English-speaking nanny.

Ski Famille   01223 363 777
www.skifamille.co.uk
Ski Famille don't charge extra for childcare. They provide fully qualified nannies to your chalet where playrooms are equipped with toys, games and arts/craft materials. When the weather allows they encourage them to play outside. For older children they ensure they are at ski school on time and pick them up afterwards. Childcare is available between 9am-4.30pm except on Saturday (arrival day) or Wednesday (staff day off). They can provide nappies at cost as well as baby bottles, sterilizers, high chairs, cots and bedding.

travel companies

Holiday with Baby   020 8930 8379
www.holidaywithbaby.com
Passionate about travel - dedicated to babies. Holiday with Baby is a dedicated website to help you find your perfect baby friendly holiday. With a comprehensive guide to help you do your research, a fantastic showcase of selected baby friendly holidays for every lifestyle and budget, holiday reviews and diaries and an essential shop - Holiday with Baby has everything you need for a perfect family holiday. Join the Holiday with Baby community and share your travel experiences by submitting a review or holiday diary.

JC Journeys   01886 812 862
www.jcjourneys.com
JCJourneys is a privately owned tour operator dedicated to uncovering a discreet, worldwide portfolio designed to delight and inspire. They specialise in luxury villas & hotels all over the world, with a wonderful collection of ski chalets.

Quo Vadis Travel   01279 639 600
www.quovadistravel.co.uk
Luxury family holiday experts providing independent advice on the best holidays available, with tailor-made solutions and a hassle free booking service. They are all parents and have travelled extensively with first-hand knowledge of recommended worldwide destinations. Their new family holiday brochure is free and well worth consulting. This is a highly personal service with no fees.

Responsible Travel   01273 600 030
www.responsibletravel.com
This website has a wide range of budget adventure holidays with an eco-friendly philosophy that gets you closer to the real country and supports local people. There are lots of "off-the-beaten track" destinations, no group hotels, and really helpful, independent traveller reviews. They have a selection of holidays that are entitled "baby friendly family adventure" - suitable for children from 1 year old. Think Morocco, Sri Lanka or Transylvania.

Tiny Tots Away   **0800 279 4433**
www.tinytotsaway.com
When you travel the last thing you want is to lug a week's
worth of nappies, toiletries and baby food. Nor do you want
to spend your first day scouring local supermarkets for your
baby's favourite branded products. Enter Tiny Tots Away,
who will send everything you need direct to your travel
destination. They'll send nappies and wipes, food and milk,
suncream and sunglasses - and many more items to holiday

Tots Too   **020 7284 3344**
www.totstoo.com
Tots Too has hand-picked the finest spa resorts with superb
facilities for children, offering a bespoke travel service to
match your family's needs. The expert team has a treasure
trove of information for a perfect escape for everyone,
whatever the age of your children. ATOL 5914.

CENTREPARCS

If you are looking to have a
long-weekend or short mid-
week family break then you should
consider the CentreParcs formula. Celebrity
mum Kim Wilde swears by her half-term breaks in
Wiltshire.

Tel: 0870 520 0300

◀ **Travel Changing Bag**
ZPM £24.50
You'll never have to think about how to squeeze a packet of nappies into your own suitcase with this all-in-one travel and changing bag. Available from www.zpm.com

▶ **Lightweight Pushchair**
Maclaren 4 Seasons £225
This pushchair folds down in seconds and has it's own travel case. It comes with 3 reversible seat liners, footmuff, reversible blanket and raincover to coordinate with all 4 seasons. Are you fashionable enough not let this pushchair down? www.johnlewis.com.

reversible liners

spring liner   summer liner   autumn liner

◀ **Pop-Up Travel Cot**
LittleLife £79.99
Weighing in at only 2.6kg this is the lightest travel cot on the market. It comes in a compact carrying case, and is structured by a series of aluminium rods. With a thick foam mattress this is a perfect place to rest and play. Free factor 30 sun shade. www.littletrekkers.co.uk

▼ **Travel Highchair**
Totseat £24
Fully washable, hand-bag sized highchair from 8mths+ which means you wont need to ask for a highchair. www.totseat.com

Tots Suitcase ▶
Trunki £24.99
We've seen these in action and they make the inevitable waiting so much more fun. Toddlers can ride on them, pull them along and pack all their favourite goodies inside. They also qualify as hand-luggage. www.trunki.co.uk

good advice

And finally… our indispensable list of contacts and helplines, to help you navigate your way swiftly to the people, places and advice you need.

adoption

Nottingham Adoption Services   **0845 301 2288**
(Forever Families)
www.nottinghamshire.gov.uk/adoption

cleaners

Chem Dry   **07961 966 424**
8 Corporation Oaks, Nottingham, Nottinghamshire, NG3 4JY

councils

DERBYSHIRE
Derby City CIS   01332 716 381

Derbyshire CIS   0845 605 8058

LEICESTERSHIRE
Leicester City CIS   0116 225 4890

Leicestershire CIS   016 265 6545

RUTLAND
Rutland CIS   01572 758 495

LINCOLNSHIRE
Lincolnshire CIS   0800 195 1635

NOTTINGHAMSHIRE
Nottingham City CIS   0800 458 4114

Nottinghamshire Childrens   **0800 781 2168**
Information Services
www.childcarelink.gov.uk/notts
Nottinghamshire Children's Information Service is a free service and can help you find: registered childcare in your area, free nursery education places for 3 & 4 year olds, information about help available with paying for childcare and details about your local Sure Start Children's Centre. Please call us for more information or visit our website.

naming ceremonies

If you want a secular naming ceremony, as opposed to a christening, then you have many options available to you. If you choose to focus the event on naming the child and making a public declaration of the commitment of parents and godparents then the following organisation will be able to guide you with a selection of formats (formal or informal).

Life Ceremonies   **01159 224 402**
6 Trafalgar Road, Beeston, Nottingham,
Nottinghamshire, NG6 1LB
www.lifeceremonies.co.uk

Naming ceremonies   **0845 004 8608**
www.civilceremonies.co.uk
Capture a precious moment in time with a beautiful Naming Ceremony at any venue including your home, delivered by a professional Celebrant or 'Script only' services available. Visit the online shop for Naming Ceremony accessories.

parenting advice

These courses can help parents expand their knowledge and techniques for effective parenting, as well as know how to set limits, foster self-esteem and maintain a happy equilibrium in the home.

Parentline Plus   **0808 800 2222**
www.parentlineplus.org.uk
Information, advice and workshops for parents on a range of parenting topics such as coping with a new baby. Excellent website and message board.

Nanny Dee   **0845 618 2509**
www.nannydee.co.uk
Feeling blue? If you are struggling to cope with your emotions and thoughts Nanny Dee can help. Nanny Dee Motherhood Mentors visit women at home who are struggling with emotional distress, anxiety and depression related to motherhood issues. Don't suffer in silence, call us today.

helplines

Abuse/Domestic Violence

Organisation that advise on how to protect yourself or your children and support given to victims.

Kidscape   020 7730 3300
www.kidscape.org.uk
Support and advice on bullying and sexual abuse.

Women's Domestic   0161 839 8574
Violence Helpline
www.wdvh.org.uk

Adoption

To adopt you need to be approved by the British authorities [at least 6mths]. The first step is to contact your local authority where a social worker will conduct a Home Study to assess your suitability to adopt. To adopt from overseas the government has to formalise the paperwork [6-9mths] and send the papers to the British Embassy in your chosen country.

Adoption UK   0870 770 0450
www.adoptionuk.org.uk

OASIS   0870 241 7069
www.adoptionoverseas.org.uk

After Adoption   0161 839 4930
www.afteradoption.org.uk

Intercountry Adoption Centre   020 8449 2562
www.icacentre.org.uk
Advice and information and workshops for parents wanting to adopt from overseas.

BAAF   020 7593 2000
www.baaf.org.uk
British Association for Adoption and Fostering. Information and advice for prospective parents; list of UK children looking for families [normally 5yrs+].

Post-Adoption Centre   0870 777 2197
www.postadoptioncentre.org.uk
Daily advice line which offers advice, information and support to all affected by adoption.

Bereavement and loss

Support and information for parents whose pregnancies fail or whose baby or child dies.

Baby Loss
www.babyloss.com
Online information and support for women who have experienced the loss of their baby.

Cot Death Society   0845 601 0234
www.cotdeathsociety.org.uk

Child Bereavement Trust   01494 446 648
www.childbereavement.org.uk

Cruse Bereavement Care   0870 167 1677
www.crusebereavementcare.org.uk
Support and advice when someone you know has died.

Child Death Helpline   0800 282 986
www.childdeathhelpline.org.uk
Open daily 7pm-10pm, 10am-1pm Mon-Fri and Wed 10am-4pm. Voluntary helpline and listening service where all volunteers have lost a child and are happy to talk to parents.

Miscarriage Association   01924 200 799
www.miscarriageassociation.org.uk

Stillbirth & Neonatal Death   020 7436 7940
www.uk-sands.org

Charities, campaigns and appeals

Charities funding research into pregnancy and birth complications as well as diseases affecting babies.

ChildLine   0800 1111
www.childline.org.uk

NSPCC   0800 800 500
www.nspcc.org.uk

CLIC Sargent   0845 301 0031
www.clicsargent.com
Care and support for families with cancer and leukaemia.

Tommy's   0870 777 3060
www.tommys.org
Information for parents-to-be to ensure a healthy pregnancy.

Education

Organisations that help parents whose children have a learning difficulty or find reading/writing difficult as well as home-educating groups.

British Association for Early Childhood Education 020 7539 5400
www.early-education.org.uk
Promoting good education for all families.

British Dyslexia Association 01189 668 271
www.bdadyslexia.org.uk
www.dyslexia-inst.org.uk

Barrington Stoke 0131 225 4113
www.barringtonstoke.co.uk
Publishers of books that entice the most reluctant readers.

British Institute for Learning 01562 723 010

Difficulties
www.bild.org.uk

British Stammering Association 020 8983 1003
www.stammering.org

Children's Information Service 0800 960 296
www.childcarelink.go.uk
Split into regional councils you can find details about childminders, pre-schools and nurseries in your area.

Daycare Trust 020 7840 3350
www.daycaretrust.org.uk
Help and support in finding and paying for high quality childcare.

Dyspraxia Foundation 01462 454 986
www.dyspraxiafoundation.org.uk

Home Education Advisory Service 01707 371 854
www.heas.co.uk

Environmental Campaigns

Organisations that care and campaign on environmental issues.

Real Nappy Network 020 8299 4519
www.realnappy.com

Womens Environmental Network 020 7481 9004
www.wen.org.uk
Campaigns on issues that link women, health and the environment. Campaigns promote positive alternatives to polluting practices and consumer items.

Families and relationships

Help for step-families, foster, single and adopting parents.

National Council for One-Parent Families 0800 185 026
www.oneparentfamilies.org.uk

National Family Mediation 020 7383 5993
www.nfm.org.uk

Parentline Plus 0808 800 2222
www.parentlineplus.org.uk
Information, advice and workshops for parents on a range of parenting topics such as coping with a new baby. Excellent website and message board.

Relate 020 8367 7712
www.relate.org.uk

Gingerbread 0800 018 4318
www.gingerbread.org.uk
Leading support group for single parents.

Single Parent Travel Club 0870 241 621
www.sptc.org.uk
Network of mums and dads joining up on holidays and days out.

Grandparents' Federation 01279 444 964
www.grandparents-federation.org.uk

Fatherhood

Information and support for fathers.

Fathers Direct 020 7920 9491
www.fathersdirect.com
Support and information for expectant, new, solo and unmarried dads.

Families Need Fathers 020 7613 5060
www.fnf.org.uk
Produces booklets and regular newsletters from its informative website.

Fertility, preconception pregnancy and women's health

Support and information if you are trying to get pregnant or have health problems during pregnancy.

Action for ME Pregnancy Network 0845 123 2314
www.afme.org.uk

Action on Pre-Eclampsia 020 8427 4217
www.apec.org.uk

Association for Improvements in the Maternity Services 0870 765 1433
www.aims.org.uk

Ante-natal Results and Choices 020 7631 0285
www.arc-uk.org
For people having ante-natal tests where there is a risk of abnormality.

Continence Foundation 0845 345 0165
www.continence-foundation.org.uk

Ectopic Pregnancy Trust 01895 238 025
www.ectopic.org

Group B Strep Support 01444 416 176
www.gbss.org.uk

Endometriosis Society 020 7222 2781
www.endo.org.uk

Infertility Network UK 0870 118 8088
www.infertilitynetworkuk.com
Confidential advice on interfility and reproductive health.

Women's Health Concern 0845 123 2319
www.womens-health-concern.org
Giving confidential advice to women on all heath matters.

Food and nutrition

Organisations that guide parents on healthy eating during pregnancy and for babies and children.

Baby Milk Action 01223 464 420
www.babymilkaction.org

British Allergy Foundation 01322 619 898
www.allergyfoundation.com
Dealing with food intolerance, allergies and chemical sensitivity.

Nut Allergy Sufferers: Anaphylaxis Campaign 01252 542 029
www.anaphylaxis.org.uk

Allergy Testing Direct 01489 581 968
Diagnostic allergy testing service and advice for parents.

Coeliac UK 01494 437 278
www.coeliac.co.uk
Information about gluten and wheat intolerances.

Diabetes UK 020 7323 1531
www.diabetes.org.uk

Food Standards Agency 020 7276 8000
www.eatwell.gov.uk
Provides the latest information on food safety.

Vegetarian Society 0161 925 2000
www.vegsoc.org
Advice and information about feeding a vegetarian diet to babies and children.

Illness and disability help

Organisations that help with disabilities and conditions affecting children. Also organisations that help parents with a disability.

Action for Sick Children 0800 074 4519
www.actionforsickchildren.org

Birth Defects Foundation 08700 707 020
www.birthdefects.co.uk
For parents whose child has a birth defect.

Birthmark Support Group 01202 257 703
www.birthmarksupportgroup.org.uk
Support and information for anyone who has a birthmark.

BLISS 0870 7700 337
www.bliss.org.uk
Support for parents of special care babies.

Brain Injured Children 01278 684 060
www.bibic.org.uk

Cerebral Palsy Helpline 0808 800 3333
www.scope.org.uk

Illness and disability help cont.

Children's Heart Federation `0808 808 5000`
www.childrens-heart-fed.org.uk
Information on all aspects of bringing up a child with a heart condition.

Cleft Lip and Palate Assoc `020 7833 4883`
www.clapa.com

Contact a Family `0808 808 3555`
www.cafamily.org.uk
Links families of children with special needs through contact lines with local parent support groups.

Cystic Fibrosis Trust `020 8464 7211`
www.cftrust.org.uk

Disability Alliance `020 7247 8763`
www.disabilityalliance.org

Down's Syndrome Assoc `020 8682 4001`
www.dsa.uk.com

Epilepsy Association `01132 108 800`
www.epilepsy.org.uk

Fragile X Society `01371 875 100`
www.fragilex.org.uk
For those with inherited learning disabilities.

Hyperactive Childrens Support Group `01903 725 182`
www.hacsg.org.uk

LOOK `0121 428 5038`
www.look-uk.org
Advice and support for parents with visually impaired children.

Meningitis Trust `0845 600 0800`
www.meningitis.org

National Autistic Society `020 7833 2299`
www.nas.org.uk

National Deaf Children's Soc `020 7250 0123`
www.ndcs.org.uk

Parents for Inclusion `020 7735 7735`
www.parentsforinclusion.org
A network of parents of disabled children and children with special needs.

Money and benefits

Government agencies, information and tax advice about employment, maternity benefits/leave and tax credits.

Citizen's Advice Bureau.
www.nacab.org.uk
Free and confidential advice on a wide range of issues such as debt management.

Inland Revenue Tax Credits `0845 300 3900`
www.taxcredits.inlandrevenue.gov.uk

Stressed, depressed and lonely parenting

Organisations providing help if you have had a bad birth experience or trauma, if your baby cries constantly, or if you children's behaviour is out of control. Also if you are feeling low and unhappy.

Association for Post-natal Illness `020 7386 0868`
www.apni.org

Birth Crisis Network `01865 300 266`
www.sheilakitzinger.com/birthcrisis.htm
Was set up to offer a listening service for mothers who have experienced a bad or traumatic birth:

Meet A Mum Association `0845 120 3746`
www.mama.co.uk
Open 7pm-10pm Mon-Fri. Helping mothers who feel depressed or lonely.

Working parents

Information and advice on how to find the right childcare when you go back to work and information for parents trying to balance career and family.

Working Families `020 7628 2128`
www.workingfamilies.org.uk

Mother @ Work `01273 670 003`
www.motheratwork.co.uk
A monthly webzine dedicated to working mothers.

Notes

Notes

Notes

Notes

Notes

Notes

Notes

Notes

Notes

READERS

If you think there is an event, product or service we should know about and include in the next edition, drop us a line, oran e-mail: editor@babydirectory.com

☐ This is a new product, service or facility.
☐ Oops! You've missed this.
☐ Change of address, new branch, etc.
☐ Please send me a media pack.

Name of event, product, service or location ....

Address ....
....

Postcode .... Tel No ....

E-mail address ....

www ....

Contact name and tel no (if different from above)
....

We would very much appreciate your comments about errors or omissions, please let us know.

You will receive a FREE copy of the next edition of The East Midlands Baby Directory for your efforts.

Page ....

Feedback..
....
....

Your own name, address, phone number, e-mail address (all optional)
....
....

Many thanks for taking the time to fill in this form Please send completed form(s) to:

The Baby Directory, Studio 7, Eurolink Business Centre, Effra Road, London SW2 1BZ
Tel: 0845 466 0262   Fax: 020 7733 4988   E-mail: editor@babydirectory.com

To order by telephone call: **0845 466 0262** or order via our secure website at **www.babydirectory.com**
or send this order form with your cheque to:
The Baby Directory, Studio 7, Eurolink Business Centre, Effra Road, London SW2 1BZ

Title	Price	Qty	Postage	Total
The London Baby Directory (All London postcodes)	£8.99		£1.50	
The Central Baby Directory (Oxfordshire, Berks, Bucks, Northants, Beds & Herts)	£5.99		£1.00	
The East Baby Directory (Essex, Cambridgeshire, Suffolk & Norfolk)	£5.99		£1.00	
The North East Baby Directory (Durham, Northumberland, Teeside, Tyne & Wear, Yorkshire)	£5.99		£1.00	
The North West Baby Directory (Cheshire, Cumbria, Lancashire, Greater Manchester, Merseyside)	£5.99		£1.00	
The East Midlands Baby Directory (Derbyshire, Leicestershire, Lincolnshire, Nottinghamshire, Rutland)	£5.99		£1.00	
The West Midlands Baby Directory (Herefordshire, Shropshire, Staffordshire, Warwickshire, W Midlands, Worc.)	£5.99		£1.00	
The South East Baby Directory (Surrey & S. Middlesex, Hampshire, Sussex & Kent)	£5.99		£1.00	
The South West Baby Directory (Somerset, Dorset, Wiltshire, Gloucestershire, Devon & Cornwall)	£5.99		£1.00	
			Total Order Value	

Please print clearly

Name . . . .

Address . . . .

. . . .

. . . . Postcode . . . .

Tel . . . . E-mail address . . . .

METHOD OF PAYMENT (please tick appropriate box)

Cheque/Postal Order ☐   Credit Card ☐

Please make cheques payable to **The Baby Directory Limited**

Card Number ☐☐☐☐ ☐☐☐☐ ☐☐☐☐ ☐☐☐☐ ☐☐☐☐

Issue No ☐☐   Expiry Date ☐☐☐☐   Valid from ☐☐☐   Security code ☐☐☐

Signature . . . .

How did you hear about the Directory? . . . . Leaflet Code ☐☐

If you would like to receive our monthly e-newsletter please tick here ☐